DERSU THE TRAPPER

RECOVERED CLASSICS

Dersu
THE TRAPPER

— *by* —

V. K. Arseniev

Translated by Malcolm Burr
Preface by Jaimy Gordon

McPHERSON & COMPANY

Published by McPherson & Company, Post Office Box 1126, Kingston,
New York 12402. This book has been issued with assistance from
the literature program of the New York State Council on the Arts.
First printing: April 1996.

For this edition the publisher extends its thanks to the University
Libraries of the State University of New York at Albany for the loan of
a copy of the original 1941 edition. The original title page, copyright
page, and two-page "Publisher's Note" have been superseded in this
edition. Except for the table of contents, pagination of the original has
not be affected; no part of the original work has been altered.

Library of Congress Cataloging-in-Publication Data

Arsen'ev, V. K. (Vladimir Klavdievich), 1872-1930.
  [Dersu Uzala. English]
  Dersu the trapper / by V.K. Arseniev ; translated by Malcolm Burr
; preface by Jaimy Gordon.
      p.   cm. —(Recovered classics)
  English ed. originally published: New York, E.P. Dutton, 1941.
  Includes index.
  ISBN 0-929701-50-X (hc : alk. paper).
  ISBN 0-929701-49-6 (pbk. : alk. paper).
  1. Ussuri River Valley (Russia and China)—Description and
travel. 2. Natural history—Ussuri River Valley (Russia and
China). 3. Dersu Uzala.   4. Arsen'ev, V. K. (Valdimir Klavdievich),
1872-1930—Journeys—Ussuri River Valley (Russia and China).
I. Burr, Malcolm, 1878-1954. II. Title. III. Series.
  DK771.U9A8   1996
  915.7'7—dc20   —dc20
  [B]
  [973'.04914]   95-52484

Printed on pH neutral paper.

Manufactured in the United States of America.
  5 7 9 10 8 6 4

PREFACE

A RUSSIAN CLASSIC little known in the west, *Dersu the Trapper* is at once a geographer's memoir of his expeditions in the Siberian Far East, and a tale of adventure on the wild frontier in the same family with the Leatherstocking Tales of James Fenimore Cooper and the Western novels of Irish-born adventure writer Mayne Reid, both of which certainly influenced it. These were the favorite books of V. K. Arseniev as a boy, and his first meeting with the astute native tracker Dersu reminds him of them. For Russian readers, Arseniev's tales of the Siberian hunter Dersu Uzala would bring the myth of the noble savage home from America to the Old World.

Dersu the Trapper, like no other work, conjoins the motif of the idealized primitive to the romance of the actual. No made-up scrapes could be more voluptuously squeaky than these recollected ones: Arseniev, his small band of Cossacks and the hunter Dersu barely escape blizzard, flood, forest fire, bandits and tigers, and even starvation when supplies do not materialize and weather turns murderously harsh. Not only the terrain and climate but every human encounter is to be feared, for, as Arseniev says, "In the Ussurian *taigá*, one must expect at times to meet with a wild beast, but the most dangerous meeting of all is with a man."

Against this background of stunning danger in the *taigá*, the vast and dense Siberian forest, the deep attachment of Arseniev to his friend Dersu, a wandering hunter of the vanishing Gold tribe who many times saves his life, makes a kind of simple good sense one seldom encounters in this literature. For the traveler from civilization to be saved by his wild companion is a stock device of the romance of the noble savage, but in most such tales, in a rite of heroic twinship, the man of civilization gets to return the favor. The message is that this deliberate fugitive from urbanized life has incorporated the wild man's powers, and thereby doubled his own.

Arseniev fashions at once a humbler persona for himself and a more tragic fragility for both Dersu and the wilderness they traverse together. In *Dersu the Trapper* the man of letters apprentices himself to his native mentor without hope of matching his abilities. He defers not only to the depth of native culture but also to the lifetime of experience in the *taigá* that Dersu alone possesses. Arseniev casts himself figuratively as Dersu's child rather than as his twin:

> Then we lay down to sleep. Now I felt afraid of nothing, neither tigers nor brigands, nor deep snow or floods. Dersu was with me, and with that thought in my head I fell asleep.

Dersu the Trapper benefits in its handsome prose from this unusual marriage of the scientist's memoir to the literary motif of the noble savage. Like those other traveling naturalists and gentlemen of letters Charles Darwin and Alfred Russel Wallace, Arseniev writes a shapely sentence, at once vivid and utilitarian. Still, at times the endless *taigá* and stony lifeless peaks of the Sihoté-Alin register on his introspective nature in distinctly Russian shades of melancholy. As in Darwin and Wallace, the Latin names and descriptions of exotic species constitute a poetic relief in the prose texture that is pleasant even to one who has no idea what he is talking about. On the other hand Arseniev and Dersu regularly undergo perils unlike anything in the accounts of the English gentlemen of science, so that, unlike on HMS Beagle, one will never be rocked to sleep. And finally it is as a natural scientist that Arseniev is best equipped to appreciate Dersu's astoundingly developed gifts for tracking. A scientist himself, he treats Dersu's knowledge of weather and tracking, plant and animal, as the indigenous science it is. And the genius of modesty which leads Arseniev to organize the narratives of his own explorations around encounters with Dersu puts this book in a literary landscape by itself.

The dates of Arseniev's travels with Dersu Uzala could not be other than what they are. The farthest eastward stretch of the Trans-Siberian Railway, the Ussuri Line north and south through Primorye, the Maritime Territory of then Imperial Russian, from Khabarovsk to Vladivostok, was among the first built; it was completed in 1897. Arseniev arrived in the Russian Far East in 1900. Arseniev's three surveying expeditions in *Dersu the Trapper*, between 1902 and 1907, all begin and end with the railroad which brings soldiers, pack animals and supplies into the wild, and many months later returns the exhausted men to civilization. In Ussuria, a region of drastic climatic extremes, tropical jungle mingles with the last reaches of the Siberian *taigá*. In Arseniev's works it is clear that the very means by which this unique wilderness is opened to scientific investigation will soon put an end to its richness and particularity.

In fact exploitation is already underway in the Maritime territory, by the Russians and by the nearer Chinese. Arseniev is aware of the volatility of the historical moment. He works his way up and down river valleys and gorges on either side of the Sihoté-Alin range, between Ussuriland and the coast of the Sea of Japan, suffering fearsome privations in a world without telegraph, road or post, and yet he knows for a certainty that all this is passing away. Dersu says: "'All round soon all game end... Me think ten years, no more wapiti, no more sable, no more squirrel, all gone.'" Dersu himself will be a fatality of change in the very purity of his resistance to it. His highly developed arts of hunting and tracking were not long ago traditional to his people, but most of the indigenous settlements of the region have already fallen victim to Chinese opium and bottomless debt to the company store. Dersu is alone because smallpox, a pestilence that outsiders bring, has wiped out his family. Even compared to other trappers he is alone; all he owns is in the knapsack on his back. So far he has been saved by his stubborn solitude, his perfect adaptation to life in the wild and his aversion to towns, but the same qualities will finish him as soon as his physical capacities begin to slip.

So fabulous—so like something in a story—are Dersu's abilities to read whirlwind and animal track in the Siberian *taigá* that one is shocked and moved to come across one of those blurred old photographs of Arseniev and Dersu in camp and suddenly realize: Dersu Uzala lived. Arseniev's house in Khabarovsk, where Dersu tried but failed to settle in for his old age, may still be visited. I wonder what has become of the wax cylinder on which Dersu recorded, for Arseniev, the poetic pidgin Russian that set the style for lesser imitators of Arseniev ever after, when Russian writers have depicted native Siberian characters.

Vladimir Klavdievich Arseniev was born September 10, 1872 (August 29, 1872, o.s.), in St. Petersburg, the son of a former serf who had raised himself from a railway office clerk to chief of the

Moscow District Railway. He received a military education; at St. Petersburg Cadet Infantry Academy, under the influence of Grigorii Grum-Grzhimailo, an earlier explorer of the Amur region, Arseniev developed an interest in the Russian Far East. At infantry outposts in Russia and Poland, he carried on scientific studies on his own until he succeeded in arranging a transfer to Vladivostok in 1900. From 1902 until his death in 1930 he led twelve major geographic expeditions in the Trans-Amur region and was involved in countless minor ones. He was in the habit of using native guides, Chinese as well as native Siberian, on all his expeditions; the actual Dersu Uzala he knew for only nineteen months, between 1906 and 1908. We may be sure that the Dersu of the books is a composite character. In 1910, Arseniev became director of the museum of regional studies in Khabarovsk where eventually were stored the rich collections from his travels. He had become a thorough *zaamurets* or Trans-Amurian, a member of the Society for Study of the Amur Region (he married the daughter of its secretary in 1918), an expatriate scholar who had no intention of returning home. The encyclopedic range of his scientific interests is often commented upon; in the course of a long and varied career, he wrote some sixty works on the Russian Far East.

Meanwhile, during Arseniev's residence, the Maritime Region experienced the Russo-Japanese War, ceased to be a territory of Imperial Russia, was occupied at its southern end by the Japanese, then by an Allied Expeditionary Force, during World War I, eventually became part of the short-lived Far Eastern Republic—in short, passed through all the convulsions of a far outlying district in the revolutionary period and succeeding Red Russian-White Russian conflict before being absorbed under Soviet rule in 1922. "Vladimir Arseniev came through revolution and civil war unscathed, quite an achievement for an Imperial Army officer with principles and a conscience," says Far Eastern scholar John Stephan. All the same the cosmopolitan scholarship of the pioneering orientalist and ethnographer was bound in time to attract the attention of zealous bureaucrats of the young police state. Among other sagacities, Arseniev had the good sense not to live to be old. There was a warrant for his arrest when he died in 1930, at the age of 57. His widow was arrested in 1937 and shot as a Japanese spy in 1938. Arseniev's personal archives were plundered. His daughter spent ten years in a labor camp. But in the 1940s the writer began to be rehabilitated; *In the Wilds of Ussuriland* (Khabarovsk, 1928), a combined edition of the Dersu Uzala chapters from two earlier books of Arseniev's memoirs, was republished in 1949, and has stayed popular in Russia ever since. The 1928 redaction was also the basis of the present book. Malcolm Burr (1878-1954), born near London, a soldier in the Balkans in World War I, geologist, entomologist, Slavic linguist and intrepid traveler, author of *The Insect Legion* (1939) and *In Bolshevik Siberia* (1931) among other books, was an ideal translator for Arseniev, and his graceful version of *Dersu the Trapper*, which has been out of print in English for over fifty years, is a recovered classic indeed.

—JAIMY GORDON

This introduction could not have been written without the help of Stephanie Peters of the Department of Slavic Languages and Literatures, The University of Michigan. Readers interested in the political and cultural milieu behind Arseniev's *Dersu the Trapper* should consult John Stephan's excellent *The Russian Far East* (Stanford U. Press, 1994). On Arseniev's creation of the Dersu type in Russian literature, see Johanna Nichols' "Stereotyping Ethnic Communication: The Siberian Native in Soviet Literature," in *Between Heaven and Hell: The Myth of Siberia in Russian Culture*, edited by Galya Diment and Yuri Slezkine (St. Martin's, 1993). —J.G.

CONTENTS

CONTENTS

THIRD EXPEDITION

First Expedition

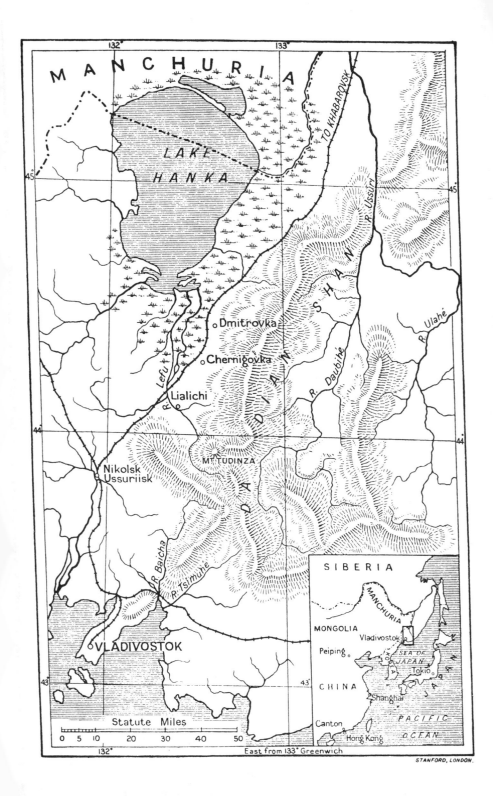

MANCHURIA

LAKE
HANKA

TO KHABAROVSK

R. Ussuri

S I K H O T A — A L I N   S H A N

Dmitrovka

Chernigovka

R. Lefu

Lialichi

R. Daubihe

R. Ulahé

Mt. TUDINZA

Nikolsk
Ussuriisk

R. Baicha

R. Tsimuhe

VLADIVOSTOK

Statute Miles

0   5 10   20   30   40   50

East from 133° Greenwich

SIBERIA

MANCHURIA

MONGOLIA

Vladivostok

Peiping

SEA OF
JAPAN

Tokio

CHINA

Shanghai

PACIFIC

Canton

Hong Kong

OCEAN

STANFORD, LONDON.

CHAPTER I : OUR NOCTURNAL VISITOR

IN the year 1902 I was engaged on a survey of the then unmapped country between the rivers Amur and Ussuri on the west and the Sea of Japan on the east, to the north of Vladivostok. It is marked on English maps as the Maritime Province, but is conveniently referred to as Ussuria, from its dominant river. My duties included the making of a reconnaissance of the chief rivers and of the central watershed, the range called Sihoté-Alin, which dominates the province. My orders covered the study of the zoology and botany of the district, and of the natives, both aborigines and immigrant. I had with me two assistants and a small detachment of Siberian Rifles and Cossacks, with pack-horses.

It is rough, steep, mountainous country where we were trekking, covered with dense virgin forest, the famous *taigá* of Siberia, in places almost impenetrable, especially where the ground is littered with fallen giants smashed down by storms.

One afternoon, when the sun was low over the horizon, it was time to stop and bivouac. There was urgent need to find water quickly, for both beasts and men. The slopes were gentle at first, but farther on the gradient became much steeper, and the horses slid down, squatting on their hocks. The packs slipped forward, and if it had not been for the breech-bands they would have fallen over the horses' heads. We were obliged to make long zigzags, and through all the windfalls that littered the ground here it was by no means easy going.

Over the pass we dropped at once into a gulch. The place was extraordinarily broken. Deep screes, encumbered with boulders and trunks, streams and rocks, all thickly overgrown with a carpet of moss; the whole scene reminded me vividly of a picture of Walpurgis Night. It would be hard to imagine a wilder and more repellent scene than that grim gorge.

Sometimes it happens that mountain and forest have such a cheerful and attractive appearance that one would be glad to linger there for ever. In others mountains seem surly and wild. It is a strange thing that such impressions are not purely personal and subjective, but were felt by all the men in the detachment. I tested this several times and was always convinced that it was so. That was the case here. In that spot there was an oppressive feeling in the air, something unhappy and painful, and the sensation of gloom and ill-omen was felt by us all.

" Never mind," said the riflemen, " we'll manage to bivouac somehow or other. We're not here for a year, and we'll find a jollier place to-morrow."

I did not want to stop there either, but what else could we do ? Night was coming on, and there was no time to lose. I could hear the murmur of a brook at the bottom of the defile, so made my way down to it and chose the nearest approach to a level spot and gave orders to pitch camp there.

The silence of the forest was at once broken by the ring of axes and by human voices as the men started collecting firewood, unsaddling the horses, and preparing supper.

Poor horses ! Among those rocks and broken branches they would find little grazing, I feared, but we would make it up for them the next day if we succeeded in getting through to some farmers' cabins.

Darkness comes on early in the forest. In the west a few spots of pale sky were still to be picked out between the black branches of the pines, but below the shades of night had already fallen. As our bonfire sprang into flame the dark clumps of shrubs and thick trunks of the trees stood out in the glare against the darkness. A little squirrel-like pica, startled among the screes, uttered a high-pitched pipe, but, suddenly frightened, slipped nimbly into its hole and did not appear again.

At length our little party quieted down. After drinking tea, each one of us was busy on his own particular job. One was cleaning his rifle, another repairing a saddle, or darning a piece of torn clothing. There is always plenty of that sort of work to be done. When they had finished, the men turned in to sleep. They pressed up close to each other for warmth, covered themselves with their greatcoats, and slept like the dead. The horses, finding no food among the rocks, came up close to our bivouac, and stood and drowsed. Only Olentiev and I remained awake. I described our road in my diary, and he patched his boots. About ten I rolled myself up in my shaggy Caucasian cloak, or *burka*, and lay down by the fire. The branches of the old fir under which we were sleeping swayed in the rising column of heat and smoke from the fire, disclosing and closing the dark sky above, all spangled in a long colonnade of stars which faded away gradually into the depths of the forest and imperceptibly merged into the blackness of the night.

Suddenly the horses raised their heads and pricked up their ears, were restive a moment, then quieted down and resumed their drowse. We paid no attention to that and continued our conversation. A minute or two went by. I asked my assistant Olentiev something and, not receiving a reply, turned towards him. He was standing in an attitude of expectancy and, shading the glare of the fire with his hand, gazing into the darkness.

" What's up ? " I asked.

" Something coming down the hill-side," he whispered.

We both listened, but all around was still, as still as it can be only in the heart of a forest on a cold autumn night. Suddenly some small stones came trickling down from above.

" A bear, I expect," said Olentiev, and began to load his rifle.

7

"No shoot . . . me man!" came a voice out of the darkness, and a moment later a man stepped into the light of the fire.

He was dressed in a jacket of deerskin with breeches of the same material. He had a sort of scarf tied round his head and on his feet *unty*, moccasins made of wapiti or elk skin. He had a knapsack of birch bark on his back and in his hands he carried an old rifle, called in Russian a *berdianka*, with *soshki*, or prop, to support it when aiming.

"'Morning, captain," he said, greeting me in the way the local tribesmen address all Russians in uniform.

Then he leant his rifle against a tree, took off his knapsack, wiped the sweat off his face with his sleeve, and sat down by the fire. I had a good look at him.

Our visitor looked about forty-five years of age. He was not very tall, but broad and thick-set, and evidently a man of great physical strength. He had a tremendous chest, his arms were strong and muscular, his legs a trifle bowed. His weather-beaten face was typical of the local tribesmen, with high cheek-bones, small nose, slanting eyes with the Mongolian fold of the lid, and broad mouth with strong, big teeth. A small reddish moustache edged his upper lip, while his chin was tipped by a short, reddish, skimpy beard. But most remarkable of all were his eyes. These were dark grey rather than hazel, with a calm but somewhat naïve expression. Through them there looked out upon the world directness of character, good nature, and decision.

The unknown did not take us in as we did him. From his breast he took out a pouch of tobacco, filled his pipe and started smoking. Without asking him who he was or whence he came, I offered him food. That is the custom in the *taigá*.

"Thanks, captain," he said; "me want eat very much; me not eat all long day."

I watched him while he ate. A hunting-knife hung from his girdle. His hands were gnarled and scarred. Similar, but deeper scars marked his face, one across his brow, another on the neck below the ear. He pulled off his scarf, and I saw that his head was covered with thick, reddish hair, all in disorder, long locks hanging down his neck.

Our guest was taciturn. At length Olentiev could contain himself no longer, and asked him right out :

" Are you a Chinaman or a Korean ? "

" Me a Gold," he answered simply.

I was interested to meet one of this disappearing tribe of natives, related to the Manchus and Tungus. I knew there were but about five thousand of them left in Russian territory and a few more in Chinese. They are mostly hunters and fishermen, and such culture as they have is more influenced by China than by Russia, and there are more Buddhists among them than Orthodox, and plenty still are heathen.

" You are, of course, a hunter ? " I asked him again.

" Yes," he answered. " Me all time go hunt ; no other work ; me no can fish, not know ; only know hunt."

" And where do you live ? " went on Olentiev relentlessly.

" Me no got house ; me all time live moving ; light fire, make tent, sleep ; all time go hunt, how have house ? "

He went on to tell us that that day he had been after a wapiti, that he had wounded a doe, but only lightly. Following her spoor, he had come across our tracks, which he had followed down into the gulch. When darkness came on he saw our fire, so came straight to it.

" Me go quiet," he explained ; " think what man go far ? Go see, captain or Cossack. Me then come straight."

" What's your name ? " I then asked the stranger.

" Dersu Uzala," he answered.

This man interested me. There was something unusual and original about him. He spoke simply, quietly, and had a modest, gentle manner. We sat and talked. He told me all about his life, and the more he talked, the more I liked the fellow. Before me I saw a primitive hunter, who had spent his entire life in the *taigá* and was exempt from all the vices which our urban civilization brings in its train. From his words I gathered that everything in life he owed to his rifle, and the results of the chase he gave to the Chinese in exchange for tobacco, lead, and powder, and that his rifle he had inherited from his father. He then told me that he was fifty-three years of age, that he had never had a house in his life, that he had always slept under the open sky and only in winter built himself a hut of bark and brushwood. His first glimmerings of childish memories were of a river, a hut, father, mother, and little sister.

" They all gone dead," he concluded, and became pensive. After a little silence he went on :

" Once me had wife and son and girl child ; smallpox kill all ; now me alone."

His face became sad at the thought of past suffering. I attempted to offer consolation, but what consolation could I give this lonesome man, whom death had robbed of his family, the only consolation of old age ? I felt I wanted to express my sympathy for him, to do something to help him, but I did not know what. Then an idea came to me, and I offered to give him a new rifle in exchange for his old *berdianka*. But he refused, saying that his was an old favourite, that he loved it for the sake of the memory of his father, that he was used to it, and that it killed well. He stretched out his arm to the tree, picked up the old weapon, and began to stroke the stock affectionately.

The stars over our heads had moved on, showing that it was after midnight. The hours sped by, but still we sat over the fire and talked. Dersu did most of the talking, while I sat and listened, and listened with very real pleasure. He told me about his hunting, and how once he had fallen into an ambush of brigands, and how he had escaped from them. He told me about his encounter with tigers, how he could not shoot them because they are gods, who protect ginseng from men ; he talked about floods and about evil spirits.

Once a tiger had severely mauled him. His wife tracked him for several days and eventually found him exhausted from loss of blood. While he was ill, she did the hunting.

Then I began asking him about the place where we then were.

He told me that it was the source of the Lefu and that the next day we should come to the first cabin.

One of the sleeping soldiers awoke, looked in astonishment at us, muttered something to himself, smiled, turned over, and went to sleep again.

On the ground and in the sky it was still dark, but on the side where new stars were rising we could detect the approach of dawn. A heavy dew was falling, a sure sign of fine weather to-morrow. Around the stillness was impressive. It seemed as though Nature herself was resting.

Another hour, and the east turned crimson. I looked at my watch; it was six o'clock, and time to wake the orderly of the day. I shook him by the shoulder. He sat up and stretched himself. The bright light of the fire dazzled him and he screwed up his eyes. Then, catching sight of Dersu, he smiled and said : " Hullo. That's rummy, a pal turned up ! " and began to pull on his boots.

The sky turned from black to deep blue, and then grey and cloudy. The shades of night began to shrink into the bushes and ravines. In a few minutes our bivouac was astir again ; men started talking; the horses stirred at their ropes ; a pica piped on one side, and lower down the gorge another answered it ; the yaffle of the woodpecker rang through the forest and the melodious whistle of the oriole. The *taigá* awoke. It grew lighter every minute, and suddenly the dazzling rays of the sun burst out from beyond the mountains and lit up the whole forest. Now our camp had a very different aspect. Instead of the blazing bonfire there lay a pile of ashes, with hardly a glimmer of flame ; on the ground there lay the empty tins out of which we had supped ; on the spot where my tent had been there stood a naked pole, and the trampled grass.

WHEN we had drunk a mug or two of tea the soldiers began to load up the horses. Dersu also began to make ready. He pulled on his knapsack and picked up his rifle and prop. In a few minutes the detachment was on the road, and Dersu came with us.

The ravine along which we went was long and winding, with similar lateral ravines running into it from the sides, down which mountain streamlets came bustling. The gulch broadened out gradually into a valley. Here the trees had been blazed, which kept us on the trail. The Gold marched ahead, keeping his eye fixed upon the ground. At times he would stoop to pick up a leaf between his fingers.

" What is that ? " I asked him.

Dersu stopped and said that the path was not intended for horse traffic, but only for men on foot, that it led to sable traps, and that a man had passed that way some days previously, probably a Chinaman.

The Gold's words surprised us all. Noticing that we looked rather incredulous, he exclaimed :

" How you not know ? Look self ! "

After this he produced such indications that my doubts were scattered at once. It was all so clear and simple that I was surprised not to have noticed it myself. In the first place there had been no sign of hoof marks, and in the second, none of the twigs on the shrubs bordering the path had been broken off, which would have been the case if horses had been that way, for the trail was narrow for them and the packs kept catching in the branches. The bends were so sharp that horses could not turn round, but were obliged to make little detours, and the tracks across the brooks always led to a tree-trunk bridge, and never into the water ; besides, the blown-down branches lying about the track were not broken. All this showed that the trail was not suitable for caravans with pack animals.

" Long time one man he go," continued the Gold as though to himself. " Man he go finish—rain come," and he began to count how many days since the last rain.

For a couple of hours we marched along the trail. Little by little the coniferous forest became mixed and broad-leaved trees more numerous—poplar, maple, aspen, birch, and lime. I wanted to halt again but Dersu advised us to go on a little further.

" We soon find hut," he said, and pointed to some trees from which the bark had been cut.

I understood. It meant that in the neighbourhood there must be something for which that bark was wanted. We pushed on and in about ten minutes saw a small hut on the bank of a brook, rigged up by some trapper or ginseng-hunter. Looking round, our new friend repeated that a Chinaman had passed that way a few days previously, and spent a night in the hut. The ashes of his fire, beaten down by the rain, the pile of grass that made his couch, and an abandoned pair of old gaiters of the coarse blue material locally called *daba*, were clear evidence of that.

I had by now realized that Dersu the Gold was no ordinary man. Before me stood a tracker, and involuntarily my thoughts went back to the delight of my boyhood, Fenimore Cooper and Mayne Reid.

It was time to feed the horses. I decided to take advantage of the opportunity to lie down in the shade of a big cedar, and dropped off to sleep at once. In a couple of hours Olentiev awakened me and I looked round. I saw Dersu splitting firewood and collecting birch bark and stacking it all in the hut.

I thought at first that he wanted to burn it down, and started dissuading him from the idea. Instead of replying he asked me for a pinch of salt and a handful of rice. I was interested to see what he was going to do with it, so told the men to give him some. The Gold carefully rolled up some matches in birch bark, and the salt and rice, each separately, in rolls of birch bark, and hung it all up inside the hut. He then started packing his own things.

" You'll probably be coming back here one of these days, I suppose ? " I asked him.

He shook his head, so I then asked him for whom was he leaving the matches, salt, and rice.

" Some other man he come," answered Dersu, " he find dry wood, he find matches, he find food, not die."

I well remember how struck I was by this. It was wonderful, I thought, that the Gold should bother his head about an unknown man whom he never would see, and who would never know who had left him the provisions. I thought how my men, on leaving a bivouac, always burnt up all the bark left at the fire. They did it out of no ill-will, but simply for amusement, to see the blaze, and I never used to stop them from doing so. And here was this savage far more thoughtful for others than I. Why is it that among town-dwellers this forethought for the interests of others has completely disappeared, though no doubt it was once there ?

" The horses are ready. It's time to be off," said Olentiev, coming up to me.

I agreed.

" Yes, it's time to be off. March ! " and I gave the word to the men, and led off along the trail.

Towards the evening we came to the confluence of two streams, where it is counted that the Lefu, the Stream of Happy Hunting, begins.

After something to eat, I turned in and fell asleep at once.

When I awoke next morning, everyone else was already up. I gave orders for the horses to be saddled, and while the men were busy with the packs, I got the plane table ready and started ahead with the Gold.

From our camp site the valley began to swing somewhat to the west. The left flanks were steep, the right sloping. With every mile the trail became broader and better. At one spot we found a tree that had been felled with an axe. Dersu looked at it and said :

" Cut in spring ; two man work ; one man tall, his axe blunt ; other man short, his axe sharp."

For this astonishing man there were no secrets. He saw everything that had taken place here, like a clairvoyant. Then and there I decided to be more observant and to try to understand tracking myself. Soon I saw another stump of a fallen tree, with a mass of chips lying about, rich in resin. I understood that someone had been collecting chips for kindling, but beyond that . . . ? Beyond that I saw nothing.

" Hut near," said the Gold, as though in answer to my meditations.

And, in fact, trees stripped of bark soon became more frequent, and by now I understood what that meant, and a couple of hundred yards farther on, on the banks of a brook, in a small clearing, stood a cabin.

It was a small building, with walls of clay covered with bark. It seemed empty, as I concluded on seeing that the door was held shut from the outside by a stake. Round the hut was a small kitchen garden, well rooted by wild pigs, and on the left a wooden temple, as always, facing south.

The interior was rough. An iron kettle, a greasy stove, from which led the flues to heat the *k'ang*, two or three wooden bowls, a wooden pitcher, an iron kitchen chopper, a metal spoon, a kettle-brush, a couple of dusty bottles, a few bits of rag, one or two chairs, an oil lamp, bits of animals' skins thrown on the ground, that formed the entire domestic equipment.

There were three trails leading up the valley of the Lefu, the one by which we had come, one leading up into the hills on the east, and a third towards the west. The last was good for horses, and we went some way up it. The men let the reins drop on their animals' necks, and let them choose their own road. The clever brutes went well, doing their best to prevent their packs catching in the branches. In the bogs and screes they did not jump, but first of all tested the ground with a foreleg before entrusting their weight to it. This dodge is characteristic of the local horses, accustomed to carrying packs through the *taigá*.

From the trapper's cabin the Lefu bends slightly to the north-east. When we had gone about half a dozen miles we came to a group of farmers' cabins, on the right bank of the river, at the foot of a lofty hill called by the Chinese Tudintsy, the earthy ridge.

The unexpected appearance of a military detachment startled the Chinese. I told Dersu to explain to them that they need not be afraid, and they went on with their work. I wanted to see what sort of a life the Chinese lived in the *taigá* and what work they did.

A number of skins stretched out to dry, a pile of wapiti horns in a shed, bags of bears' bile, used by the Chinese as medicine for trachoma, deers' fœtus, also used for medicine, lynx, marten, sable, and squirrel skins, and implements for traps, all showed that the local Chinese were engaged not so much in farming as in trapping. Round the cabins were a few plots of cultivated ground, where the Chinese sowed wheat, maize, and millet. They complained of the damage done by wild pig, and said that lately whole herds of them had come down from the hills and begun to ruin their fields. Consequently they were obliged to take their crops before they were ripe, but now the acorns had fallen the pig had gone back to the oak forests.

The sun was still high, so I decided to walk up Mt. Tudintsy, to have a bird's-eye view of the country. Dersu came with me. We travelled lightly, taking only our rifles.

Mt. Tudintsy is a big hill falling steeply down to the Lefu valley, and cut by deep gorges on the northern side. The foliage had already turned yellow, and the ground was strewn with fallen leaves. The forest was getting thin, only the oaks still clad in their full attire, though sere and faded.

It was a steep pull. Twice we sat down for a breather, and then resumed our climb.

The ground all round was torn up. Dersu often stopped to examine the spoor. By it he could tell the age of the animals, and their sex ; he could see the tracks of a lame boar, and found a spot where two boars had fought and one driven the other off. From his words I could clearly picture the scene, and it struck me as strange that I should not have observed those tracks myself sooner, and that even if I had seen them, I should have learnt nothing but the direction in which the animals were travelling.

In an hour we reached the top, covered with scree. We sat on a stone and had a look round.

" Look, captain ! " said Dersu to me, pointing to the opposite side of the ravine. " What that ? "

I looked in the direction where he was pointing and saw a dark spot. I thought it was a shadow of a cloud, and told him so. Dersu laughed and pointed to the sky. I looked up and saw that it was cloudless, without a speck upon the whole blue expanse. A moment later the dark spot changed its shape and moved a little to one side.

" What is it ? " I asked the Gold in my turn.

" You know nothing," he said. " Must go see."

We started down. Soon I noticed that the dark spot was coming towards us. Ten minutes later the Gold sat down on a stone and signed to me to do the same.

" Must sit here," he whispered. " Must sit quiet, no break twig, no talk."

We waited. Before long I caught sight of the dark spot again, and noticed that it had grown considerably, and I could distinguish its component parts. It was some living creatures, coming gradually towards us.

" Pig ! " I exclaimed.

It was in fact a herd of wild pig, over a hundred of them. Several of them kept straying to one side, but quickly rejoined the main body. Before long we could distinguish individual animals.

" One man very, very big," whispered Dersu.

I looked at him uncomprehendingly, wondering to what ' man ' he was referring.

Standing out like a dark lump in the middle of the herd was one immense boar. He was far greater than the others and could not have weighed less than about 560 lb. The herd came nearer every moment and now we could clearly hear the rustle of the dry leaves trampled under hundreds of hooves, the crack of broken twigs, the snorting of the boars, the grunting of the sows and squeaking of the pigs.

" Big man no come near," said Dersu, and again I failed to understand him.

The big boar was in the middle of the herd, but a number of the brutes wandered about on one side and the other, some to quite a distance from the main herd, and when any of these individuals came quite close to us, the big boar was still out of range. We sat immovable. Suddenly one of those nearest to us raised his snout. He was chewing something. I remember as though it were yesterday the huge head, the pricked ears, the cruel eyes, the mobile jaws with the wide open nostrils and great white tusks. The brute stopped munching and froze, fixing on us his inquiring, malicious eyes. At last he understood the danger and uttered a piercing snort. Instantly the whole herd, snorting and grunting, dashed to one side, and at the same instant a shot rang out, one animal rolled in the dust, and I saw the rifle smoking in Dersu's hand. For a few seconds the forests resounded with the crash of broken branches, and then all was still.

The wild boar of the Ussurian district, *Sus leucomystax continentalis*, Nehring, is related to the Japanese wild boar, and attains huge dimensions. In weight it runs to well over 600 and even 660 lb., with a length of 6 ft. 6½ in. and a height of 3 ft. 3 in.

The boars are armed with a pair of powerful tusks that may reach a length of almost 8 in. As they are fond of rubbing themselves against the trunks of firs, cedars, and spruce, their bristles are often smeared with resin. In the cold autumn weather they are fond of wallowing in mud, so that the water freezes on to their bristles. In the sows the udders become enormous, and sometimes form such an immense lump of ice as to impede the animals' movements.

The wild boar is an extraordinarily active and powerful brute, with sharp eyesight, keen hearing, and wonderful sense of smell. When wounded he is formidable indeed, and woe to the unwary sportsman who incautiously approaches one ! When followed, a wounded boar will lie down on his tracks and face his pursuer.

Then, directly he sees a man, he will charge with such ferocity and violence that the latter hardly has time to get his rifle to the shoulder.

The pig killed by Dersu was a two-year-old sow. I asked the old man why he had not shot a boar.

" Him old man," he explained, speaking of the huge tusker. " Him bad to eat ; meat much smell."

I was struck that Dersu spoke of the boar as a man, and asked him why he did so.

" Him all same man," he said, " only different shirt. Him know everything, know traps know angry, know all round . . . all same man."

Suddenly I understood. The attitude of this primitive soul to nature was animistic, and he humanized his whole environment.

We spent some time up the mountain, and the day imperceptibly drew to its close. The clouds, piling up on the west, glowed as though of burnished bronze. Through them broke the beams of sunlight, spreading fanwise across the sky.

Dersu paunched the pig, humped it on to his shoulders, and we started home. In an hour we were back at camp.

In the Chinese cabins it was close and suffocating with smoke, so I decided to sleep out in the open with Dersu.

" Me think," he remarked, looking up at the sky, " to-night be warm, to-morrow night rain."

I could not fall asleep. All night long I could see nothing but boars' muzzles with distended nostrils, nothing else but those red nostrils. They looked at first like small points, and then suddenly grew immense. Then it was not the head of a boar, but a mountain, and the nostrils were caverns, and then again a boar's muzzle. . . .

What a strange thing is the human brain. Out of all the impressions of an eventful day, out of the mass of varied things seen and noted, one in particular, by no means necessarily the most important but often a quite subsidiary matter, makes a more vivid impression, and leaves a stronger memory than all the others. Some places, even where I had no adventures at all, remain graven in my memory far more clearly than others where there were quite important happenings. For some reason or other, perhaps a particular tree, in no way different from a thousand other trees, or an ant-heap, a yellow leaf, a lump of moss, and so on. I really think that I could sketch these things quite accurately, in all their details.

CHAPTER III : IN A KOREAN VILLAGE

NEXT morning I awoke later than the others. The first thing that struck me was the absence of sun, as the whole sky was covered with cloud. Noticing that the men were packing the things carefully to keep them dry, Dersu said :

" No need hurry ; day go fine, to-night rain."

I asked him why he was so confident.

" Look-see self," answered the Gold. " Look-see little birds go come here there, play, sing, eat. Rain come soon—birds sit still quiet all same sleep."

As a matter of fact I remembered that before rain everything is quiet and dull, but now it was just the opposite and the forest seemed alive. Woodpeckers could be heard on every side, and the harsh scream of the jays, the croaking of the nutcrackers and busy little nuthatches were whistling cheerfully.

We asked the Chinaman about the road, and started.

Beyond Mt. Tudintsy the river Lefu broadens out at once from four or five furlongs in width to a couple of miles, and was the first inhabited district. About two o'clock we came to the hamlet of Nikolaevka. After a short rest, I told Olentiev to buy some oats and give the horses a good feed, as they deserved, and myself went on ahead with Dersu. I was in a hurry to reach the Korean village of Kazakevichevo and get my men a night's lodging with a roof over their heads.

It grows dark early on dull autumn days. About five it began to drizzle, so we hastened our steps. Soon the road forked, one branch going to the river, while the other seemed to lead up into the hills. We chose the latter. Presently we came upon some more paths cutting ours in various directions, and by the time we reached the Korean village it was quite dark.

At that time the riflemen reached the cross-roads and, not knowing which direction to take, fired a couple of shots. Afraid that they might take the wrong road, we replied in the same way. Then from the nearest cabin there came a yell, and a shot rang out through the window, followed by another and another, and in a few moments the whole village was blazing away merrily. I was bewildered, with the rain, the yelling, and firing. What was all the fuss about? Suddenly from behind one of the cabins a light appeared, and a Korean came out, carrying a kerosene torch in one hand and a *berdianka* in the other. He was running and calling out something in his own language, so we ran to meet him. The flickering reddish light of the torch flashed in the puddles and lit up his terror-stricken face. Directly he caught sight of us, he flung down the torch, fired point-blank at Dersu, and bolted. The spilt kerosene burst into flame and burnt out in a column of smoke.

" You're not hit, are you? " I called to Dersu.

" No," he answered, and picked up the torch.

I saw that they were shooting at him, but he stood there erect, waving his arms, and calling out something to the Koreans.

Hearing the firing, Olentiev jumped to the conclusion that we had been attacked by a band of brigands, so, leaving a couple of men in charge of the horses, he came running to the rescue with the others. At last the firing from the nearest cabin ceased, and Dersu opened talk with the Koreans, but they would not open their doors to us at any price. No amount of persuasion on our part was of the slightest effect. The Koreans swore, and threatened to start firing again.

There was nothing to do but bivouac once more in the open. We started a bonfire on the bank of the river and began to pitch our tents. On one side was an old tumble-down cabin, on the other a huge stack of firewood that the Koreans had prepared for the winter. Meanwhile the shooting went on in the village itself and from the outlying cabins the firing continued all night. Who was it? The Koreans themselves did not know. The riflemen were shooting, swearing, and laughing.

The next day I ordered a rest. I told the men to overhaul the saddles, to dry the wet things, and clean the rifles. The rain stopped, a fresh north-westerly breeze cleared away the clouds, and the sun peeped out.

I dressed and went to have a look round the village. One would have thought that, after last night's little battle, the Koreans would have come to have a look at our camp and see who it was they had been shooting at, but nothing of the sort. Out of the nearest cabin there came two men, both dressed in white jackets with broad sleeves, white wadded baggy trousers, with plaited string sandals on their feet. They never even looked at us, but walked right past. By another cabin was sitting an old man, spinning. When I approached him he raised his head and looked at me with eyes which expressed neither surprise nor curiosity. A woman came out to meet us, dressed in a white petticoat and jacket, open at the breast. She was carrying an earthenware pitcher on her head and walked at a steady, even pace, keeping her eyes on the ground. When she drew level with us she walked past, without raising her eyes. On every side, wherever we went, I witnessed that astonishing impassiveness, for which the Koreans are famous, and thought of the name given the country, the Land of the Morning Calm. It is a calm, however, that is exceedingly like dullness. It would seem as though there were no life here, but only mechanical movement.

The Koreans are small farmers. Their cabins are built at a considerable distance from each other, and each is in the midst of its own fields and gardens, which explains why a quite small Korean village occupies an area of a square mile or so.

Returning to camp, I went into one of the cabins. The thin walls were smeared with clay both within and without; there were three doors, with openwork windows covered with paper; the rectangular roof was thatched with dry grass.

The Korean cabins were all alike. Each had a clay *k'ang* inside, a clay platform occupying more than half the area of the building, and under the *k'ang* are the flues which conduct the heat that warms the floors and distributes the warmth throughout the house. The flues connected with the open air by means of a huge hollow tree in place of chimney. In one half of the cabin, where the *k'ang* was, lived the family ; in the other, with floor of beaten earth, the poultry, horses, and cattle. The dwelling half was divided by board partitions into separate rooms, the floors strewn with clean matting, one room for the women and children, another for the menfolk and guests.

In the cabin I saw the same woman who had walked past with a pitcher on her head. She was squatting on her heels, pouring water into the kettle with a wooden mug. She was doing this slowly, raising the mug high into the air and pouring the water in a strange way across her arm on the right side. She looked dully at me and went on with her work in silence. On the *k'ang* was sitting a man of about fifty, smoking a pipe. He never stirred, nor answered my greeting. I sat for a few moments, and then went out, back to my companions.

After a meal I went for a walk round the district. Crossing over to the other bank of the river, I went uphill, and strolled about for a couple of hours and at last came on to the cliff.

The day was approaching its close. Across the sky there slowly crept wisps of pink cloudlets. The distant hills, lit by the last rays of the declining sun, glowed with a violet light. The trees, stripped of foliage, assumed a monotonous grey tint. In the Korean village reigned the customary calm ; out of the clay chimneys rose whitish columns of smoke which dissipated quickly in the cool evening air ; here and there on the paths flitted the white figure of a Korean. Down below, by the river bank, I saw the light of a fire. It was our camp.

By the time I returned it was growing dark. The water of the river looked black, and its smooth surface reflected the flames of our fire and the stars twinkling overhead. Round the fire sat the riflemen ; one was talking, and the others were laughing.

" Supper ! " cried the cook.

The laughter and joking at once stopped.

After some tea, I sat by the fire and entered my observations in my diary. Dersu arranged his knapsack and attended to the fire.

" Little cold," he muttered.

" Better go and turn in in the cabin," I advised him.

" Me no want—me all time sleep so," he replied.

Then he stuck some branches of willow into the ground, stretched the fly of a tent across, flung a goat skin on the ground, sat on it, pulled a leather jacket across his shoulders, and lit his pipe. In a few minutes I heard a gentle snore. He was asleep. His head bowed forward on his chest, his arms dropped, and the burnt-out pipe fell from his mouth on to his knees.

' And to think that he has slept like that all his life ! ' I thought.

And then I thought of the effort, at the cost of what privations, this man earned his living ! And at the same moment caught myself in another thought, that he would never consent to give up his liberty.

In his own way Dersu was happy.

Behind me the river murmured gently. Somewhere in the distance a dog barked. In one of the cabins a child was crying. I rolled myself in my *burka*, lay on my back, and dropped into a sweet slumber.

The next morning we were all afoot directly it was light. The horses, not finding any grazing in the Koreans' meadows, had strayed off to the hills to glean what they could. While the men were hunting for them, the camp cook brewed tea and *kasha*, our Russian gruel. By the time the men returned with the horses I was ready, and by eight we were on the road again.

From the Korean village two trails lead down the valley of the Lefu, one to a village ; the other, little used and boggy in places, followed the left bank.

We chose the latter. The farther we went, the more the valley was filled with meadowland. We had come to the end of the mountains. They had dropped behind, and their place was taken by broad, gently rolling hills covered with scrub. Oaks and limes with frozen tops grew here and there in groups and singly. By the river itself there were thickets of willows, alders, and bird-cherries. Our path bore to the left towards the mountains, and took us two or three miles from the river.

That day we failed to reach Lialicha, and stopped to camp about four miles from it on the bank of a small, winding stream.

In the evening I sat by the fire and discussed with Dersu the rest of our journey down the Lefu. I very much wanted to have a look at Lake Hanka, discovered by N. M. Przewalski. The Gold told me that there were extensive swamps ahead and pathless bogs, and advised us to take a boat, and leave the horses and some of the men at Lialicha. His advice struck me as sound, and I followed it, only choosing another place for the men and horses to wait.

THE next morning I took Olentiev and Rifleman Marchenko with me and sent the rest to the village of Chernigovka with orders to await my return there. With the help of the *starostá*, or head-man, we soon succeeded in finding a tolerable flat-bottomed boat, for which we paid twelve roubles in cash and a couple of bottles of vodka. The entire day was given up to equipping our craft. Dersu himself made the oars, rigged up rowlocks out of props, made the seats, and got ready the poles. I loved watching him at work, so swiftly and efficiently was it all done. There was no fuss, and all his movements were deliberate and consequential; everything went smoothly and without interruption. It was obvious that he had grown up in a stern school which had taught him to be energetic, active, and economical of time. We happened to come across some biscuits in one of the huts, and there was nothing more we wanted. Everything else, tea, sugar, salt, groats, and tinned food we had in plenty. In the evening, on the Gold's advice, we put all the stores on board and ourselves spent the night on the bank.

The night was cold and windy. We had not enough wood to make up a big fire, and we hardly slept for the cold. However I tried to roll myself up in my *burka*, the cold wind managed to find a chink, and one minute my shoulder was frozen, then my side, or else my back. The wood was wretched stuff, cracking and throwing out sparks all over the place, but giving very little heat. Dersu had a hole burnt in his blanket. Through my drowse I could hear him swearing at the log in his own lingo and, in his funny pidgin-Russian, calling it ' bad man.'

" Him burn all time like that—cuss him all same," he was saying to some imaginary person, and imitating the cracking of the logs. " Need throw him."

Then I heard a splash and the hiss of the chunk of wood. Evidently the old man had thrown the offending log into the river. After that somehow I felt a little warmer and dozed off.

While it was still night I awoke and saw Dersu sitting by the fire. The wind had fanned it into a blaze, blowing the flames in all directions. I felt something on top of my *burka*. It was Dersu's coat. That meant that he had covered me with his own coat, and that was why I had felt warmer and been able to go to sleep. The soldiers too were covered with his piece of tent. I invited Dersu to change places with me for a time, but he refused.

" No need, captain," he said. " You go all same sleep—me watch fire. Him very naughty," and he pointed to the wood.

The more I saw of this man, the more I liked him. Every day revealed some new fine trait in his character. Formerly I had thought that egoism was characteristic of savages, and feelings of charity, humanity, and love of one's neighbour were a speciality of Europeans and Christians. Was I not mistaken ? Lazily chasing these thoughts, I dozed off and slept till morning.

When it was quite light, Dersu awakened us. He brewed tea and roasted a piece of meat. After breakfast I despatched the men with the horses to Chernigovka, and then we launched our boat and started.

Punting with our poles, we pushed the boat down-stream at

a fine pace. After about four miles we came to the railway bridge, and stopped for a breather. Dersu told us that he had been in that district as a child with his father to shoot goats. He had heard of the railway from the Chinese, but never before seen such a thing.

After a short rest we resumed our journey. The hills came to an end near the railway line. I went ashore and climbed the nearest one to have a last look round the district, and my eyes were gladdened by a beautiful panorama. Behind us, to the east, were the mountains nestling together ; to the south rolling hills, studded with larches ; to the north, as far as the eye could reach, an endless expanse covered with grass. However I strained my eyes, I could see no end to the steppe, which extended far away beyond the horizon. Every now and then a puff of wind came, making waves through the grass like those at sea. Here and there, singly and in small clusters, stood a few stunted birches and some other trees. From the hillock on which I stood the course of the Lefu could be followed by the belt of alders and willows growing in abundance along its banks. At first it keeps its north-easterly bearing, but, without reaching the hills visible about five miles away to the west, it bends to the north with a dash of east. These lowlands seemed lifeless and desert. The pools glistening in the sun in several places showed that the valley of the Lefu is subject to floods during the rainy season.

During the second half of the day we travelled as far again, and stopped to camp fairly early.

We were cramped from sitting so long in the boat and all of us were glad to get ashore and stretch our legs. The plain attracted me. Olentiev and Marchenko undertook the camp, while Dersu and I went out to see if we could bag something for the pot.

From the very first step we found ourselves in the grip of the exuberant grass on every side. It was so dense and high that a man felt drowned in it. Beneath our feet, grass ; before and behind us, grass ; on either side of us, grass ; even over our heads, grass. We seemed to be swimming through a sea of grass, and this feeling was even stronger when we came across a hummock, and we were able to see how the steppe undulated into the distance. With a certain feeling of apprehension I plunged again into that green sea, and started ahead. In places like that it is as easy to lose one's way as in a forest, and the danger of being bushed is real. We strayed from the path several times, but quickly corrected our mistakes. When we came across a tuft or a hillock, I tried to get a look round, to get my bearings. Dersu took a bunch of reeds and mugwort and bent it down as a patteran. I looked ahead and all round. Everywhere, on every side, extended the endless, waving ocean of grass.

Animal life in these swamps was mostly feathered. He who has not been in the lower reaches of the Lefu at the time of migration can have no conception what an amazing sight that is. Thousands and thousands of birds, both great and small, stretch in endless wisps away to the south. Some were travelling in a northerly direction, and some were crossing the main line of flight. The festoons of birds now rose, now dipped, but all, both far and near, stood out against the blue of the sky, especially those near the horizon, that looked as though entangled in a vast cobweb. I gazed fascinated. High above all were the eagles. Sailing on their mighty pinions, they soared in immense circles. What did distance mean to them? Some were weaving their circles so high that they were barely visible. Below them, but still high above the earth, flew the geese. These wary birds flew in regular gaggles, beating their powerful wings, sending their *honk honk* ringing through the air. Alongside them flew the brents and the swans. At a lower level bustled the duck. The flocks of mallard were easy to distinguish by the whistling noise made by their pinions. Nearer the surface of the water skimmed the teal, garganey, and other smaller duck in their thousands. Here and there against the sky I could pick out a rough-legged buzzard, and a kestrel or two. These pretty hawks described beautiful circles, hanging hovering over one fixed spot by the rapid beating of their wings, keenly scanning

the ground. Every now and then one would swing to one side, and start circling and hovering over another spot. Then suddenly one would close his wings and dive to the ground, but swiftly swing up aloft again, just skimming the grass. The graceful gulls and elegant terns stood out in relief like dazzling white stars against the azure sky, while curlews sped by in swift easy flight, performing marvellous evolutions. The golden plover clung to the swampy lowlands, evidently steering by the pools of standing water. And all those birds were speeding southwards, a magnificent sight !

Suddenly, quite unexpectedly, we burst upon a pair of roedeer. They were about sixty paces from us and in that high grass scarcely visible. We caught only a glimpse of their heads with protruding ears and the white flash on their rumps, as they dashed off a hundred paces or so, and then stopped to look at us. I fired and missed. The roar of the shot re-echoed afar down the valley, and thousands of birds rose screaming from the water, flying off in all directions. As the roe in their terror moved off in great bounds, Dersu took aim, and directly a head appeared above the grass he let the hammer fall.

When the smoke had wafted away, there was no sign of an animal. The Gold reloaded unhurriedly and advanced, while I followed in silence. Dersu looked round him, then turned back, then aside, and back again. He was evidently looking for something.

" What are you looking for ? " I asked.

" The roe."

" But it's gone ! "

" No," he replied confidently. " Me hit him on head."

I started looking for the body too, but, I must admit, a little incredulously, as I thought he must be mistaken. But in about ten minutes he found it, and I saw that the bullet had in fact passed right through its head. Dersu lifted it on to his shoulders and quietly started back. By the time we reached camp it was dusk.

The twilight was still struggling with the advancing darkness, but could not vanquish it; it yielded, and vanished over the horizon. At once the stars started winking at us from the sky, as though glad that at last the sun had set them free. Near a little tributary I could just see a thicket, standing out as a dark spot, but it was not possible to distinguish the trees. They all looked alike. Through them twinkled the light of our camp fire. The night was still and cool. We could hear a flock of duck alight noisily upon the water not far from us. By their manner of flight we could tell that they were teal.

After some supper, Dersu and Olentiev set to work to dress the roe, while I attended to my own affairs. When I had written up my diary I turned in, but could not go to sleep for a long time. As soon as I closed my eyes, there danced before me visions of waving cobwebs, that undulating sea of grass and the uncountable flocks of geese and duck. At last, just before dawn, I dropped off.

The next morning we were up early, and as soon as we had swallowed our tea we put our things into the boat and were off again down the Lefu. The farther we went the more winding became the stream. The loops sometimes described almost complete circles, and, doubling back, swung forward again, and there was not a single straight stretch.

The stock of provisions we had brought with us was running low, and it was necessary to reinforce them. So we tugged the boat up on to the bank and went to the village of Halkidon, the last Russian settlement. A broad street ran down the middle, and the houses stood far apart from each other. Almost all the peasants had been there a long time and had allotments of 250 acres. I called at the first house. I cannot say the yard was clean, and I cannot say that the inside was clean. Rubbish, things flung about, the tumbledown fence, the door hanging on

its hinges, and a wash-basin black with age and dirt, all showed that the owners were not exactly house-proud. As we walked into the yard, a woman with a baby in her arms came to meet us. She answered my greeting timidly, and nervously stood aside.

I could not help noticing the windows. They had double frames with four panes, and the space between the two frames was filled almost half-way up the lower panes with something greyish yellow. At first I thought the space was packed with sawdust, and I asked the woman why.

" Sawdust ! " she exclaimed. " That's not sawdust ; that's mosquitoes."

I went closer and saw that it was in fact a mass of dried mosquitoes, and there must have been at least a pound of them.

" It's the only way we can deal with them, by having double windows," explained the woman. " They get in between the panes and die there. Indoors we burn smoke-sticks, and sleep under mosquito-curtains."

" But you could have burnt the grass in the bog," said Marchenko to her.

" We burnt it, but it didn't do any good," she replied. " The 'squitoes come out of the water. Fire doesn't worry them. And in the summer the grass is moist and won't burn."

At that moment Olentiev arrived and told us that he had bought some bread. We strolled round the village and returned to the boat, to find that Dersu had roasted a joint of venison and had tea ready. Some village urchins ran along the bank behind us, and stood and watched us with curiosity.

In half an hour we were off again. I looked round. The children were clustered on the bank, watching us still. The river made a bend, and the village was hidden from view.

It is hard to follow the channel of the Lefu through the maze of its feeders. The breadth of the stream here varies from twenty to a hundred yards. It gives out backwaters, from which run long, deep streams which connect up with pools and swamps or with brooks that fall back into the Lefu some distance lower down. The nearer we approach Lake Hanka, the slower the current. The poles which the men used for punting in the prow often stuck in the mud, sometimes so tightly that they were snatched out of their hands. The depth of the Lefu here was very uneven. At one moment the boat was bumping on the bottom in the shallows, and at another the men could dip the pole wholly into the water without touching bottom.

The ground on the banks is fairly firm, but if you go even a little away from them, you are in a bog at once. There are long pools hidden among the thickets of willow and alder, which, growing in rows, show how the Lefu formerly had a different course and has changed its channel several times.

Towards the evening we came to the river Chernigovka and

bivouacked on a small neck of land between it and a small tributary.

To-day the migration had been very strong. Olentiev shot several duck and so provided an excellent supper. As soon as it was dark the birds stopped their flight and stillness reigned around. One would have thought that the steppe was lifeless, but in reality there was not a pool, not a backwater nor a stream where there were not flocks of swan, geese, mergansers, duck, and other water-fowl roosting.

CHAPTER V : IN THE SWAMPS

IN the evening Marchenko and Olentiev turned in before us,
as usually Dersu and I sat and chatted. The kettle sang
merrily on the fire to remind us of its existence. Dersu
moved it a little, but it continued to sing. He moved it farther
off still, and then it hummed on a low note.

" How him cries ! " exclaimed Dersu. " Him bad man,"
and he jumped up and poured the water on the ground.

" How ' man ' ? " I asked him, puzzled.

" Water," he answered simply. " Him can cry, him can sing,
him can play."

This primitive soul saw in water a living force ; he saw its
quiet flow and heard its roar in time of flood.

" Look-see," said Dersu, pointing to the fire. " Him too all
same man."

I looked at the fire. The wood was crackling and sparkling.
The fire would burst into long tongues of flame, and then drop
back into short flamelets, one moment be bright, another dull ;
out of the embers were formed castles and grottoes, and then
everything collapsed and began again. Dersu sat silently, and
I gazed into the ' live fire.'

A fish splashed noisily in the river. I started, and looked at
Dersu. He was sitting brooding. Out on the steppe everything
was as still as before. The stars above told us that it was midnight. I flung some more wood on the fire and aroused the
Gold, and we both turned in for the night.

The next morning we all awoke very early, by chance,
spontaneously.

Directly the dawn began its task, the feathered kingdom rose
again into the air and with noise and hubbub resumed its journey

southwards. First up were the geese, then went the swans, then the duck, and after them the rest of the birds. At first they flew low, but the lighter it grew, the higher they flew.

We had made a good five miles down stream before the sun was up, and reached the hill called Firewood Hill, covered with elm, rowan, and aspen. Here the Lefu broadens out to more than twenty-five miles. On the left bank for an immense distance is continuous swamp. The Lefu splits into numerous branches, tens of miles in length. These divide again into smaller streams and these in turn are forked. These streams extend in a broad belt on both sides of the river and form a labyrinth in which one can easily lose one's way, unless you keep to the main stream, or if you flatter yourself that you will find a short cut up one of them.

We followed the main stream, turning up a lateral branch only in case of actual need, and took the first opportunity of getting back to the main river. These feeders are thickly grown with osiers and reeds, which completely hid our boat. We rowed quietly, and often came within easy gunshot of birds. Sometimes we refrained from shooting, and enjoyed watching them.

First of all I noticed a white heron with black legs and yellowish-green beak. He was stalking along near the bank with great dignity, bobbing his head in time with his pace, scanning the river bottom. Noticing the boat, he sprang up into the air, ponderously raised himself on his wings, flew a short distance, and came down in a neighbourly stream. Then we saw a bittern. The greyish-yellow colour of the plumage, the dirty yellow beak, yellow eyes and legs make it an extraordinarily unattractive creature. This sulky bird walked along the sand,  bent forward, all the time persecuting an active, fussy oyster-catcher. The oyster-catcher flew off a little way, and directly

37

it settled again the bittern at once walked straight up to it, and as soon as it was near enough, it rushed at it and tried to stab it with its dagger-like beak. Noticing the boat, the bittern faded into the grass, stretched up its neck, raised its head upwards, and simply disappeared completely against the background. When the boat had passed, Marchenko had a shot at it with his rifle, but did not hit it, though the bullet cut the reeds just alongside. The bittern never stirred. Dersu smiled.

" Him very sly man. All time deceive," he commented.

And, in fact, it was now impossible to pick out the bittern, so completely did his plumage and his head raised upwards blend with the background of reeds.

Farther on we saw another scene. Low above the water on a branch of a willow was perched a kingfisher. The little bird  with its big head and beak seemed asleep, but all of a sudden it plunged into the water, dived, and came up to the surface with a small fish in its beak. Swallowing its prey, it once more took its perch upon the willow and seemed buried in thought, when the noise of the approaching boat disturbed it and with a shrill whistle it flew down the river. We watched the flash of its brilliant blue back, and saw it settle on a bush, and then disappear round a bend.

Twice we shot coot, which run easily about on the water-weeds but are rather helpless in the air, which is clearly not their proper element. They give the impression of being beginners, who have not yet learnt to fly properly, and their legs dangle in a comical way.

Here and there in the meres were grebes, with their brightly coloured frill standing out round their heads. These did not fly away, but hurriedly hid themselves among the rushes, or else dived.

The weather favoured us. It was one of those mild autumn days which we often have in the southern Ussurian region in October. The sky was cloudless and bright, and a gentle breeze blew from the west. Such weather is often deceptive, and followed by the cold north-westerly winds; the longer the fair weather lasts, the more abrupt the change.

About eleven in the morning we made a long halt near a feeder. After a meal the men lay down for a siesta, but I went for a stroll on the bank. In whichever direction I looked, I could see nothing but swamp and reeds. Far away to the west I could faintly distinguish the misty outline of the hills. In the treeless valleys here and there, like small oases, dark spots marked the presence of clumps of bushes.

As I made my way to one of these, I flushed a big marsh owl, the 'night bird of the wide open spaces,' which by day hides in the grass. It fluttered timidly aside, flew a little way, and settled again in the bog. By the bushes I sat down to rest when suddenly I heard a faint rustle. I was startled, and looked up quickly, but my fears were groundless. It was only a few reed-warblers, fluttering about among the reeds, flicking their tails. Next I saw a couple of wrens. These delightful little birds kept hiding in the thickets, then suddenly popped out on the other side and again vanished in the dry grass. With them was a reed-bunting. It kept climbing about the reeds, cocking its head on one side, and looking at me inquiringly. And I saw many more little birds that I could not name.

After an hour I rejoined the others. Marchenko already had tea ready and was waiting for me. When we had satisfied our thirst, we started down-stream again. As I wanted to make my diary complete, I asked Dersu what animals' tracks he had noticed in the valley of the Lefu since we left the hills and came into the swamps. He answered me that there were roe, racoons, badgers, wolves, foxes, hares, polecats, otters, water-rats, voles, and shrews.

In the second half of the day we did another eight miles or so, and then bivouacked on one of the numerous eyots.

To-day the sunset was in particularly bright colours. At first it was pale, then became emerald, and on this green background, like diverging columns, there rose from the horizon two pale-yellow beams of light. In a few minutes they faded away. The green colour of the sky turned to orange, and then to red. As a closing phenomenon the purple-red horizon darkened, as though by smoke. Simultaneously with the sunset, on the east appeared the shadow of the earth, one end reaching the northern horizon, the other the southern. The outer edge of this shadow was purple, and the lower the sun descended the higher rose the shadow. Soon the purple band fused with the crimson sunset on the west, and then a dark night came on.

I gazed in admiration, but at that moment heard Dersu grumble :

" No understand."

I guessed that he was alluding to me, and asked him what was the matter.

" That bad," he said, pointing to the sky. " Me think will be big wind."

That night we sat long over the fire. We had been up early and worked hard all day, so we turned in to sleep directly after supper. We slept heavily. In all my body I felt listless and weak, and my movements were laboured. As the symptoms were felt by us all alike, I was alarmed, fearing that we all had caught fever or some other infection, but Dersu reassured me, saying that it was always the case with abrupt change of season. We forced ourselves to start and forced ourselves to go on rowing. The weather was warm ; there was not a breath of wind, and the reeds stood motionless, as though asleep. The distant mountains, hitherto quite visible, were now lost in haze. In the sky there were long, narrow clouds, and a halo appeared round the sun. I noticed that there was nothing like the life about the place that we had observed the previous day. The geese and duck and all the little birds seemed to have vanished. In the sky only the eagles could be seen, perhaps because they were above those atmospheric changes which were producing such a relaxing effect and feeling of lassitude among the earth-dwellers.

" No mind," said Dersu. " Me think when half sun gone, big wind come."

I asked him why the birds had stopped their flight, and he gave me a long lecture on migration.

According to him, birds like flying against the wind. In quite calm and hot weather, they sit in the marshes. If the wind blows from behind, they feel the cold, because it blows up under their feathers. Then they take shelter in the grass. Only an unexpected fall of snow will then force them to take to the wing again, regardless of the wind and cold.

The nearer we came to Lake Hanka, the more swampy became the valley. The trees along the banks became fewer and fewer, yielding place to a few bushes and shrubs. The slowing-up of the current was reflected in the vegetation. Flags put in an appearance, water-lilies, *kuroslep*, *Cornus alba*, and *Trapa natans*, that we Russians call the water-nut. Sometimes the weeds were so thick that we simply could not force the boat through them and had to go round. In one place we lost our way and got caught in a backwater. Olentiev wanted to go ashore to have a look round, but directly his foot touched the bank he sank in up to the knee. Then we turned back, made our way into a pool, and by chance hit on the stream again. The weed-grown maze was now behind us and we could congratulate ourselves on having got out of it so cheaply. Every day it became harder and harder to find our way.

Formerly it had been easy to follow the course of the river for a long way by the trees that grew along the banks, but now there were no longer even any bushes, with the result that one could not tell what happened to the stream only a few yards ahead.

Dersu's prophecy was fulfilled. At midday the wind began to blow from the south. It grew stronger and stronger and then veered to the west. The geese and duck took to the wing again and flew low.

In one place there was a tangle of flotsam, washed down in flood-time. On the Lefu we could not afford to miss that, or we might have been left without any firewood. In a few minutes the men had loaded the boat to the full, and Dersu pitched tent and lit a fire.

It was not much farther to Lake Hanka. I knew that here the river swings to the north-east and falls into the eastern corner of the Swan Gulf, so called from the quantities of swan that are always to be found here at the time of migration. The gulf is four or five miles deep and about a mile wide. It is very shallow and connects with the lake by a narrow stream. In order to reach the lake by boat we had still nearly ten miles to row, but the distance as the crow flies was not more than a couple of miles. We decided that the next day Dersu and I would go on foo and come back in the evening, while Olentiev and Marchenko would wait for us in camp.

In the evening we all had plenty of spare time. We sat over the fire, drank tea, and yarned. The dry wood burnt with a long bright flame. The reeds swayed and rustled, which made the wind seem stronger than it really was. A mist obscured the sky, through which only the larger stars were just visible. The sound of the surf reached us from the lake. Towards morning the sky was covered by layers of cloud. It was now blowing from the north-west. The weather became rather worse, but not bad enough to spoil our expedition.

LAKE HANKA, in the Gold language Kenka, is shaped like an egg. The greatest width is about thirty-seven miles, the least about half that. It is 162 miles round the coast and about fifty miles in length.

When we had made the necessary arrangements, Dersu and I started out for the lake. We were expecting to be back in the evening and so travelled light, leaving everything we could spare at the camp. To be on the safe side I put on a jersey, and Dersu took his piece of tenting and two pairs of moccasins. On the way he kept looking at the sky, saying something to himself; at last he turned to me with the question :

" How, captain, us soon go back or not ? Me think will be bad night."

I answered that it was not far to the lake and we would not stop there.

Dersu was easily persuaded. He considered it his duty to give warning of impending danger, but if no notice were taken of his warning, he did not argue, but accepted the situation and walked on in silence.

" All right, captain," he replied. " You look-see self; if all right, all right to me."

Walking was possible only along the banks of the streams and pools where the ground was a little drier. We took the left bank of the stream alongside which we had pitched camp. It went in our direction for a long way, but then suddenly turned sharply back, so we left it, and crossing a bit of bog, came to another narrow but very deep stream. We jumped across, and went on among the reeds. Then I remember that still another stream appeared on our left, so we followed its right bank. Noticing

43

that it bent towards the south, we left it, and went on some time in a straight line, skirting the pools of standing water, jumping from tuft to tuft. Like that we walked about a couple of miles. At length I stopped to take my bearings. The wind was now blowing from the north, that is from the lake itself, and the reeds were bending and rustling. Sometimes the wind beat the reeds down to the ground, which made it possible to see a little distance ahead. Across the horizon on the north was a sort of fog, like smoke. The sun shone vaguely through the clouds and I took that for a good sign. At last we saw Hanka. The water was rough, covered with white horses.

Dersu called my attention to the birds. He noticed that something was upsetting them. It was not a steady migration, but a headlong flight. They were flying in disorder. The geese were flying low, just over the ground. They looked very odd when flying towards us and were in the direct line of vision, like fabulous flying dragons. Neither feet nor tail were to be seen, but only a bob-tailed sort of thing, rapidly beating great long wings and coming on at terrific speed. Catching sight of us, they swung up, but, directly they had passed the danger spot, they dipped again.

We reached the lake about midday. The great freshwater sea now had a menacing aspect; the water lashed into foam as though boiling in a kettle. After the long walk through the reeds and rushes of the swamps, the view of the open expanse of water was refreshing. I sat down on the sand and gazed at it. There is a peculiar fascination about the surf, and I could sit by the hour and watch the waves breaking on the shore.

The lake was deserted. There was not the sign of a sail of a boat. We strolled about the shore for an hour and shot a few birds.

" Duck stop go," said Dersu aloud.

Then I noticed that the flight had suddenly ceased.

The black fog which I had seen on the horizon suddenly began to rise into the air. The sun was now completely hidden. Scattered, whitish clouds were chasing each other across the dark sky, their edges torn and hanging in tufts, as it were, like dirty cotton-wool.

" Captain, us must go back quick," said Dersu. " Me little afraid."

And in truth it was time to think of returning to camp. We changed our moccasins and started back. When we came to the thickets I turned back to have a last look at the lake. It was lashing its shores like a savage hound on a leash, throwing a yellow foam high into the air.

" Water him rise," said Dersu, looking at the stream.

He was right. The strong wind had driven the water up the mouth of the Lefu, with the result that the river had overflown its banks and begun to invade the plain. Before long we came to a big stream cutting across our road. The place seemed unfamiliar to me, and Dersu did not recognize it either. I stopped, considered a moment, and went to the left. The stream began to wind and turned off on one side. We left it and walked straight southwards. In a few minutes we came to a bog and were obliged to return to the stream. Then we turned to the right, came on to another stream, which we were able to ford. Then we went towards the east, but came to a quagmire, though we succeeded in finding a firm strip of ground that crossed it like a bridge. Feeling the ground carefully with our feet, we cautiously made our way forward, and about half a mile farther on reached some firm ground covered with grass. At last we had left the bog behind.

I looked at my watch. It was about four in the afternoon, and it seemed as though darkness were coming on. Black clouds dropped low and scudded southwards. I calculated that it was only another couple of miles to the camp. An isolated hummock opposite our camp served as a landmark. We could not lose our way ; at the worst we might be late. Suddenly and quite unexpectedly there appeared in front of us a good-sized lake. We decided to go round. But it seemed a long way, so we went to the left. A couple of hundred yards farther on we came to another stream, flowing at right angles to the lake. We crashed across to the other side, and soon found ourselves back at the quicksands. Then I decided to try our luck on the right side. Before long we felt water squelching under our feet, and farther on we could see big pools. Evidently we had lost our way. The situation was taking a serious turn. I suggested to the Gold to turn back and look for that firm isthmus which had brought us to the island where we now found ourselves. Dersu agreed. We went back, but could not find it again.

Suddenly the wind dropped. Behind us we could hear the sound of the waters in the lake. It was growing dark, and at the same time some snow-flakes were fluttering in the air. The stillness lasted only a few minutes, and then came the blizzard.

' We're in for it for the night,' I thought, and suddenly realized that on the island there was no wood, not a single branch or twig, nothing but water and reeds. I felt a tug of fear.

" What shall we do ? " I asked Dersu.

" Me very much afraid," he replied.

Then I realized the full horror of our position. We had to face the night in the midst of those swamps, without fire or warm clothing, through a raging blizzard. My only hope was in the resourcefulness of Dersu. In him alone I saw salvation.

" Listen, captain," he said. " Listen well. We now need work, need much work. If not much work, then we all go die. Need quick cut much reed."

I did not ask him why. It was enough for me that he said ' need quick cut reed.' We slipped off our packs and set to work feverishly. While I was cutting as many reeds as I could carry under one arm, Dersu managed to cut enough for both arms. The gale blew in gusts, at times so violently that it was almost impossible to stand up against it. My clothing began to freeze. Directly I flung an armful of reeds on the ground it was covered with snow. Dersu told me not to cut reeds in a few places, and was very angry when I did not obey him.

" You not know nothing ! " he cried. " You obey and work ; me know, me understand."

Dersu took the strap off the guns, his girdle, and a piece of cord that happened to be in my pocket. He rolled it all up and thrust it into his jacket. It was growing darker and colder. Thanks to the fallen snow we could see something. Dersu was working with tremendous energy. If I eased off for a moment, he called to me to hurry. In his voice I detected the note of fear. Then I grasped my knife again and cut till I was exhausted. My shirt was filled with snow, which began to melt, and I could feel the icy water trickle down my back. I thought I had been collecting reeds for over an hour. The piercing wind and burning snow cut my face unendurably. My hands were numbed. I started blowing on to my hands to warm them and in so doing dropped the knife. Noticing that I had stopped for a minute, Dersu again called out to me :

" Captain, work ! Me very much fear. Soon all go die."

I said I had lost my knife.

" Tear reeds with hand," he shouted to me, trying to make himself heard through the gale.

Automatically, almost unconsciously, I started breaking off the reeds, and cut my hands badly, but I was afraid to stop, and went on tearing off reeds until I collapsed. I saw wheels spinning before my eyes, my teeth chattered as in a rigour. My drenched clothing began to shrink and split. Drowsiness overwhelmed me.

' This is what it's like to be frozen to death,' I thought, and became unconscious.

How long I remained in that condition I do not know. Suddenly I came to, with the feeling that I was being shaken by the shoulder. Dersu was leaning over me.

" Stand on knees," he ordered me.

Obediently I propped myself on my arm. Dersu covered me with his piece of tent canvas and started piling reeds on top of me. I felt warmer at once. Water began to trickle. Dersu for a long time kept walking round, piling up snow, and trampling it underfoot.

I began to feel a little warmer, and then fell into a heavy, drowsy condition. Suddenly through it I heard the voice of Dersu :

" Captain, move up."

I mastered myself by an effort, and squeezed a little aside. The Gold crept in under the canvas, lay down by my side, and started covering us both with his leather jacket. I stretched out my hand, and on my feet felt a pair of fur moccasins that I knew.

" Thank you, Dersu," I said. " Cover yourself up."

" No matter, captain," he replied. " Now no fear ; my reed now strong ; wind no break him."

The more the snow piled up on us, the warmer it became in our improvised hut. The trickling from above stopped. We could hear the howling of the gale outside. It sounded like the droning of bagpipes and the tolling of the knell for the dead. Then I began to dream of queer dances, that I was slowly falling somewhere, down . . . down . . . and at last was overwhelmed by a long and overpowering sleep.

Like that we slept, I dare say, twelve hours. Suddenly I awoke, and noticed that I was alone.

" Dersu ! " I called out in fear.

" Bear ! " I heard his voice outside. " Time bear come out of den ; time go own den ; sleep long time in strange den."

I crawled out as quickly as I could and involuntarily shaded my eye with my hand. All around was white with snow. The air was fresh and clear. It was freezing. Across the sky there floated ragged clouds. Here and there the blue sky could be seen. Although it was all dusk and murky around, I felt that the sun would soon be out. The reeds, beaten down by the snow, lay in rows. Dersu managed to collect a few dry bits of rubbish and succeeded in getting a small fire alight, on which he was drying my boots.

Now I understood why Dersu had forbidden me to cut the reeds all round. He had twisted the uncut places into bunches, and with the girdles and bit of cord lashed down our reed hut to prevent it being blown away by the gale.

The first thing I did was to thank him for saving my life.

" Us go together, us work together ; no need thank," and then, as though wishing to change the subject :

THE BLIZZARD ON THE LAKE

" Last night many man die."

I knew that the ' men ' he meant were feathered.

After the blizzard the plain really seemed lifeless. The geese, gulls, duck, and all the birds had disappeared.

After that we broke up our shelter, took our guns, and went to look for the isthmus. It turned out that our camp was not very far away. In crossing the swamp we had passed it a little on the lake side, and then turned towards the east, towards the Lefu.

The swamps showed up as big white pools against the dark yellow background, covered with snow. It was splendid going, as the wet ground was frozen enough to support a man's weight. We soon came out on to the river and within an hour were in camp.

Olentiev and Marchenko had not worried about us. They thought that on the side of the lake we had probably found some houses and got shelter for the night. I changed, drank some tea, lay down by the fire, and fell into a sound sleep. I dreamt that I was again out in the storm among the swamps, with the blizzard raging round me. I called out in my sleep and flung my blanket off me. It was evening. In the sky the stars were brightly shining, and the Milky Way stretched clearly across the heavens. The breeze had freshened during the evening, fanned the flames of the fire, and was scattering sparks about the place. Dersu was asleep on the other side of the fire. Marchenko was getting supper ready, and was just about to arouse us both.

The next morning there was a sharp frost, and all the water was frozen, while lumps of frozen snow, *shuga* as we call it, were floating down the river. It took us the whole day to cross the streams of the Lefu. We were constantly finding ourselves in backwaters, and obliged to turn back. Going for nearly a couple of miles along our stream we ran into another, narrow and winding. At the point where it joined the main river was a conical hill, covered with oak scrub, and there we had our last bivouac. From there was a straightforward journey to Chernigovka, where we should find the rest of the expedition with the horses.

When we left the camp, Dersu asked Olentiev to help him drag the boat ashore. He then cleaned it thoroughly, wiped it down with bunches of rush, turned it upside down, and left it. I realized that he did that to provide for the chance arrival of some wayfarer who might need it.

In the morning we said good-bye to the Lefu, and the same afternoon came to the village of Dmitrovka, on the far side of the Ussurian railway. As we crossed the track, Dersu stopped, touched the rails with his hand, looked up and down the line, and said :

" Hm ! Me heard this. Men all round much talk ; now understand."

In the evening we found billets. The Gold did not want to go indoors, but preferred to stay outside to sleep in the open as usual. In the evening I missed him and went to look for him.

Although the night was dark, thanks to the fallen snow it was possible to distinguish things. The stoves were alight in all the houses, as I could see from the whitish smoke that rose from the chimneys and mounted slowly to the heaven. The whole village was smoking. Through the windows beams of light lit up the masses of snow. On the other side, near the stream, a fire was visible. I guessed it was Dersu's camp, and walked towards it. The Gold was sitting over the fire, pensive.

" Come inside and have some tea," I said to him.

He did not answer, but put a question himself :

" Where go to-morrow ? "

I replied that we were going to Chernigovka, and from there to Vladivostok, and invited him to join us. I promised to return to the *taigá* before long, and offered him a salary. We were both pensive. I do not know what he was thinking, but I felt my heart sink. I started telling him how comfortable and convenient life is in the towns. Dersu listened in silence. At last he sighed, and said :

" No thanks, captain. Me no can go Vladivostok. What

work me do there? No shooting; no trap sables; town life —me soon die."

As a matter of fact, I thought, the woodsman cannot live in towns, and was I not doing wrong in trying to seduce him from the life in which he had grown up?

Dersu was silent. He was evidently pondering over what he was going to do next. Then, as though answering his thoughts, said:

" To-morrow me go straight," and he pointed to the east. " Go four suns; come Daubihé, then come Ulahé, then Fuzin. Dzub-Gin, as we Golds call Sihoté-Alin, and the sea. He hear that side by sea much things; sables there, deer too there."

Long we sat and chatted by the fire. The night was still and cold. Afar the gentle breeze rustled the foliage of the oak clump, that had not yet fallen. In the village all were asleep long since, except in the house where I was stopping with my companions; there was still the light of a fire. The constellation of Orion pointed to midnight. At last I arose, said good-bye to the Gold, and went back to my hut to sleep. I felt a restless disquiet overcome me. In that short time I had become so attached to Dersu that now it hurt me to part from him. And with that thought I dozed off.

Next morning the first thing that I remembered was that Dersu was going to part from us. After a glass of tea, I thanked our host and went outside. The riflemen were ready to start, and Dersu was with them.

At first glance I saw he was prepared for a long journey. His haversack was packed tight, his girdle stretched to the utmost, and his moccasins already on his legs.

When we had gone about a mile from Dmitrovka, Dersu stopped. The moment of parting had come.

" Good-bye, Dersu," I said to him, pressing his hand. " God grant you everything of the best. I can never forget what you have done for me. Farewell! Perhaps we shall meet again one of these days."

Dersu said good-bye to the soldiers, nodded his head to me,

and started off into the clumps to the left. We stood there a moment, and I watched him disappear. A couple of hundred yards from us was a hummock covered with scrub. In five minutes he had reached it. His outline stood  out sharply against the light background of the sky, with his haversack on his shoulders, and his gun and prop in his hand. At that moment the sun came out from behind the hills and lit up the Gold. He walked up to the top, where he stopped a moment, turned towards us, waved his hand, and disappeared over the brow. I gulped. I felt that I had lost someone near and dear to me.

" A good fellow, that," commented Marchenko.

" Yes, pity there aren't more like him," said Olentiev.

' Farewell, Dersu ! ' thought I. ' You saved my life. That I can never forget.'

By dusk we reached Chernigovka and rejoined the detachment. The same evening I left for Vladivostok, to go back to my headquarters.

Second Expedition

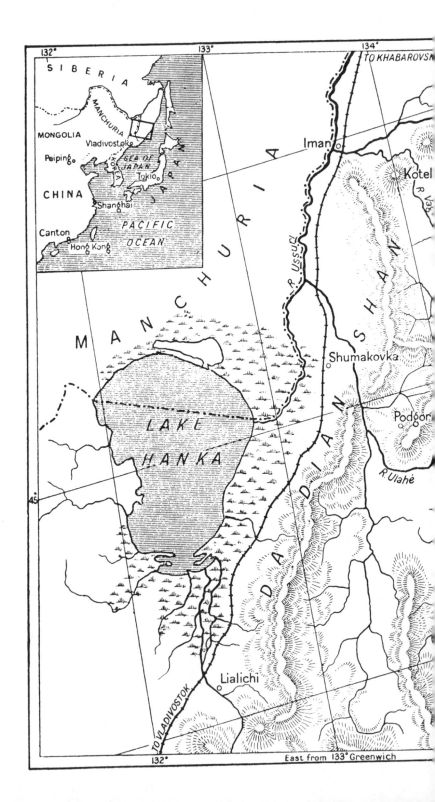

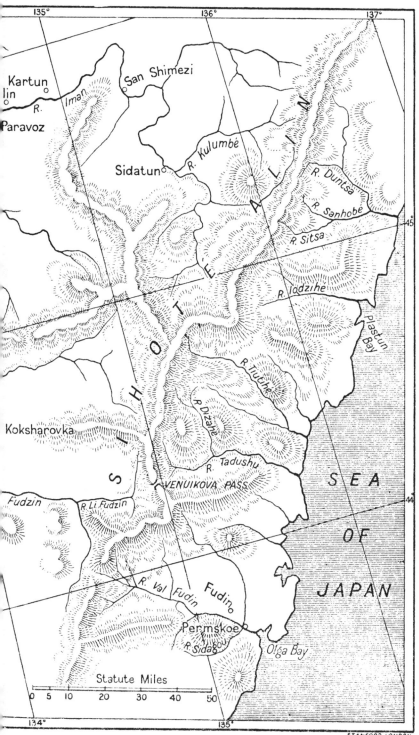

CHAPTER VII : IN THE *TAIGÁ* AGAIN

FOUR years rolled by. I had been moved from Vladivostok to Khabarovsk, and soon after I had taken up my new duties I was invited by the Russian Geographical Society to organize an expedition to explore the Sihoté-Alin, the ridge which runs down between the river Ussuri and the coast, and the coastal belt from Olga Bay northwards as far as time would permit, and also the upper reaches of the rivers Ussuri and Iman.

The object of the expedition was the study of the natural history of the region, of which our information was confined to the casual observations of a handful of travellers. All that was known of the shore to the north of Olga Bay was from naval officers who had been surveying the coast.

The selection of personnel and material and organization in general took a good couple of months. I had a staff of three assistants, and was permitted to select ten soldiers from the garrison. I chose half a dozen Siberian riflemen and four Ussurian Cossacks. The Siberians were selected not for their social qualifications, but because they were resourceful men accustomed to roughing it. There took part in the expedition also Forest Officer N. A. Palchevski as botanist.

I received my instructions in the middle of March 1906, and on 17 May we left in a special wagon by rail for the station of Shmakovka, which was to be our starting-point, and on the 19th we set forth into the field. It was a brilliant sunny day with a cloudless sky, although the air was heavy with moisture. Everybody was in the best of humour.

This part of the river Ussuri is extraordinarily winding, and if all the meanders were straightened out on the map it would probably take up double as much distance. It was a wet summer, and the low-lying ground was all heavily flooded. We started off along the muddy village road from Shmakovka to Uspenka. All the bridges had been washed away by the spring floods, so it was no easy job crossing the numerous brooks on the road, now swollen into torrents. On arrival at the settlement of Uspenka we billeted ourselves in the school, as it was holiday-time, and the next day came to the Ussuri itself.

The whole valley was under flood, the slightly higher ground standing out as islands, and we could distinguish the river itself only by the swift current and rows of trees protruding from its banks. The villagers who accompanied us to the river told us that they were often isolated by the floods. On consultation, we decided to follow up-stream until we came to a point where the river was confined to one bed, and there to swim across with the horses.

The morning had been overcast and threatened to be wet, but about ten it cleared up. Then we found what we were look-ing for. About three miles from us the river was flowing in a single channel. A number of dry hillocks made it possible for us to make our way right up to the bank.

The horses by now were settled down and had stopped kicking and biting each other. Only the leader was on a halter, the rest following freely, while one of the riflemen brought up the rear to prevent any straying.

When we were level with Mt. Kabarga we turned to the east, to a Chinaman's cabin on the bank of the Ussuri, just where a feeder joins it. By dodging the bogs and working our way from hillock to hillock we managed to reach the woods growing on the bank of the river. By a stroke of luck we found an old boat by the cabin. It was about as watertight as a sieve, but at all events it was a vessel, and considerably helped our crossing, when we had spent about an hour patching it up. We caulked up the cracks somehow or other, nailed the boards together, and improvised rowlocks with pegs and loops, and then launched our craft.

We took over first the packs with the baggage, and

then the men, but the horses had to swim. They would not face the water alone, so someone had to go in and swim across with them. This risky job was taken on by one of the Cossacks, Kozhevnikov. He stripped completely, mounted the best horse of the lot, a grey, and rode boldly into the water, when the riflemen drove all the rest of the animals in after him. Directly the Cossack's horse was out of its depth he slipped off its back, gripped its mane with one hand, and swam across by its side. The other horses then followed. From the bank we could see that Kozhevnikov was cheering his horse on and patting his neck. The swimming horses bared their teeth as they swam, snorting and puffing with distended nostrils. The current was carrying them down stream fairly strongly, but still they made good progress across. Still, it was a question whether or not Kozhevnikov would succeed in getting them all across at the point selected. Lower down there were bushes and trees and the bank was steep and covered with fallen trunks and broken branches.

In ten minutes his horse touched bottom on the far side, then its shoulders appeared out of water, then its back, and its hocks. The water streamed off its mane and tail. The Cossack jumped on to its back again, and rode ashore.

As the horses varied in strength they were strung out across the river, and when the Cossack was riding out on the far bank the last horse was only half-way across. We could see that it was being carried down stream, although it was exerting all its strength to beat the current. Kozhevnikov saw that. He waited till the rest were ashore, and then galloped hard along the bank down-stream. Then, choosing a place free from broken branches, he pushed out into the river and pulled up below the swimming horse, and began to call out to cheer it, but the roar of the water drowned his voice. The grey he was riding pricked up its ears, stretched out its head, and its loud, penetrating neigh sounded across the waters. The swimming animal heard it, changed direction, and in a few minutes struggled out on to the bank. The Cossack gave it a breather, slipped a halter over its nose, and led it back to the others. In the meantime the boat had carried across the rest of the men and baggage.

We continued our march up the river, avoiding the bogs, and soon came to the hills. Relieved at finding terra firma under the feet again, both men and beasts stepped forward with renewed vigour. We passed a small settlement of twenty-five houses called Podgornaya, inhabited by Old Believers, but as it was early we did not stop. The track followed the stream, with forest on the left and floods on the right. We came to another stream to cross, flowing through a narrow but very swampy valley. The men crossed by jumping from tussock to tussock, but it was hard going for the horses. It made me miserable to see the poor brutes plunging up to their girths, and often falling, so that we were obliged to unload them and manhaul the packs across.

When we had got the last horse over, it was late. We marched but a short distance farther, and then stopped to bivouac on the bank of a swift, clear brook.

In the evening the riflemen and Cossacks sat round the camp fire singing. Someone produced an accordion. Looking at their carefree faces, no one would have thought that but a couple of hours previously those men had been fighting their way through a swamp, winded and exhausted. It was evident that they never worried their heads about to-morrow and lived only in the present. But round another fire another group of men were poring over maps, working out the next day's march.

The next morning we decided to give them all a day's rest. There was plenty to do, drying all the things, cleaning the saddles, and resting the horses. The riflemen were busy from the morning; every man of them knew what was wanted, what was not in order, what needed repair.

That day we had an interesting experience watching how the Cossacks catch bees. When we had done tea, one of them took a cup with a little honey left in it, and almost at once a bee appeared, then another, and another, until there were quite a number of them. Some came flying up, while others, loaded with honey, flew off on their return journey. A man named Murzin undertook to find their store of honey. He carefully watched the direction taken by the returning bees, and took up his position on it with a cup of honey. Presently a bee appeared, and when it flew off Murzin watched it carefully till out of sight. Then he moved up in that direction, and repeated it, and so on, step by step, until he, slowly but surely, came to the hive. The bees themselves showed him the way. A job like that calls for patience.

In about an hour and a half Murzin came back and reported that he had found the bees, and round their hive there was so strange a scene that he had come back for his companions. It was a battle between the bees and ants. In a few minutes we were on the path, armed with a saw, an axe, a kettle, and matches. Murzin went ahead and showed the way, till we came to a huge lime growing at an angle of forty-five degrees. Round it were humming the bees, almost the whole swarm. The entrance to the hive was down below, by the roots. On the sunny side they were all clinging together in a sloping mass, and they were also massing round the opening that led into their home, and just opposite them, also in a dense mass, was an army of big black ants. It was interesting to see how these two enemy forces stood facing each other, neither deciding to open the attack. The ants threw out a few scouts, which the bees attacked from the air. The ants squatted, opening their jaws, and put up a vigorous defence. Sometimes they tried a flanking movement in order to attack the bees from the rear, but bees' scouts found them, and a detachment of bees at once flew up to head them off.

We watched the battle with intense interest. Would the ants force their entrance into the hive? Which would give in first? Probably at sunset the two forces would return from the field, to renew the war the next morning. Perhaps it was not the first day of the siege.

It is not known what the issue would have been if the Cossacks had not come up as allies for the bees. They lit a fire, and started

pouring boiling water on the ants. These shrank under this fearful attack, lost their heads completely, and perished in thousands. The bees were in a state of tremendous excitement, and when someone chanced to spill some boiling water on them, the whole swarm rose into the air.

The Cossacks turned and bolted. The bees pursued them, overtook them, and stung them on the head and neck. In a moment not a soul was left within hundreds of yards of the tree. The men stopped a long way off, and stood there, swearing and cursing as Cossacks can, roaring with laughter and chaffing each other. Then suddenly a look of terror came over their faces, and they turned and bolted further still, as hard as they could go.

We decided to leave the bees in peace till they settled down. Towards evening a couple of the men went back to the hive, but

found neither bees nor honey. The nest had been robbed by a bear, and that was the end of our hunt for wild honey.

That night it rained hard till morning, and then the sky remained grey and overcast; heavy clouds crept by, low-lying, covering the hill-tops as with a shroud. More rain was inevitable.

On a long expedition one does not pay attention to the

weather. You are wet through one day, dry the next, and soaked again the next. In fact, if you stopped in camp every wet day, the party would not get veɪy far. We decided to try our luck, and did well. About ten it cleared up a bit, but all day there was alternate rain and sun. The trail, which had dried tolerably, was sodden again and covered with puddles.

Presently we came to some sable traps, some old and some quite freshly made. One was right across the track. Kozhevnikov dragged off the beam and flung it aside. Something was lying under it. It was a cluster of sable bones. Evidently there had been a fall of snow just after the animal had been caught. I wondered why the Chinaman had not come back to inspect his trap before leaving the *taigá*. Perhaps a storm had prevented him reaching it, or perhaps he had been taken ill, and could no longer go on hunting. Long had that captured sable waited its captor, and then when the spring came and the snow thawed, the crows had come and pecked out the eye of the precious little beast, and now all that was left of that valuable creature was a bunch of fur and a few bones.

I thought of Dersu. If he had been with us now he would have told us the whole story, why the sable had been abandoned in the trap.

The dense, mixed forest through which we were so painfully making our way was handsome and picturesque. Some of the trees were immense, real giants of the forest, from 70 to 100 ft. in height with a girth from 7 to 10 ft. The undergrowth was a tangle of *Spiræa chamædrifolia*, L., hazel, *Corylus heterophylla*, Fisch., and the veitch, *Lespedeʒa bicolor*, Turc., and many a trunk covered with moss and lichen. In the damp spots was a mass of luxuriant ferns, some of them a yard across. They looked just like huge green lilies.

The Ussurian *taigá* is rich in flowering plants. Most noticeable is the poisonous white hellebore, *Veratrum album*, L., with coarse, sharp-pointed leaves, the dittany, *Dictamnus albus*, L., with oval, pointed leaves and bright pink flowers, rich in essential oil. Among the grass the deep blue aconite, *Aconitum kuʒnetsovi*, Rehub., stood out boldly, and the lady's slipper, *Cypridedium ventricosum*, Sw., with its big, lancet-shaped leaves, the delicate meadow rue, *Thalictrum filamentosum*, Max., with its bright flowers, fiery red catch-fly, *Lychnis fulgens*, Fisch., with its sessile leaves, and groups of orange globe-flowers, *Trollius lebedaurii*, Reich.

In spite of all our troubles, we could not remain indifferent to the beauties of nature. Artists, botanists, and mere lovers of nature would find here a source of inexhaustible delights.

Before evening that day there put in its first appearance the curse of the *taigá*, flies. The settlers call them *gnus*, horror or abomination, and they are indeed the plague of the forest. Their bite draws blood and the wound itches desperately, and the more it is scratched the worse it becomes. When there are many biting flies about, it is impossible to expose the head for an instant. The flies blind your eyes, become entangled in the hair and ears, crawl up your sleeve, and savagely bite your neck. Your face swells up as though with erysipelas. After a few days the organism acquires a certain immunity and the inflammation subsides.

The men could protect themselves against the flies with netting, but the poor horses had a bad time. The flies bit them on the lips and eyelids. The wretched animals tossed their heads and lashed their tails, but were helpless against their tiny tormentors.

The best protection against the flies is a mosquito-net, worn as a veil. One should never wear a metallic gauze, as that is so readily heated by the sun, and it is better to put up with the flies than to be baked, especially in an atmosphere saturated with moisture. Ordinary kitchen gauze is not strong enough and easily torn ; insects then find their way in through the holes, and then the only way to get rid of them is to take the whole thing off. The best net is made of hair ; it is strong enough and neither tears nor is heated by the sun. Some recommend smearing oneself with vaseline. I have tried it and found it useless, or worse. In the first place insects stick to it, struggle to get free, and tickle like mad. Another inconvenience is that the vaseline melts and trickles down the face and neck, mixing with the perspiration. Various aromatic greases have been recommended, such as oil of cloves or lavender, but they are worse still. They penetrate into the open pores and start stinging like a nettle. The best remedy of all is patience. The *gnus* may drive an impatient, nervous, or irritable man to distraction.

CHAPTER VIII : THE BANDIT

ABOUT midday we came to a point where the river makes a sharp bend to the north, and again turns back towards the east. On the far bank stood a Chinaman's cabinhouse, where a couple of old Chinamen lived, one lame, the other blind. As the river was in flood, we could not ford it, but the Chinamen found us a small boat and we made the horses swim across.

During the past few days the horses had lost a lot of flesh, as they had been working all day and tormented by the flies at night. They were off their feed and clustered round the smoke fires. To ease things for them I decided to send forward part of the baggage by boat in charge of a couple of riflemen, and the Chinese were glad to let us have the boat very cheaply. Directly the boat was in mid-stream, one of the men overbalanced and fell, with the result that the boat capsized. The men could swim, and had no difficulty in making their way to the bank, but the rifles, axes, horseshoes, saws, and smith's tools went to the bottom.

The boat was easily righted, but in the confusion no one marked the spot where the shipwreck occurred.

In our party there were two men who could dive. They spent the rest of the daylight groping with poles and fishing with lines and hooks to pick up the things again, but all in vain.

The next day was spent hunting for the guns in the water. We counted that if only the sun would come out we should be able to see the bottom, but the weather, as luck would have it, was bad. The sky was covered with clouds and it began to drizzle. In spite of that in the afternoon one of the men succeeded in recovering two guns, the smith's tools, horseshoes, and nails. Satisfied with this, I gave orders to resume our march.

Every cloud has its silver lining. As compensation there were fewer flies, so the horses had a rest and were able to take a good feed. We returned the unlucky boat to the Chinamen and at two o'clock were on the road again.

The weather then improved, becoming dry and cool, although the sky remained overcast and clouds hid the sun.

Farther on the Fudzin makes a big loop, and the trail makes a short cut over the hills, crossing a couple of low ridges and a bubbling spring. We halted for lunch by the brook at midday. After a mug of tea, without waiting for the horses to be loaded, I gave my orders and started off ahead along the trail.

In the second half of the day the weather remained grey, but we felt it would not rain, and it is always advisable to take advantage of weather like that. One can get a great deal done and a good distance covered, as it seems to stimulate energy and one does not feel fatigue. The hated *gnus* too disappeared. Flies cannot stay on the wing when there is a wind, but come out in clouds on a still, sunny day, though it is not the sun that they need, but a warm, saturated atmosphere, which accounts for their appearance in swarms about dusk and before rain.

On the second ridge the trail forked. The left branch seemed to me little used, so I chose the right one, leading straight into the forest.

I was amused by the antics of a spotted woodpecker. The lively and nimble bird with his pretty chequered black and white plumage and scarlet cap kept flying from one tree to another, often tapping with his beak on the bark and seeming to listen, as though trying to decide whether it were hollow or not. Seeing me, the artful bird hid behind a trunk and peeped out cautiously with one eye from the other side. On seeing me approach, he flew off with a scream and disappeared among the trees.

Not far off I heard a cuckoo. This sly and wary bird did not sit in one place, but flitted from branch to branch, bobbing his head and flirting his tail in time to his song. Not observing any danger, the cuckoo flew silently past quite close to me, settled on a tree and began again, but suddenly took fright, broke off his monotonous song abruptly, and flew off.

A little farther on I flushed a woodcock. He let me approach quite close, and then suddenly slipped off and flew away close above the ground, skilfully dodging among the treees. In places where the thickets were denser there were grey shrikes. Directly they saw me coming near they started a terrific chattering. They are not big birds, but have a cold, cross expression

and a beak like that of a hawk. They sat one moment on a branch, and at another dropped to the ground and seemed to be pecking at something in the grass, and then again flew up and cleverly hid among the foliage. Near water at the edge of the forest were Chinese orioles and Siberian warblers, both of which betray their presence by their song. The orioles, handsome orange-yellow birds as big as pigeons, sat on the highest trees, but in spite of their size and brilliant plumage, they are very hard to see. The warblers, or Siberian nightingales, preferred the thickets near the water. They are greyish with a red throat, but their voice is not as rich as that of their European cousins, and quickly drops into a chuckling and chatter.

My trail kept bearing to the south. I crossed another brook and started climbing. At one spot I came across an old camp, probably of a Chinese trapper.

The forest became denser, the trees bigger, the occasional thick crown of a Korean so-called cedar, *Pinus koraiensis*, and pointed firs, *Picea ajanensis*, lending it a sombre look. I crossed another low ridge without noticing it, and dropped into a valley with a bubbling brook at the bottom. Tired, I sat down for a breather under a big cedar, and noted the trees around me. Here were the Daurian buckthorn, *Rhamnus dauricus*, with its pointed, oval leaves and small white flowers, the spiny briar, *Rosa pimpinellifolia*, a small shrub with very thorny branches, and a yellow acacia, *Caragana arborescens*, sometimes called the Siberian pea tree, with bright golden corolla. Among the shrubs stood out the giant hemlock, *Angelica daurica*, the herb paris, *Paris quadrifolia*, which we call crow's eye in Russian, with its diverging, narrow, lanceolate leaves, and a special kind of fern, *Pteridium aquilinum* with fronds like the outstretched wings of an eagle, whence its local trivial name of eagle-fern.

Suddenly I heard behind me monotonous, mournful sounds. They came closer and closer, and then suddenly I heard quite close to me, immediately over my head, the noise of wings and a dull cooing. Very quietly I raised my head and saw our East Siberian dove. Inadvertently I let something drop from my hands, and the bird was startled and disappeared at once into the wood. Next I watched the Eastern grey woodpecker, with greyish-green plumage and the scarlet cap of his tribe, wary, nimble, and fussy, obviously anxious because I sat there without moving. The bird kept fluttering from one spot to another, also hiding behind the trunk, as the other pecker did. Then I caught a good view of it, a speckled, big-headed, clumsy bird. It scampered nimbly up the trunks, shelling cedar-nuts, and uttering a penetrating screech, as though to warn the denizens of the forest that there was a man sitting there.

At last, tired of sitting in one place, I started back to meet my party. As I moved, my ear caught a faint, rustling sound. It sounded as though some big animal was cautiously making its way through the wood. I shot the bolt of my rifle. The sound approached.

Holding my breath, I tried to peer through the dense vegetation to catch sight of the approaching creature, when my heart stopped. I saw it was a man.

In the Ussurian *taigá* one must expect at times to meet with a wild beast, but the most dangerous meeting of all is with a man. An animal will bolt from a man, or at least attack only if first attacked itself, and in such cases both beast and hunter know what to do.

But with a man it is different. In the *taigá* there are no witnesses, and for that reason custom has worked out its own technique. When a man sees another man in the forest the first thing he does is to hide behind a tree, and the second to have his rifle at the ready.

For in the *taigá* all carry arms, natives, Chinamen, Koreans, and trappers. Trappers are men who live exclusively by the chase. In most cases their home is maintained by a father, brother, or some other near relative. With such a man it is most interesting to travel in the forest, to have the benefit of the experience of a lifetime. He knows where the animals have their lairs and how to circumvent them. The art of finding his way, of fixing a dry lodging for the night in all weathers, of silently and swiftly finding his quarry, of imitating the cries of animals, all these arts the trapper has at his finger-tips.

But there is another type of man in the *taigá*, the so-called 'business man,' like the *chevalier d'industrie* of the French. Just

as the true trapper is always a good fellow, so is the business man dangerous and to be avoided. He creeps through the *taigá* not on the trail of animals but 'for business.' Besides his rifle he usually carries a shovel and a bottle of acid in his knapsack. He is hunting for gold, but ready at a moment's notice to hunt also 'blackcock,' that is Chinamen, and 'swans,' that is Koreans, nor is he squeamish about stealing a boat or shooting a cow and selling the meat for venison.

An encounter with such a 'business man' is far more dangerous than with any animal, and one must at once be on the defensive. The slightest inadvertence may be fatal. Experienced trappers can tell at a glance whether they are dealing with a respectable fellow or a bandit like that.

There was no mistaking the bandit in the man I saw before me. He was wearing a strange blend of costume, half Chinese, half Russian. He was walking obliquely across my path, stooping, and glancing round on all sides. Suddenly he stopped, slid the rifle off his shoulder, and at the same moment slipped behind a tree. I realized that he had seen me. In that situation we stood for several minutes, and then I decided to retreat. Slowly and cautiously I crept back, and in a minute was taking cover behind a big tree. The bandit also withdrew, hiding among the bushes.

I realized then he was afraid of me too. He would not believe that I could be alone, and imagined that he was being watched by a party. I knew that I could shoot him through the scrub where he was hiding, and kill him. I was thinking of doing so, when another thought passed through my mind. He was retreating, afraid, and if I shot him it would be murder. I withdrew a little farther, and looked out. I just caught a glimpse of his blue clothing between the trees, and drew a breath of relief as he faded away.

Carefully, from tree to tree, from stone to stone, I crept back from the danger spot, and as soon as I felt out of range I stepped out openly and hurried back to meet my party.

Within half an hour I came to the spot where the trail forked. I remembered the lesson Dersu had given me, and carefully examined both. The fresh spoor of horses went to the left.

I quickened my pace and in another half an hour came to the Fudzin. Beyond the river I saw a Chinese house surrounded by a fence, and by it my detachment was resting.

The place was called Iolaiza. It was not a trapper's house, but a farm. Beyond stretched the *taigá*, wild, deserted, inhabited only in winter, the sable-trapping season.

The detachment was awaiting my return. I gave orders to unsaddle and pitch camp. This was our last opportunity of laying in stocks of supplies.

After a short rest I went to have a look at the home of a family of natives near the Chinese. The aborigines of Ussuria, inhabiting the central part of the mountain district of the Sihoté-Alin and the coast to the north of Cape Uspenika, call themselves *Ude-hé*. Those who used to live in the southern part of the country have in the course of time become assimilated with the Chinese, and cannot now be distinguished from them. Chinese call them *da-tsy*, which means foreigners, that is neither Russian, Korean, nor Chinese, which has been corrupted by the Russians into *taẓi*, the name our people generally know them by. The characteristics of these assimilated natives are poverty and slovenliness, poverty in their home, poverty in their clothing, poverty in their food.

When I walked up towards their cabin, an old Taz came out to meet me. Clad in tatters, with swimming eyes and sores on his head, he greeted me, and in his voice I could hear fear and submissiveness. Near the cabin some children were playing with the dogs. Their bodies were completely unclothed.

The cabin was old and tumbledown ; here and there the clay had peeled off the walls ; the old paper on the window, yellow with age, was torn ; on the dusty *k'angs* lay a few fragments of matting, and on the wall hung some smoke-begrimed, discoloured rags. On every side neglect, dirt, and squalor.

Formerly I had thought that all this was from sloth, but I have since come to the conclusion that the poverty of the natives is due to other causes, in particular their position among the Chinese settlers. From what I heard on inquiry, I learnt that the owner of the Chinese farm of Iolaiza was a *tsai-dun*, that is lord of the river, in other words a capitalist. All the natives living on the Fudzin get things from him on credit, opium, spirit, provisions, and clothing. In return they are obliged to pay him in the proceeds of their hunting, sables, antlers, ginseng, and so on. The result is that the natives have fallen into a bottomless debt. It has happened more than once that, as a result of such a debt, they have lost their wives and daughters, and it has happened that they have sold themselves into other hands. These aborigines having adopted Chinese culture could not absorb it, and succumbed to the influence of the Chinese themselves. As farmers and tillers of the soil they could not live, and they forgot the arts of the hunter and trapper. The Chinese have taken advantage of their spiritual poverty and made themselves indispensable to them. From that moment the natives lost all independence and became converted into slaves.

On my way back I missed the path and came to the Fudzin, where I saw two Chinamen fishing for pearls. One stood on the bank and with all his might drove a long pole into the bottom of the river, and then the second climbed down it into the water. With his left hand he clung to the pole and with his right collected mussels. They found the pole necessary owing to the force of the current. The diver does not stay under longer than half a minute, not because of any difficulty in holding his breath for longer, but owing to the low temperature of the water which makes him come up quickly. For that reason the Chinese dive with their clothes on.

I sat on the bank to watch them at work. After his short stay under water the diver warms himself in the sun for five minutes. As they take it in turns, it works out that each of them goes under not more than ten times in an hour. In that time all they succeeded in fishing out were eight shells of the pearl-bearing freshwater mussel, *Margaritana margaritifera*, L., in which lot they did not find a single pearl. In reply to my questions the Chinamen explained that on the average one shell in fifty contains a pearl. In the course of the summer they get a couple of hundred pearls for a sum of five or six hundred roubles. These Chinamen did not confine themselves to the Fudzin, but travelled about the country, looking for old, shady streams. The best river for pearls, they said, was the Vaku.

Presently they stopped their diving, put on dry clothes, and drank some hot spirit. Then they sat down on the bank and started smashing the shells with a hammer to look for pearls. I remembered then that I had previously come across piles of smashed mussel shells on the banks of rivers, and wondered how they came there. The process is, of course, most wasteful. They smash the shells and throw them away on the spot, and out of eighty shells put aside only two as of value. However carefully I examined them, I could not find the pearl until they showed it to me. They were little lumps of shining, dirty-grey colour. The layer of mother-of-pearl was far brighter and prettier than the jewel itself.

When the shells were dry the Chinamen carefully detached the little gems from the valve and put them in a little leather bag.

While I had been to see the natives and then watched the Chinamen fishing for pearls, the evening had crept on. In our house the lamp was lit.

After some supper I asked the Chinese about the road to the sea. Either they did not want to tell me where the trapper's cabins were, or they had some other motive for concealing the truth, but I noticed that they gave evasive answers. They told me that it was ages since anyone had been to the sea by the river Li-Fudzin, that the trail was all overgrown and filled with fallen trees. They thought that we should turn back, but seeing that we were decided to continue on the road, they started telling us all sorts of impossible things, and to frighten us with stories about bears, tigers, and bandits. In the evening Granatman went to the Tazi to try to induce one to come as a guide, but the Chinese forestalled him, and forbade the natives to show us the way. Consequently we were thrown upon our own resources, and for guidance had nothing but unsatisfactory replies to our questions.

The next morning we left Iolaiza fairly early. We followed a narrow trail at first by the hills on the left bank of the Fudzin and then, avoiding a small, marshy bit of woodland, we dropped back into the valley. The eroded soil, the banks of gravel, and the holes, all pointed to the fact that the river often overflows its banks and floods the valley.

The day turned out hot and oppressive, and we all felt languid. There was not a breath of wind, and the saturated atmosphere seemed petrified, and all living things inert and hidden away.

By the side of the track sat a kind of raptorial bird, sitting with its beak open. He too felt the heat.

The further we left the houses, the worse became the trail. Near the forest it divided into two ; one fork, somewhat rather more trodden, went straight ahead ; the other, clearly less used, turned into the *taigá*. We stopped in indecision. Which should we take ?

While we were thus considering, suddenly there stepped out of the wood a Chinaman. He looked about forty years of age, and from his sunburnt face, torn clothing, and worn-out sandals, we judged he had come from afar. On his back hung a heavy knapsack, on one shoulder he carried a rifle, and in his hand a stick to use as an aiming-prop. Catching sight of us, he was startled, and started to run away, but the Cossacks called out to him to stop. The Chinaman cautiously and timidly approached them, but soon he was reassured and began to answer our questions. From his words we learnt that the more trodden track would lead us to the river Tadusha, which falls into the sea a good long way north of Olga Bay, but the track on which we were standing went first to the stream Chao-Sun, and then, crossing a lofty ridge, comes out onto the river Sinantsa, which falls into the upper reaches of the Fudzin. At Sinantsa the track again divides. One fork, available for horses, goes to the Yan-mut-hou-zu, a tributary of the Ulahé, but the old track goes up into the mountains after six fords. That was ours, and we must be careful not to overlook it.

So we thanked the Chinaman for his information and stepped out with confidence. Human habitations, meadows, fields, open valleys, all that was now left behind.

Every time I enter a forest which stretches for several miles I have an involuntary feeling of something like humility. Such a primitive forest is a kind of elemental force, and it is not to be wondered that even the aborigines, these simple nomads of the forest, before crossing its threshold which separates it from the inhabited world, first utter prayers to their gods and beg protection against the evil spirits which haunt the wooded wastes.

The farther you go in, the more the ground is encumbered with fallen trunks. In the mountains the layer of productive soil is very thin, so that the roots cannot strike deep but spread along the surface, with the result that the trees cannot stand up against the gales and are easily blown over. That is why the *taigá* of the Ussurian district is such a mass of prone trunks. A fallen tree raises its roots into the air, all entangled with earth and stones, and when these are alongside each other they make formidable barricades five or six yards in height. That explains why the forest tracks are so winding, as the wayfarer is con-

stantly making detour round these obstacles. All this must be taken into account in estimating distances, which work out in fact at least half as long again as they appear on the map. Down in the valleys the trees are more firmly rooted.

Here one can see monsters standing from eighty to over a hundred feet in height, with a girth from twelve to fifteen feet. Often enough old poplars are chosen by bears for their winter quarters, and sometimes a hunter will find two or even three bears hibernating in a single hollow tree.

In the valleys the forest is sometimes so dense as completely to screen the sky, and then there is perpetual twilight, always damp and cool. Dawn and dusk do not synchronize in the forest and in the open. Within, if but a cloudlet veil the sun, the forest forthwith becomes gloomy and the weather seems grey and overcast, and that is why on a bright and sunny day, when the trunks are illuminated by beams of sunshine, and the bright green foliage and shining pine needles, the flowers, the moss, and variegated lichens all have so decorative an effect.

Unfortunately, all the beauties of fine weather are poisoned by the biting flies. It is difficult to convey an idea of the torment suffered by men in the *taigá* from the *gnus*. It cannot be described. It must be felt.

We marched for three hours without a halt, till we heard the sound of water on our left, probably the Chao-Sun mentioned by the Chinaman. The sun had reached its peak and was blazing mercilessly. The horses dragged their paces, with drooping head and laboured breathing. The atmosphere was so heated that even in the shade of the mighty cedars there was no cool air. Not an animal, not a bird made a sound. The only living things visible were the insects, whose liveliness increased with the heat.

I had intended resting at the top, but the horses refused their feed and crowded to the smoke-fires. Sitting in such a place under such circumstances is worse than marching, so I gave orders to saddle up and carry on. About three in the afternoon the trail brought us to a hill covered with screes, where began the rise to the crest. It was all as the Chinaman had described.

At the top of the pass was a joss-house, not a decent stone building, but so ramshackle an affair that, but for some red rags tied to a tree nearby, one would not have noticed its existence. It consisted merely of a couple of flat stones set up on edge and a bigger one across the top, and nothing more. Inside were some crude carvings of gods and some wooden boards with religious inscriptions. Careful search round the stone showed the charred remains of paper candles, ashes, a pinch of rice, a little piece of sugar, and a few other simple sacrifices to the God of the Forests and Mountains, the guardians of the growth of wealth.

On the far side of the ridge the trail brought us to a trapper's cabin on the left bank of the Sinantsa. The owner was not at home, so I decided to stop and wait for him, and gave orders to pitch camp.

About five in the evening the owner arrived. Directly he caught sight of the soldiers he was terrified and tried to run away, but they caught him and brought him to me. He soon saw that

77

we wished him no harm and willingly answered our questions. He was a native, Taz as we call them, about thirty years of age, his face heavily pitted with smallpox. I gathered from his words that he was in the employment of our friend at Iolaiza, or rather deep in his debt. He had not an idea of the amount of his debt, but knew it was an outrage. Our suggestion that he should come with us to the Sihoté-Alin as a guide he rejected on the grounds that the Chinese would kill him if they heard of it. I did not insist, but gathered that we were on the right road. To put the Taz in a good humour with us, I made him a present of twenty-five cartridges for his old *berdianka*, which so delighted him that he started a song and dance, and then said he would show us the way as far as the next cabin, where there were two Chinese trappers.

It was still long before dark, so I took my rifle and went for a stroll round. About a mile from the camp I sat on a stump and listened. In the hours of dusk bird life is always more alert than during the day. The small birds perch on the highest twigs so as to catch the last glimpse of the dying sun and bid it good night. I was quickly absorbed in the contemplation of nature and completely lost sight of the fact that I was quite alone and far from the bivouac.

Suddenly I heard a rustle by my side. In that still air it seemed loud and threatening. I was alert instantly, expecting to see some big animal come by, ready to be on the defensive if necessary, but it turned out to be only a badger. He was jogging along at a gentle trot, stopping every now and then to nose about in the grass, passing so close to me that I could have touched him with the end of my rifle. He made his way down to the brook, lapped a drop or two of water, and waddled along farther. Again all was still.

Suddenly a sharp, penetrating, spasmodic whistle rang out behind me. I turned and saw a pica, *Lagomys hyperboreus*, a little rodent with a wide distribution all over eastern and north-eastern Siberia. It is rather like a small rabbit, without the long ears, of a greyish-brown colour. It haunts the screes and talus of the mountain-sides, and is diurnal in habits, though extremely wary and shy. It is very hard to kill it without spoiling the skin, as it would be torn to ribbons by a single shot.

My movement started the little chap, and he bolted at once into his earth, which showed how alert he constantly was, not lulled into security by the stillness of the forest. Then I saw a chipmunk, *Tamias asiaticus orientalis*, which we call *burunduk*, a little striped ground-squirrel, lively as a kitten. The little fellow popped about the log, slipped up into a tree, down again, and vanished in the grass. It is yellowish in colour, with five black stripes down the back and flanks.

I noticed that the chipmunk kept returning to the same spot and every time carried something. When he went off his cheek pouches were crammed, but when he appeared on the surface again his mouth was empty. That interested me, so I crept closer to watch. On the big log there were lying some dried fungi and nuts.  As it was too early for either, it was evident that the *burunduk* had brought them out of his burrow. Why? Then I remembered that Dersu had told me that chipmunks lay in big reserves of food, sometimes enough to keep them for two years. To prevent them rotting, they bring them out and air them in the sun every now and then, taking them back into their burrow in the evening.

After sitting a little while longer, I moved on a little distance farther. I kept coming across freshly overturned logs, in which I recognized the work of a bear. That is a favourite trick of theirs. On his rambles about the forest, when he comes upon a fallen trunk, he rolls it over to find some dainty beneath. The Chinese pretend that he wants to dry the logs, exposing first one side to the sun and then the other.

On my way back it so happened that I came back on to my

own trail. I recognized the huge cedar where I had stopped, crossed the brook by the same fallen tree, and came to the same fallen log where I had seen the chipmunk. But this time in the place of it slittle burrow was a yawning hole. The nuts and fungi were scattered all over the place, and on the freshly turned ground I saw the tracks of a bear. The story was plain as a pikestaff. Bruin had looted the chipmunk's nest, swallowed up his stores of food, and very likely the owner himself.

Meanwhile evening was drawing on. The light went out, the air darkened, and the trees, both near and far, all assumed a common tint that cannot be described as green, as grey, or black. All around was so silent that I could hear my ears tingling. A beetle hummed by. I walked carefully to avoid stumbling. Suddenly on one side of me I heard a loud noise. Some large animal was standing ahead of me, sniffing. My instinct was to shoot, but I controlled myself. The startled brute might bolt, but also might charge. I waited a minute, and it seemed an eternity. I recognized it as a bear, energetically sniffing the air. I stood quite still, not stirring a finger, till I could not bear it any longer, and I carefully stepped to the left. I had not gone two paces when I heard the heavy breathing of the animal and the crackle of broken twigs, and my heart stopped beating. Instinctively I raised my rifle and fired in its direction. The crashing noise, becoming fainter, told me that the brute was bolting. A moment later I heard an answering shot from the camp.

Then I turned and went on in my former direction, and in half an hour saw the bivouac. The bright flames showed up the ground, the shrubs, and the trunks of the trees, and men were sitting round the fire. The pack-horses were peacefully grazing, with smoke-fires smouldering near them. As I approached the dogs raised a din and dashed forward, but, seeing me, stopped their row and slunk back.

When the sun went down the big flies disappeared and the little night flies came out, tiny, biting midges, hardly visible to the naked eye. The first symptom of their presence is a burning feeling in the ears. Then it feels as though a prickly cobweb were stretched across the face, but the itching is most maddening on the forehead. The little brutes find their way into the ears, the hair, the nostrils, the mouth. Men swear and spit, and wipe their faces with their sleeves. The soldiers put handkerchiefs under their caps to give at least some protection to their neck and brow. I was tormented by thirst and begged for a mug of tea.

" You can't drink," said one Cossack, Epov by name, as he handed me a mug.

I raised it to my lips and then saw that the surface was covered with a sort of dust.

" What's that ? " I asked.

" *Gnus*," he answered, " overcome by the steam and fallen into the tea."

At first I tried to blow the dead flies away; next I tried to take them out with a spoon, but the moment I stopped the mug was filled up again with the little brutes. The Cossack was right. I did not succeed in getting my drink, so poured the tea on to the ground and crawled into my mosquito-net.

After some supper the men tried to fix themselves up for the night. Some of them were too lazy to put up their mosquito-nets and lay down to sleep on the open ground, covering themselves up with their blankets. For a long time they kept tossing and cursing, and smacking their heads, but it did not avail them against the myriads of flies, which penetrated into the slightest crevice. At last one of them could stand it no longer.

" The devil take you ! " he called out, flinging out his arms and uncovering himself.

A general laugh burst out. He was not the only one who could not sleep, but nobody wanted to be the one to get up and make the smoke-fires. In a couple of minutes the bonfire was blazing. The riflemen were laughing and chaffing each other, and grunting and swearing at the same time. Little by little peace was restored and once again silence reigned. Millions of mosquitoes and midges crowded on to my netting, and the sound of their humming lulled me into a deep sleep.

The noise of conversation awoke me next morning at five.

From the snorting of the horses and the noise they made when whisking their tails, and the oaths of the Cossacks, I divined that there were plenty of flies about. I dressed hurriedly and stepped out of my net, when an interesting picture met my eyes. Over the whole camp there circled uncountable clouds of midges. The unfortunate horses, thrusting their muzzles right into the heart of the smoke-fires, were whisking their tails and frantically throwing their heads about.

In the place where there had been the fire, on the ash was a thick layer of dead flies. They had fallen into it in such uncountable swarms that they had actually put it out.

There are only two ways of escaping from fly, by big smoke-fires or quick movement. As sitting in one place is not to be recommended I gave orders to load up the horses, and went up to a tree to pick up my rifle, which I had leant against it. I did not recognize my own weapon. It was covered with a thick, ashy-grey coating of tiny flies and midges, which had stuck to the oil. I hurriedly grasped my instruments and, without waiting for the horses, started off at a brisk step along the trail.

Presently the road forked. Here the native stopped. He pointed to the road for us to follow, and turning to me, said :——

" Captain ; look-see road well ; horses go, you go ; horses no go, you no go."

To the unaccustomed ear this statement would have sounded a mere collection of words, but I understood his pidgin-Russian at once. He meant that we should follow the broad trail used by horses and avoid the narrow path.

When the horses arrived the Taz turned back, and we followed the new trail up the Sinantsa.

In this district the hills are covered with a dense mixed growth, the cedar predominating. The washed banks of the stream, the quantity of fallen trunks carried down by the current, the holes and cavities, overturned trees with clods of earth, stones, and grass still clinging to their roots, all spoke eloquently of the recent floods.

The rivers of the Ussurian region have one feature in common, that after a flood they change their channel. This made it difficult to find the path that had been washed away, so I sent out men to make casts on all sides, and eventually the trail was found and we carried on.

On the road we came across the spoor of animals, including plenty of tracks of tiger. Twice we moved deer and pig, but, firing hurriedly, we always missed and interfered with each other.

The forests of Ussuria appear deserted, mainly owing to the absence of song birds. Here and there I saw the Ussurian jay. These cheeky and restless birds kept flitting from one branch to another, accompanying us with their raucous screams. As I wanted to have a good look at one, I tried to come up closer to it. The jay at first tried to hide in the foliage, and did not fly away until they realized that I was stalking them. The flash of the blue wing feathers and the white rump produce the impression of a handsomer bird than it really is.

From time to time we heard a strange sound, like a sort of drumming, and it did not take me long to identify the bird that made it. It was the great black woodpecker. Wary and timid, black as a raven, with a scarlet cap, it looks at first glance like a small crow. With harsh cries it flew from tree to tree, hiding behind the trunk as do its congeners.

In a moist thicket near the river there were some hazel-hen. Frightened by the dogs, they flew off into the thick bush and began whistling to each other. Diakov and Melian wanted to try to shoot a few, but the birds would not let them come within gunshot, and I persuaded the men not to waste time on them.

On one tree was sitting a large bird of prey, as though for its portrait. It was the lord of the night, the great Ussurian eagle owl. It was sitting on a dead branch of a fir, gazing round with startled eyes. As soon as we approached it flew off and we did not see it again.

The geology of the valley of the Sinantsa is very simple. It is a tectonic valley, running at first from the south-west and later turning to the north along the Sihoté-Alin.

The deeper we went into the hills, the more frequent were the rapids. The trail kept crossing the stream, which was rendered easy by the frequent fallen trunks which made natural bridges. That showed that it was only a footpath, so, remembering the warning of the Taz, I doubled my attention, and soon noticed that we were bearing more and more to the south. There was no doubt that we had made a mistake, and that our proper trail had turned aside, and this one, more used, was undoubtedly taking us to the source of the Ulahé.

We reached the trapper's cabin towards evening. The owner was not at home and there was no one to ask. On a council of war we decided to leave the horses there to camp for the night, and to throw out scouts to make a reconnaissance. Granatman went ahead, Merzliakov to the east, while I turned back to try to pick up the trail we had mislaid.

Towards evening, when the breeze dropped, again fly appeared. The tiny bloodsuckers savagely attacked both man and beast.

The day was over. The last rays of daylight had flickered out from the sky, but it was no cooler, for the heated earth continued to radiate its warmth even after dark. The air was fragrant from the forest herbs, and dense vapours rose from the stream. The Cossacks lit a ring of smoke-fires round the camp, and both men and horses crowded to the smoke and avoided the fresh air. When all essential duties were finished I told them to put up my mosquito-house, and took refuge beneath its saving walls. In an hour it was quite dark. Then out came the moon and with its gentle, as though phosphorescent, light lit up the forest. Soon after food the whole camp turned in to sleep, only the dogs, horses, and sentries staying awake.

Next morning before it was light I took a Cossack and started off. It soon grew light, the moon turned pale and feeble, the shadows vanished, and softer tones appeared. The dawn breeze fluttered the tree-tops and aroused the feathered inhabitants.

The sunlight climbed higher up the sky, and then suddenly the life-giving rays of the sun itself burst out from behind the crest, and at once lit up the whole scene, trees, bushes, and grass, all glistening with dew.

Near the first cabin we did in fact find a small track leading to the side, which brought us to a second, similar cabin, where we found a couple of Chinamen, one young, the other an old man, the former a trapper, the latter a hunter for ginseng. The younger was a strongly built fellow of about five-and-twenty, and from his face it was clear that he enjoyed life, was happy and contented with his lot. He was constantly laughing, and all the time playing some prank. The old man was tall, cadaverous, and more like a mummy than a living man. From his heavily lined and wrinkled skin and weather-beaten face and grey hair I guessed he was in his seventies. Both were wearing blue jackets, blue trousers, gaiters, and *uly*, but the younger man's clothes were new and cared for, while the old fellow's were old and crumpled. The first wore a straw hat that he had bought somewhere, the other a home-made one of birch bark.

They were frightened at first, but reassured when I explained what was the trouble. They gave us some gruel and tea. From our inquiries I gathered that we had come to the foothills of the Sihoté-Alin, that farther on there was no road at all to the sea, and that the trail which the detachment had followed led to the basin of the upper Ulahé.

Then I climbed up a tall tree, and what I saw there amply confirmed the plan the old man had sketched for me in the dust with a stick. In the east I could see the jagged outline of the crest of Sihoté-Alin, about two days' trek, I should estimate it. To the north as far as the eye could reach there was a gently rolling lowland covered with immense virgin forests. In such vast growths there is always something mysterious and grim. Man seems so small, so lost and insignificant. To the south and further to the west the country became more hilly. A second crest ran parallel to the Sihoté-Alin, behind which probably flowed the Ulahé, but it could not be seen. I was not a little surprised at the type of country I had seen. I thought that the nearer we approached to the water-shed, the more marked would be the character of the country. I had been expecting to see lofty mountains and sharp outlines of isolated peaks. In reality it was the reverse. Round near Sihoté-Alin there were sloping hills, cut by a few small streams. It was the result of erosion.

Orientating myself satisfactorily, I came down the tree and at once sent my Cossack back to Rutkovsky with the news that I had picked up the trail, while I waited with the Chinamen. These, knowing that the detachment could not arrive till the evening, started on their day's work. I did not feel inclined to stop behind all by myself, so went with them.

The old man carried himself with great dignity and talked little, but his companion was a regular chatterbox. He told me that in the *taigá* they had a ginseng plantation and that was where they were then going. I was so interested in what he was telling me that I lost my sense of direction, and without their help I doubt if I could have found my way back to their hut. We walked across the flanks of the hills for an hour, crossed a cliff, and then dropped into a valley. On the way we passed several mountain torrents and deep gullies, with snow still lingering in them, and then at last we reached our destination. It was a northern slope of a mountain, covered with thick woodland.

The reader will be quite wrong if he pictures to himself a ginseng plantation in the form of a garden with regular sown crops. A place where some roots of ginseng have been found is looked upon as suitable, and here they bring all their other roots. The first thing that I saw were screens of cedar bark to protect the precious plant from the scorching rays of the sun, and to keep the soil cool there were beds of ferns planted at the sides, and a small irrigation canal brought water from the brook.

On arrival at the garden the old man fell on his knees, folded his arms with the palms together, pressed them to his brow, and twice bowed low to the ground, all the time muttering something to himself, no doubt prayers. Then he stood up, placed his hands on his head, and then started work. The younger man meanwhile had been hanging some red rags on the trees with inscriptions on them.

There is no other plant in the world round which has gathered so many legends and stories. Under the influence of literature or of the stories of the Chinese, I do not know why, but I myself felt some sort of respect for this ordinary-looking representative of the *Araliaceæ*. I knelt down so as to have a closer look at it. The old man understood this in his own way, that I was praying, and from that moment he was entirely at my service.

Both Chinamen set to work. They removed dry branches fallen from the trees, planted a few twigs and watered them. Noticing that too little water was reaching the nursery, they admitted more. Then they started weeding, not taking out all the weeds, but only some. The kind that annoyed them most was *Eleutherococcus*.

Leaving them to their work, I went for a stroll in the *taigá*. Afraid of losing my way, I followed down the stream, so as to be able to come back the same way. When I came back to the ginseng garden the Chinamen had finished their work and were waiting for me. We arrived at their cabin from the other direction, so had evidently returned by another route.

The detachment arrived not long before dark. The Chinamen gave us a little food, although they were rather short themselves. In the evening I succeeded in persuading them to come with us to the Sihoté-Alin and source of the Vai-Fudzin. The old man agreed to come with us, but was not strong enough to go farther than the water-shed, beyond which point the young man would be our guide. It was absolutely necessary for them to go back to the farm and buy some flour and grain. The old man made it a condition that we should not shout at him and quarrel. There was no question of the first, and the second condition was easy to grant.

No sooner was it dark than out came the flies again. The Chinamen lit smoke-fires inside the cabin, and we tucked ourselves up in our nets. With the consoling thought that with the help of our guides we should be able to cross the Sihoté-Alin, we soon fell asleep. Our only care now was the question, would our supplies hold out?

The next morning we were ready and off by eight. The old man led the way, followed by his young companion and a couple of riflemen with axes, and then came the rest of the caravan. The old man carried a long staff in his hands, and marched in silence, pointing out the way and any log that required moving from the path. In spite of frequent delays, our cavalcade made fairly good progress. The Chinamen kept a south-westerly direction for some time, and only after midday turned to the south.

In Ussuria one seldom finds dry, coniferous forest, with pine needles covering the ground, where grass will not grow. Here it was all damp and humid, everything covered with moss, ferns, and osiers.

To-day for the first time we were obliged to halve the rations, and even then our supplies were enough only for a couple of days, and if we failed to find human habitations on the far side of the Sihoté-Alin, we should go hungry. According to the Chinamen there used formerly to be a trapper's cabin at the source of the Vai-Fudzin, but they did not know if it still existed.

I wanted to stop and shoot some food, but the old man refused to be delayed and insisted on carrying straight on. Remembering my promise, I did as he asked, and I must say that the old man kept his word and led us very well. At one place he stopped and pointed out an old track overgrown with grass and shrubs. That was the old route, he told us, by which the Ussurians used to go through to Olga Bay. It was by that route that, in the sixties of the last century, Budishchev and Maximovich had come, and at the thought their portraits rose before my eyes and their description of their journey. Judging from the well-trodden appearance of the trail, there must at one time have been a fair amount of traffic along it, but when the military port was transferred from Nikolaevka to Vladivostok, the Chinese trappers stopped using this trail; it lost its significance and became overgrown.

During these past days our men had been severely tried.

Patches had appeared on ther clothing; their veils were torn and useless; their faces scarred and bleeding, with eczema on their foreheads and round their ears.

The shortage of supplies compelled us to hasten. We cut down the main halt to thirty minutes, and in the afternoon marched till dusk.

Such long spells tired the old man. Directly we stopped to bivouac, he dropped to the ground with a groan, and could not get up again without help. I had a few drops of rum which I carried as an emergency, and this was a good occasion to make use of it. It was for us that the old man had come, and he would have to march all to-morrow, and then face the return journey. I poured the whole flaskful into a mug and handed it to him. His eyes showed gratitude indeed, but he did not want to drink alone, and pointed to my companions. We all combined to persuade him to drink the lot, which he did, and he rolled himself up in his net to sleep. I followed his example.

Listening to the hum of the midges and mosquitoes, I thought of the Biblical story of the plagues of Egypt: ' and there came grievous swarms of flies into the house of Pharaoh.' In a dry country where there are no mosquitoes, the appearance of a swarm would seem a catastrophe, but here in our moist Pri-Amur region, the accursed *gnus* is an everyday phenomenon.

At the first touch of dawn the old man woke me.

" Time go," he said laconically.

Hurriedly munching some cold gruel left over from the last evening, we set off. Now our guide turned sharply to the east. We found ourselves at once in the district of eroded mountains, forerunners of the Sihoté-Alin. They were low hills with gentle slopes. A number of brooks ran in different directions, so that at first it was not easy to find one's orientation and the true direction of the flow of water.

The nearer we came to the crest, the denser was the growth and the more the ground littered with *burelom*, that storm-felled timber which is such a nuisance on the trail. Here for the first time we met with the yew, *Taxus cuspidata*, a relic of the days of sub-tropical flora, which was formerly widely distributed over the whole Pri-Amurian region. It has red bark and reddish wood, red berries, and is like a fir, but the branches grow as in broad-leaved trees.

The undergrowth here consists mainly of *Actinidia kolomikta*, which for some reason the Russian colonists call *kishmish*, which really means compressed, stoneless raisins; then there is honey-suckle, *Lonicera maakii*, a berberis, *Berberis amurensis*, the Manchurian hazel, *Corylus manshurica*, with uneven, or dentate leaves, and the mossy myrtle, *Chamœ daphne calyculata*, with white scales on the leaves and white flowers. Of the flowering plants the most noticeable were pink peonies, *Pœonia albiflora*, collected by the Chinese for medicine, and the Okhotsk hop, *Artagene ochotensis*, with palmate-dentate leaves and violet flowers, and *Clintonia udensis*, the big juicy leaves of which are arranged in a rosette.

Towards dusk we came to the water-shed. The men were all very hungry, and the horses, too, needed rest. The whole livelong day they had gone without either food or halt. Near the camp there was no grass at all. The poor creatures were so dead beat that directly the packs were taken off they lay down. No one would have recognized in them those strong and well-fed beasts with which we had started out from Shmakovka. Now they were scraggy, worn-out old crocks, half starved and tormented to death by flies.

The Chinamen shared with the soldiers the scanty meal they eked out by roasting ferns, with the crumbs of some old grain.

After so light a supper all turned in, so as to forget the pangs of hunger. And they did well, for the next morning our start was fixed for an earlier hour even than to-day.

The next day we broke camp at five in the morning and immediately started climbing the Sihoté-Alin. The rise was gradual and slow. Our guide kept a straight road as far as possible, and we zigzagged only in the stepped places.

The higher we climbed, the more slender became the stream, until it died away completely, though the dull murmur beneath the rocks showed that the springs were still rich in water. Gradually even this began to die down. We could still hear the water trickling in rivulets, like tea out of a teapot, until it fell away to mere drops, and then that stopped too.

In an hour we reached the top, the final slope being short but steep.

At the crest itself, at the foot of an immense cedar, stood a joss, built of bark. The old Chinaman stopped in front of it and bowed to the ground. Then he stood up and, pointing towards the east, pronounced two words :

" River Vai-Fudzin."

That meant that we had reached the divide. Then our old guide sat down on the ground and gave a sign that it was time for a rest.

I took advantage of that to have a stroll over the crest towards the south, and climbed to the top of one of the piles of stones that protruded from the ground in many places, and had a good look round.

The divide here ran from south-west to north-east, the highest point rising to some 3600 ft. above the sea.

To the east, as far as the eye could reach was entirely bathed in fog, from which protruded the higher peaks like islands, while waves of fog advanced towards the mountain crest. To the west the air was pure and clear, which, according to the Chinese, is usually the case. So I satisfied myself that the ridge of Sihoté-Alin acts as a real climatic boundary between the coastal region and the basin of the right affluents of the Ussuri.

I must have stayed up there a good time, for the men were calling for me. The Cossacks had brewed tea. When it was poured out someone exclaimed :

" If only we had some sugar . . ."

" Here's a bit," answered a burly Cossack, and, rummaging in his pocket, produced a grimy lump.

" Where did you wangle that from, my man ? " I asked.

" See-hot-tea all-in-divide,"[1] answered the Cossack promptly with a grin.

The drop on the far side into the Vai-Fudzin was, as I have said, steep. Below us was a deep ravine littered with boulders and fallen trees. The water, tumbling in cascades, had in many places washed out deep cavities, which were hidden by thickets of ferns and formed regular pitfalls. I gave one boulder a push. It rolled down, sweeping away with it a mass of stones, and made a real avalanche.

It was hard work making our way down that gulch, particularly for the horses. The descent took us two hours. At the bottom ran a brook, hardly visible in the tangle of ferns and undergrowth. The water splashed away merrily down the valley, as though rejoicing in its new-found freedom. In the lower reaches it was calmer.

Then appeared another such gully on our right. The ravine had now opened into a narrow valley.

Beyond the divide the coniferous trees became fewer. On the sunny slopes the dominant tree was the Mongolian oak, *Quercus mongolica*, Fisch., but down in the valley the growth was more varied and richer. I noticed the small-leafed Amurian lime, *Tilia amurensis*, Kom., a lover of the skirts of forests and glades ; there was the yellow maple, *Acer ukurundense*, Traut. and Mey, with deeply incised pale leaves, the ashen willow, *Salix cinerea*, L., half tree, half shrub, the winged spindlewood, *Euonymus alata*, like a bush with wings of cork on the trunk and branches. Among the shrubs there was the willow-leafed *Spiræa salicifolia*, L., with bright pink flowers, a special kind of thorn, *Cratægus sanguinea*, Pall., with few and short spines and leaves whitish on the underside ; there was Maak's honeysuckle more than

[1] With apologies, but the pun in the original Russian is just as bad.— Trans.

thirteen feet high, and Our Lady's Herb, as we call thyme in Russian, with recumbent stalk.

The night was warm and still, just such a night as insects love. But the sight that met my eyes made me oblivious to flies, as I gazed enchanted at the fairy scene. The whole air was filled with countless bluish sparks. It was our eastern fire-fly, *Luciola mongolica*, giving its display.

The light they emit is interrupted, each flash lasting not more than a second, but by watching the flashes I could trace the flight of an individual insect. Fire-flies do not all appear at once, but

separately. They say that when the first Russian settlers arrived in this country and saw this flickering light for the first time, they shot at it with their rifles and ran away in terror.

That night the fire-flies were in countless thousands, in millions, it seemed. They were flying about the grass, low near the ground, swarming on the bushes and floating high above the trees. The fire-flies were flashing and the stars were twinkling, a regular fairy dance of light.

Suddenly there was a blinding flash which for an instant lit up the whole country-side, as a large meteor trailed its blazing tail across the sky, scattering into a thousand sparks and vanishing behind the mountains. As at the wave of a magic wand the illumination of the insects went out, and for several minutes there was darkness. Then suddenly in the herbage there appeared a spark again, and in half a minute the air was again filled with the thousands of elfin lanterns weaving their ethereal dances.

But, beautiful as was the night, entrancing as were the fireworks of the insects and the sky, to stay one more minute in the open was impossible. The biting midges plastered themselves upon my neck, my face, my hands, and swarmed into my hair. I bolted back into the house and lay down upon the *k'ang*. Fatigue claimed its own, and I fell asleep.

The next day we rested, which was necessary for both man and beast, the latter in fact being so exhausted that they needed more than a mere night's sleep. The young Chinaman who had brought us across the Sihoté-Alin made a few purchases and started on his homeward journey.

The evening of our arrival we were far too exhausted to take any notice, and observations were out of the question. But the next morning, after a good breakfast, I went to have a look round the district.

It was yet spring upon the coast, and the cheerful song of our East Siberian larks filled the air. At one moment they dropped to the ground and at another rose again singing into the air. Among the willow shrubs a tiny woodpecker was busy, our really tiny Ussurian species, but as brightly coloured as its congeners. Japanese warblers flitted about among the bushes, never still, perpetually and cheerfully hunting for insects. By the roadside were numerous green buntings which took their dust baths with the sparrows and with them pecked at the horse-dung.

CHAPTER IX : A HAPPY MEETING

THE Tadusha ! It was this very river that L. Veniukov was the first to explore, but the Chinese had stopped him and compelled him to turn back. That was in 1857 when he put up a big wooden cross to mark his farthest point, but I could find no trace of it. No doubt the Chinese had destroyed it as soon as the Russians had left. Later there came Maximovich, Budishchev, and Przewalski, all famous men of science.

Sunset caught us still upon the road. Long shadows stretched across our path. Soon everything would be swathed in darkness.

Presently we reached a cabin and the owner appeared in the doorway. He was a tall old man with a slight stoop and a long grey beard and well-cut features. One had but to glance at his clothes, home, and servants' quarters to see that he had long been living here in comfort. He welcomed us in his own way. Every movement bespoke hospitality. We entered his home, to find everything within as clean and tidy as without. I did not regret having accepted the old man's invitation.

After supper we sat and chatted. At first the old man answered our questions rather unwillingly, but gradually he livened up, and when he began to recall the past his conversation became interesting. It appeared that he was not a Chinaman, but a Manchu, his name was Kin Dshu, and he was born in Ninguti. He had been living more than sixty years on the Tadusha and was contemplating returning to leave his bones in the place where he was born. He then told us about life when he first came in this strange country, and interesting stories of the history of Ussuria. There had been a war between the Emperor Kuan Yun, who lived on the Suchan, and Prince

95

Yatai-Tsi of Ninguti, and he told us of a big battle on the Daubihé and the place where Post Olga now stands. He spoke at length and very vividly, and while listening to him I was completely carried away to that remote past, oblivious to the present, that I was now upon the river Tadusha. Nor was I alone thus carried away, for I noticed that all the other Chinese were silent, had stopped their gossip, and were listening attentively to the old man's yarns. He told us that there came a fearful pestilence, which wiped out almost all the population left after the war, and then the country became a wilderness.

The first Chinese who appeared in the region were hunters for ginseng, and he was among them. On the Tadusha he was taken ill, so he stopped among the native Udehé, married one of their women, and lived among them right into his old age.

At last the old man stopped. I awoke, and found myself once more in this workaday world. In the house it was stifling, and I went outside for a breath of fresh air. The sky was black, the stars glistening brightly in all the colours of the rainbow. On the earth it was black. The horses were snorting in the stable alongside. A bittern boomed in the adjoining marsh, and the crickets were chirping in the grass around.

Long I sat on the bank of the river. The night was magnificent, harmonizing with the stillness of nature. My thoughts went back to Dersu, and I felt melancholy. I stood up, went back into the house, and lay down, but for long I could not fall asleep.

Next morning I bid the old gentleman farewell and we started up-stream. The weather was kind to us, and although there were clouds in the sky, the sun was shining brightly.

There are many Chinese along the Tadusha. I counted no less than ninety-seven of their houses. They are better off here than in other parts of Ussuria. Every house was a little still. The local Chinese were better dressed than the others, were cleaner, with a better-fed and healthier appearance. There were gardens round all the houses, fields of wheat and extensive fields of opium poppy.

In the upper part of the river there are many natives, as usual, crowded into little huts of the local type. The Chinese exploit them mercilessly. Filth in their homes, filth in their clothes, filth on their bodies is the cause of much disease that is bringing them to extinction. The Chinese come into the country alone and take the natives' women by force, with the result that the children are neither true Chinese nor natives. The greater part of the native population of Ussuria to-day, including those on the Tadusha, are of such mixed blood. Many of them, especially the women, are opium addicts, and that is a further cause of their impoverishment. All smoke tobacco, including the tiny children. I often noticed tiny tots that could scarcely walk, clinging to their mothers' breasts and . . . smoking !

The next afternoon the weather changed and the sky became overcast. The clouds came down low and covered the tops of the mountains, so that the valley at once assumed a gloomy look. The crags which had looked so splendid in the rays of the sun now seemed grim, and the very water in the river seemed surly. I knew what that meant, so gave orders to pitch camp and collect firewood.

When that job was done, the men asked permission to go for a little shooting. I advised them not to go far from camp, and to return early. One Cossack went along the valley of the Dinzahe and the other up the Tadusha. The rest stayed in camp.

The sun hid behind the horizon, for it suddenly became dark. The daylight fought a losing battle with the darkness for a little time, but it was clear that night must win, and overcome both earth and heaven.

In an hour one of the Cossacks came back and reported that he had come across the camp fire of a hunter a couple of miles from our bivouac. The man had asked who we were, where we were bound, had we been long upon the road. Directly he heard my name he began hurriedly to collect his few belongings into his haversack.

This made me wonder. Who could it be ?

The rifleman told me it was not worth while going there, as the stranger had promised to come to me at once. A strange presentiment came over me, and something urged me to go to meet the stranger. I took my rifle, whistled the dog, and started off down the path at a brisk pace.

At first the glow of the fire made the darkness seem blacker than it really was, but my eyes soon adapted themselves and I could pick out the track. The moon came out. Heavy clouds scudded across the sky and for a moment veiled its face. It looked as though the moon were hurrying to meet them and simply went right through them. All life around was still but for the faint chirping of the crickets in the grass.

I looked behind me. The fire was already out of sight. I stood a moment, and then walked on.

Suddenly my dog dashed ahead and began to bark savagely. I looked up, and not far from me saw a figure in the darkness.

" Who are you ? " I called out.

In reply I heard a familiar voice that sent a thrill through me :

" What man go ? "

" Dersu ! " I called out. " Dersu ! " and sprang forward to welcome him.

If any third person had seen our meeting he would have thought that two men had flung themselves upon each other in deadly combat. Alpa, not understanding, savagely attacked him, but almost instantly recognized him, and her angry bark turned into an affectionate whimper.

" Morning, captain ! " said the Gold.

" Where have you come from ? How did you turn up here ? Where have you been all these years ? Where are you off to now ? " I overwhelmed him with questions.

He could not answer all at once.

At last our excitement subsided, and we began talking sensibly.

" Me come Tadusha not long," he explained. " My hear four captains and twelve soldiers at Post Olga. My think better go there. To-day see one man. Now understand."

We chatted a moment and then returned to my bivouac. I was gay and cheerful, and how could it be otherwise, for I was extremely fond of Dersu.

In a few minutes we reached the camp. The soldiers stood up and stared with curiosity at the Gold.

Dersu had not altered at all and did not look a day older. He was dressed in the same old things, a leather jacket and deerskin breeches. His head was still wrapped in a scarf, and he held the same old *berdianka* in his hand, but the prop looked like a new one.

The men realized at once that Dersu and I were old friends. He hung his rifle on a tree, and then had a good look at me. By the expression on his face and the smile upon his lips I could see how glad he was to see me again.

I told them to throw plenty of wood upon the fire and brew tea, while I started questioning Dersu and asking him what he had been doing these years since our parting.

He told me that after leaving us near Lake Hanka he had made his way through to the River Noto, where he had trapped sable all the winter, and in the spring crossed over to the upper reaches of the Ulahé to hunt deer for the antlers, and in the summer gone down to Fudzin. Chinamen arriving from Post Olga had told him that our detachment was making its way northwards parallel to the coast, so then he had come to the Tadusha.

The soldiers sat over the fire for a time and turned in early, but Dersu and I sat yarning late. I vividly remembered the Lefu, when he had first come to our camp, and, now as then, I sat looking at his picturesque figure and listening to his stories.

The dark night approached its end. The air began to take a bluish tinge, and one could see the grey sky, the mist on the hills, the sleepy trees, and the path, all glistening under the dew. The light of the fire died down, and the glowing embers turned pale. In nature one sensed a kind of strain ; the mist rose higher and higher, and at last there fell a steady, fine rain.

Then we lay down to sleep. Now I felt afraid of nothing, neither tigers nor brigands, nor deep snow nor floods. Dersu was with me, and with that thought in my head I fell asleep.

I awoke at nine. The rain had stopped, but the sky was still overcast. In weather like that going is bad but sitting is worse, so I ordered the horses to be loaded, and the order was welcome. In half an hour we were on the road. Dersu came with us by tacit understanding, as was quite natural. In fact nothing else had entered my head. On the way we came to a stony hill and there picked up Dersu's property, which, as before, could be packed away completely in his knapsack.

The trail brought us to the cabin of Ludeva, situated just at the crossing of the tracks to Noto and Li-Fudzin. Previously the inhabitants had gone in for hunting deer by pitfalls, which accounts for the name of the cabin, which means game fence with pitfalls. Then it served as a wayside inn, where one could always meet passing Chinamen on their way from the sea into Ussuria and back. The owner provided them with stores for cash, and so earned substantial profits. The store was situated at the foot of a high terrace, boggy on top, covered with clumps of thick birch.

We passed the store and held the road towards Sihoté-Alin. The gloomy weather of the morning began to improve somewhat. The fog covering the mountains began to roll up and rise, while the heavy curtain of clouds began to disperse and let through a little sunshine. Nature assumed a smile once more. At once everything awoke. The crowing of cocks came downwind to us from the cabin and the birds of the forest started fussing again, and insects once more put in an appearance on the flowers.

The Manchu name Sihoté-Alin has been twisted by the

Chinese into Si-ho-ta Lin, meaning the Pass of the Big Western Rivers. The Golds call the crest Dzub Gin and the Udehe Ada-Sololi.

At the foot of the pass we halted. Some dried fish with salt, a couple of biscuits, and a mug of boiling hot tea formed our dinner, which out in the *taigá* we found excellent.

The climb up the ridge is stiff near the crest. The pass itself is in the form of a broad saddle, boggy, and covered with burnt-out forest. The altitude is 1584 ft., and it ought really to be named after the pioneer, M. Veniukov, who passed this way in 1857, breaking the way for the men who followed.

On the top, on the right-hand side of the trail, stood a small joss-house, built of logs. Within was a crude carving illustrating Chinese gods, and in front of it two wooden boxes with the stamps of paper candles. On the other side were a few leaves of tobacco and a couple of pieces of sugar, sacrifices to the God of Forests. On a tree nearby fluttered a red rag, with the inscription : ' Shan men dzhen vei Si-zhi-tsi-go vei da suay Tsin tsan da tsin chezhen shan-lin,' which means : ' To the True Spirit of the Mountains. In antiquity in the dynasty of Tsi he was commander-in-chief for the dynasty Da Tsin, but now he guards the forests and mountains.'

That is to say, the tiger.

The descent from the crest is long and gradual. Walking on grass, we kept coming upon fallen trees all charred by fire. From this point begin bogs, covered with young pine forest.

About three in the afternoon we came to a confluence of two streams, and pitched camp on a gravel spit.

The mountains round here are so heavily weathered that one gets the impression of walking over gently rolling lowlands covered with coniferous forest of spruce, fir, cedar, with birch, yew, maple, larch, and alder. There had been a forest fire here not long ago, and now the whole valley was one great ' gar,' as we call such a burnt-out forest. By here passes the trail that the local people use for communication with the river Noto. Along the trail, at a day's march from each other, are four cabins, the owners of which are engaged in trapping and hunting.

The first thing we did was to light smoke-fires and collect wood. The riflemen wanted to sleep inside their mosquito-nets, but Dersu persuaded them to pitch a tent.

Towards evening the weather became once more overcast, and the mist rose to form clouds. Dersu helped the soldiers in all their work and they learnt at once to appreciate him. He wanted to pitch his own tent separately, but they persuaded him to turn in with them. Then he took his axe and went off into the *taigá* to get some cedar bark. First, he cut notches in the bark above and below, and then sliced it downwards and began to strip off with a pointed stick. Like that he cut six sheets of bark. Two of these he placed on the ground, two he used for a roof, and the rest he put up at the sides as wind-screens.

With dark came heavy rain. The flies and midges disappeared at once. After supper the men turned in, while Dersu and I sat late yarning, and he told me about the Chinese on the Noto, how badly they treated him, taking his skins without paying him.

CHAPTER X : AMBA !

THE next day a dense fog lay heavily over the whole place. It was dull, grey and overcast, cold and damp.

While the men were packing up the kit and loading the horses, Dersu and I, after swallowing a mug of tea and thrusting a handful of biscuits into our pockets, started ahead. As a rule I left camp in the morning before the others. As I was making a survey of our route as I went, my progress was very slow, and in a couple of hours the party would overtake me, and by the time I arrived at the midday halt they had already finished their meal and were starting on again. It was the same in the afternoon, when I would get away before them and arrive at the evening camp just in time for dinner.

The previous evening Dersu had warned me that there were tiger about in the district, and advised me not to stray far from the party.

Our road lay along the right bank of the Li-Fudzin. Sometimes the trail would take us aside, right into the forest, far enough to make us almost lose our sense of direction, and then unexpectedly we would come on to the river again and trek along the high banks.

Those who have never been in the *taigá* of Ussuria can have no conception of the density of those jungles. It was literally impossible to see more than a few paces ahead. Often I would disturb an animal at a distance of not more than four or five yards, and only the noise of its crashing through the thicket would show in what direction it had bolted. We had now been marching for two solid days through thick jungle like that. The weather was depressing, with steady drizzle all the time, filling the track with puddles, drenching the grass, and making the trees so wet that water was dripping down our necks all the time. The forest was surprisingly still, like the stillness of death. Even the woodpeckers were quiet.

"The devil knows what kind of weather you call this," I commented to my companion. "It isn't quite fog, and it isn't quite rain. What do you think about it, Dersu? Will it clear up, or is it going to be worse still?"

The Gold looked at the sky and around, and walked on in silence. After a minute he stopped and said:

"Me think so: ground, hill, forest . . . all same man. Now sweating. Hark!" and he listened. "Hear him breathe, all same man."

He walked on, and for long entertained me with his views on nature, explaining how it was all alive, just like men.

It was about eleven in the morning, quite time for the caravan to have overtaken us, but from the forest behind us not a sound could be heard.

"We'd better wait a bit," I said to my companion.

He stopped, slipped his rifle off his shoulder and leant it against a tree, stuck his prop into the ground, and began to look for his pipe.

"Oh, dear! Me lost pipe!" he exclaimed in anguish.

He wanted to go back to look for it, but I advised him to wait, in the hope that the men would notice it and pick it up as they came. We waited about twenty minutes. I could see the old chap was simply dying for a smoke. At last he could not bear it any longer, picked up his rifle, and said:

"Me think pipe near; must go back look-see."

As I was feeling a little anxious that the party was so long coming, and fearing that something may have happened to the horses, I went back with Dersu. He, as usual, went ahead, wagging his head, and keeping up a running conversation with himself.

"How me lost pipe? Means me got old, or head now no good, or what . . . ?"

He did not finish his phrase, stopped in the middle of a word, stepped back, stooped, and examined something on the ground at his feet. I stepped up to him. He was looking round with a rather worried air, and whispered :

"Look-see, captain! That is Amba ! He go behind us. That very bad, very. Track quite fresh. Him quite near now."

I looked, and there saw the perfectly distinct and fresh impressions of an immense cat's paw, standing out sharply printed in the muddy track. That I remembered clearly, and, besides, Dersu could not have missed them. It was clear that the brute had come along since we had passed, in the same direction as ourselves, that he was following on our heels.

"Him near, hid there," said Dersu, pointing towards the right. "He stood still here long time, when we stopped hunt pipe. We come back, he jump quickly one side. Look-see, captain, no water in track."

I looked. Although there were puddles all round, the water had not yet found its way into this quite fresh pug-mark. There could be no doubt that the great brute had stood there and then, hearing our returning steps, had sprung into the thicket and vanished behind some fallen tree.

"Him not go far. Me know well. Wait, captain ! "

We stood there silently a few minutes in the hope that some sound would betray the presence of the tiger, but there was the silence of the grave. In that silence I felt mystery, and fear.

"Captain," at last said Dersu, turning to me. "Now must look well. See rifle loaded. Go softly, softly. Any hole, any tree on ground, look-see well. Go slow, softly, no hurry. This is Amba. . . . Understand ? Amba ! "

As he spoke, he was looking attentively at every tree, at every branch. Like that we walked on, Dersu all the time ahead, never taking his eyes off the path.

At length we heard voices. One of the Cossacks was swearing at his horse. In a few minutes the men appeared with the caravan. Two of the horses were covered with mud and their loads plastered with clay. It turned out that in fording a brook both the horses had stumbled and rolled in the mud, which was the cause of their delay. As I had hoped, they had picked up Dersu's pipe and brought it along.

Before going on it was necessary to re-arrange the loads and clean some of the muck off the horses, so I suggested a halt and brewing tea. But Dersu advised simply re-arranging the loads a little and carrying on, as not very far away we should come to a trapper's hut where we could bivouac. After a moment's thought I agreed.

The men started lifting the loads off the poor brutes of horses, so Dersu and I again started ahead. We had not gone more than

a couple of hundred yards before we came upon the spoor of the tiger again. Once more the great brute was tracking us and, as the first time, scenting our approach, had sprung aside to avoid meeting us. Dersu stopped and, turning to the side where the tiger was hidden, called out loudly, in a voice in which could be heard a note of irritation :

" Why you go behind, Amba ? What you want, Amba ? We go our way, you go yours ; you no bother us. Why you keep come behind ? *Taigá* big place, room for us and you, what ? "

He brandished his rifle in the air.

I had never seen him in such an excited state. In his eyes I could clearly read his unshaken belief that the tiger heard and understood his words. He was convinced that the tiger would either accept his challenge or leave us in peace.

We waited about five minutes, and then the old man heaved a sigh of relief, lit his pipe, slung his rifle over his shoulder, and started off down the trail with a carefree stride. He had put the tiger to shame and it had gone away.

We trekked on through the jungle for about an hour. Suddenly the thicket began to thin out and we came out into an open clearing. The track crossed it diagonally.

The long tramp through the forest had wearied us. The eye craved for rest and space, so it was an immense relief to come out of the forest and be able to look round in an open space.

" This Kvandagou," said Dersu. " Now we soon find hut."

The broad glade into which we had come was covered with a thick growth of *Osmunda* fern. Behind the forest, to our right, through the mist I could vaguely distinguish lofty, tree-clad mountains; in the lower ground there stood isolated trees, chiefly maple, oak, and Daurian birch. On the right of the clearing was a strip of bog with salt pools where, according to Dersu, wapiti and pig came at night to enjoy the marsh crowfoots and lick the salt black earth.

" Must go hunt here to-day," said Dersu, pointing to the bog with his prop.

About three in the afternoon we came across a hut with a gable roof. It was built by Chinese trappers with pieces of cedar bark, in such a way that the smoke from the fire inside found its way out on both sides, to prevent the mosquitoes finding their way in. A brook near by again gave us trouble with the horses, but eventually this obstacle was overcome.

All this time the weather continued, to use Dersu's expression, to sweat. Since the morning the gloomy sky had given a slight promise of clearing. The mist rose higher, some light found its way through, the rain had eased off, but the ground was still saturated.

I decided to stop here for the night, as I was very anxious to do a bit of shooting in the bog, especially as we had been a long time without meat, living for the last four days on nothing but biscuit.

In a twinkling our bivouac was bustling with that quick and cheerful work so familiar to all who have been long in the *taigá* and become accustomed to the strange manner of life that evolves. The unloaded horses we set at liberty. Directly their loads were removed, the first thing they did was to have a good roll and then, after a shake, wander off for some grazing.

If it were raining the loads were piled in one place and covered with a tarpaulin.

While the men were busy with the horses, someone had succeeded in getting a good fire going and the kettle was already slung over it.

At such times Dersu always showed astonishing energy. He dashed from one tree to another, slicing off strips of bark, cutting poles and prongs, pitching his tent, drying his clothing and the other men's too, and trying so to arrange the fire that we could sit inside the hut without getting the smoke in our eyes. I always wondered how it was that this extraordinary man, no longer young, could do several things at once. When we had flung off our things and been resting quite a long time Dersu was still busy about the hut.

An hour later an onlooker would have seen a strange picture : horses grazing by the brook, their backs drenched with rain. The smoke from the fire not rising into the air, but clinging to the ground, almost immovable. The men crowded into the hut to get away from the mosquitoes and midges. Only one figure outside, busy out among the trees. It was Dersu, laying in a good stock of firewood for the night.

In August, especially on a dull day, it grows dark very early. The mist clings to the tops of the hills, wisps creeping like ghosts among the scrubs.

We had some supper, and then Dersu and I went to see if we could get some meat. Our track took us across the clearing to the salt-pans near the edge of the forest. The ground was covered with the spoor of wapiti and pig. The salt black earth was almost completely devoid of vegetation, and the stunted trees growing near it had a gnarled and withered look. Here the ground had been trampled hard. Evidently the wapiti came here both singly and in herds.

Choosing a suitable spot, we sat and waited for the game to arrive. I leant against a stump and had a good look round. The darkness soon became deeper round the shrubs and under the trees. Dersu was a long time settling down. He broke off branches, so as to clear himself a field of fire, and for some reason bent down a young birch growing behind him.

Around reigned a silence as of death, broken only by the monotonous buzz of the mosquitoes. Such silence has a depressing effect upon the soul. You find yourself involuntarily bathed in it, and you think you have not strength enough to break it by a word or some incautious movement.

In the air and on the ground it became darker and darker. The trees and bushes began to assume vague outlines; they seemed to take on life, to move from one spot to another. For a moment I took them to be deer, and fancy did the rest. I slipped my rifle to my shoulder, and was ready to fire, but each time a glance at the serene face of Dersu brought me back to reality. The illusion was dispelled, and the dark silhouette of a stag once more took the shape of a bush or tree. Dersu sat like a marble statue. He kept his eye on the shrubs near the salt-pans and quietly awaited his prey. Once he suddenly stiffened, quietly picked up his weapon, and began to take aim. My heart thumped. I too stared in that direction, but saw nothing.

Then I noticed that he was quiet again, so I too became quiet.

It was soon quite dark, and at a few paces one could not distinguish either the black earth on the salt-pans or the silhouettes of the trees. The mosquitoes continued mercilessly to bite both hands and neck. I pulled the veil over my face. Dersu sat motionless, apparently oblivious of the stings.

Suddenly my ear caught a rustle. I was not mistaken. The rustle came from the bushes on the far side of the salt-pans, exactly facing us. I glanced at Dersu. I could just distinguish how he had thrust his head forward, and it seemed as though he were straining the whole power of his vision to peer through the darkness and pick out the cause of the sound. At one moment it became quite loud and distinct, at another ceased completely. There was no doubt about it. Something was cautiously coming our way. It must be a wapiti come for its salt-lick. In my imagination I could see the graceful stag with his splendid branched antlers. I flung back the veil and began to listen and stare, now quite forgetful of the mosquitoes. I tried hard to pick up the outline of the wapiti which, I judged, should be by now not more than seventy or eighty paces from us.

Suddenly through the air there hit our ears a threatening growl like distant thunder.

Grrrrrrr !

Dersu gripped me by the arm.

" Amba, captain ! " he exclaimed in a startled voice.

Dread gripped my heart. I would like to describe my feelings at that moment, but can hardly do it.

I felt a kind of faintness overcome me, and a tremendous weight seemed to press me to the ground. My knees seemed to collapse, as though filled with lead. The emotion is familiar to everyone who has ever unexpectedly and suddenly felt the shock of fear. At the same time there was mingled with it another feeling, a blend of insatiable curiosity, of awe for the splendid and formidable animal, and the passion of the hunter.

" Bad ; we done wrong come here ; Amba angry. This him place," I heard Dersu whisper, and I do not know if he were speaking to me or talking to himself. I had the idea that he was afraid.

Grrrrrrr ! again resounded through the still night air.

Suddenly Dersu stood up. I thought he was going to shoot.

But to my intense astonishment I could see that he did not hold his weapon in his hand, and I was more surprised than ever when I heard him speak to the tiger.

" All right, Amba. No be angry . . . no need be angry. This your place. We not know. We go now quick to another place. *Taigá* big ; plenty room. No be angry ! "

The Gold stood there, holding out his arm towards the brute. Suddenly he fell upon his knees, bowed twice to the ground, and in an undertone muttered something rapidly in his own tongue. I felt sorry for the old man.

Then at length Dersu slowly raised himself, stepped up to my stump, and took his rifle.

"Come, captain," he said in a decisive tone, and without waiting for my answer, quickly strode off through the scrub.

I followed him without replying.

Dersu's serene expression, the confidence with which he strode on without glancing around, reassured me. I felt sure that the tiger would not follow or attack us.

When we had gone a couple of hundred yards, I stopped him and suggested waiting a little longer.

"No," he replied. "Me no can do. Me tell you now, in company will now never shoot Amba! Never! You hear this well, captain. You shoot Amba . . . you not my comrade."

Again he strode forward in silence. I wanted to stay there alone, but that feeling of apprehension overcame me, and I ran after the Gold.

The moon began to show. Suddenly both sky and earth were bathed in light. Yonder, at the far end of the open space, twinkled our camp fire. Now it died down, now it flickered up again into bright flame.

We walked the whole way in silence. Each of us was filled with his own thoughts, his own memories. I was sorry that I had not seen the tiger. I said so out loud to my companion.

"Oh, no!" answered Dersu. "Bad see him. We say that. Men never see Amba . . . happy, lucky men. Live always well."

Dersu heaved a deep sigh, and after a moment's silence continued:

"Me see Amba much. One time shot, miss. Now me very much fear. For me now one day will be bad, bad luck."

In his words I heard such emotion that again I felt sorry for him, and tried to console him and change the subject.

We reached the camp in an hour. The horses, startled by our approach, shied, and began to neigh. Figures were moving about the fire. Two Cossacks came to meet us.

"To-night the horses are all nervous," said one of them. "They seem to be afraid of something and off their feed; they keep staring at something. There must be some animal about."

I gave orders to bring the horses in and put the halters on and make them fast, to build up a big fire and set an armed watch.

All that evening Dersu sat in silence. The encounter with the tiger had had a profound impression upon him. Immediately after supper he turned in, and I noticed that he was a long time falling asleep, tossing from side to side and apparently all the time talking to himself.

I told the men what had happened. The Cossacks were interested, and began to bring out reminiscences of their life in Ussuria, their hunting adventures, what they had seen and whom they had met. Our yarns lasted late into the night, till at last fatigue claimed its own. Someone yawned, another began to spread his blanket, and in a few minutes in that hut all were asleep. Silence reigned, broken only by the regular breathing of the sleeping men, the crack of a branch in the fire, the whinny of a horse, and an occasional hoot of an eagle owl in the forest.

THE moment it began to lighten the mosquitoes again attacked our camp, and there was no more thought of sleep. As though at the word of command, all arose. The Cossacks quickly loaded the horses and we started off without even stopping to drink our morning tea. When the sun came out the mist began to clear and here and there some blue sky peeped out.

Here in the valley of the Li-Fudzin the forest is splendid, with representatives of the whole Manchurian flora. Apart from the cedar, larch, spruce, fir, elm, oak, ash, walnut, and cork trees, there are too here the yellow birch, *Betula costata*, with its yellowish-green foliage and fluffy, yellow bark, which is of no use ; there is a special kind of maple, *Acer barbinerve*, a well-branched tree with smooth, dark grey bark and yellowish shoots and deeply incised leaves. Then an elm, *Ulmus montana*, a tall, handsome tree with a broad, spreading crown and sharp, hairy foliage. Then there is a hornbeam, *Carpinus cordata*, recognizable from the other trees by its dark bark and flowers hanging in tufts ; there is Maximovich's cherry, *Prunus maximovicsii*, with branches bent to the ground which form an impenetrable tangle, and a spindlewood tree, *Euonymus macroptera*, a stumpy, stout tree, the bark covered with whitish scales arranged in rows and long, oval leaves. Near the streams and generally in moist places there grows the goat willow, *Salix caprea*, half bush, half tree ; the Manchurian currant, *Ribes manshuricus*, with three-lobed, sharply dentate leaves ; a silky *Spiræa*, *S. media*, a bushy shrub easy to recognize by its narrow leaves and preference for stony ground ; there is a jasmine, *Philadelphus tenuifolius*, a shady tree with pretty, heart-shaped, pointed leaves and white flowers, and a creeper,

Schizandra chinensis, with the fragrance of lemon, with large, dark leaves and red berries, clinging to the bushes and trees.

The trees growing near the water tend to break the banks down rather than strengthen them. When a big tree is under-mined by the stream, in crashing it brings down with it a huge mass of earth and a number of other trees and shrubs growing near it. The mass then floats down-stream until it is stranded, and then at once the current piles up sand and gravel against it. Often enough one may see regular cascades formed across the fallen trunk of a monster cedar or poplar. If ever such a tree happens to break away and be carried down-stream, by the time it reaches the mouth all that is left of it is the bare trunk, stripped of both bark and branches.

In its middle reaches the Li-Fudzin crosses the foot of the so-called Black Rocks, and here it splits into a number of separate streams, with muddy bottoms and sticky banks. As the main channel is so plugged, the water cannot find its way through the streams and floods the whole forest, interrupting communica-tions. Travellers caught here in wet weather are obliged to climb over the rocks and often spend a whole day in making not more than two or three miles.

At midday we stopped for a good rest and brewed tea.

When we were leaving a friend had given me a bottle of rum which I had held as a ' hospital comfort ' and issued to the men in bad weather. Now there were only a few drops of rum left in the bottle, so I poured them into the tea and flung the bottle away. Dersu pounced on it.

" Why throw bottle ! " he cried. " Where find more bottle in *taigá*? No bottle in *taigá*! " and he undid his knapsack.

And, as a matter of fact, for a townsman like me a bottle was a trifle of no value, but for this wild man of the woods it was a precious thing.

I watched him take his treasures out of his sack with growing astonishment. Here is the inventory: an empty flour-bag; two old shirts; a roll of narrow straps; a ball of string; old moccasins; cartridge-cases; a powder-horn; lead; a box of percussion-caps; a breadth of tent canvas; a goatskin; a chunk of brick tea and some leaves of tobacco; an old pickle-jar; an awl; a hatchet; a tin box; matches; a flint, steel, and tinder; a bit of resin for kindling birch bark; a little jar; a mug; a little kettle; a curved native knife; thread made of sinew; a couple of needles; an empty reel; some sort of dry herb; a boar's gall-bladder; bear's teeth and claws; hooves of a musk-deer; lynx claws strung on a thread; two copper buttons, and a quantity of other odds and ends. Among them I recognized several things that I had thrown away on the road. Evidently he had picked them up and treasured them.

I looked through his things, sorted them into two piles, and advised him to throw away a good half of them. Dersu implored me not to touch them, and assured me earnestly that they would all come in useful some day. I did not insist, and decided not to throw away anything in future without asking him first.

As though apprehensive that somebody might take away some of his treasures, he stuffed them hurriedly back into his bag, and took particular trouble to hide the bottle.

At the Black Rocks the trail divides, one track leading into the hills to avoid the dangerous place, the other leading somewhere across the river. Dersu, who knew the locality well, pointed to the right-hand track, into the hills, saying that the other led only to a trapper's cabin where it came to an end.

Immediately after the rest we started climbing, but the track did not reach the top. It flanked the hill and within a mile dropped back into the valley.

Towards evening the sky was once more overcast, and I feared more rain. Dersu said it was not a cloud but a mist, and that the next day would be sunny, and even hot. I knew that he was weather-wise and his forecasts always came true, and so asked him what the signs were.

" Me look so, think—air light, not heavy." The Gold took a deep breath and pointed to his chest.

The man lived so close to nature that his very organism was sensitive to changes of weather. It seemed to be with him a sort of sixth sense.

115

Dersu was really astonishingly adapted to life in the *taigá*. As a couch for the night he would choose a spot under a big tree between two big roots, so that they would protect him from the wind ; as a mattress he would put down a strip of bark off a cork tree, and hang his moccasins on a branch so that they dried over the fire without being burnt. He would keep his rifle by his side, not on the ground itself, but supported on a couple of forked sticks stuck in the ground. His firewood always burnt better than ours, never scattering sparks, and the smoke always blew to one side. If the wind changed, he fixed up a screen on the weather side. With him everything he wanted was on the spot and at hand.

Nature is merciless to man. She will flatter and caress him one moment, and then suddenly fall upon him, as though driving home his helplessness. The wayfarer has constantly to brave the elements, rain, wind, flood, flies, bogs, cold, snow, and ice. The very forest itself is an element. Dersu did not feel himself under the influence of nature, but rather in intimacy with his surroundings, a part and parcel of them.

The next day was 7 August. Directly the sun came out, the mist began to scatter, and in about half an hour there was not a cloud to be seen. A heavy dew had soaked the grass, bushes, and trees. Dersu was not in camp. He had gone out shooting, but without result, and came back just as we were ready to start. We set off at once.

On the road Dersu told how that in former days Golds lived on the west of Sihoté-Alin and Udehé on the east, but then the Chinese had appeared and lorded it over everything. In fact, their huts were so numerous in the woods that it was possible to arrange one's journey in such a way as always to reach one of them to sleep in.

After about six miles we had to ford the river again at a place where it split into several streams, leaving a number of eyots covered with scrub. The layer of mud, the crashed timber, the wash-outs, and bent bushes, all pointed to recent heavy flooding.

Suddenly the forest came to an end and we came out on to

open country, called by the Chinese Siayen Laza. We stopped to camp on the bank in a grove of oaks.

The Cossacks went for a look round, came to report plenty of tracks of game, and asked leave to do some shooting.

By day the four-legged inhabitants of the *taigá* bury themselves in the thickest tangles, but before dusk begin to stir and leave their lairs. At first they wander about the edge of the forest, but when it is quite dark they come out to graze in the open. The Cossacks did not wait for the dark, but went off directly they had unloaded the horses. Only Dersu and I were left alone in camp.

That day I had noticed that the Gold seemed somehow occupied. Every now and then he would sit apart and appear plunged in thought, dropping his hands and staring into the distance. When I asked if he did not feel well, the old man shook his head, picked up his axe, and became busy, evidently trying to dispel some gloomy thoughts.

Two hours and more went by. The shadows stretching out to immense length upon the ground showed that the sun had reached the horizon. It was time to go out shooting. I called Dersu. He seemed somehow to be afraid.

" Captain," he said to me, and I could detect an imploring note in his voice, " me no can go hunt to-day. There . . ." and he pointed to the forest, " there die my wife and babies."

Then he started telling me that according to their custom they must not go near the grave, or shoot near it, or fell timber, collect berries, or trample the grass. He must not disturb the repose of the departed.

I understood then the cause of his sadness, and felt very sorry for the old man. I told him I would not go out, but would stay in camp with him.

After dark I heard three shots and was glad the sound did not come from the direction of the graves.

When it was quite dark the Cossacks came back bringing a roe. We had supper and turned in early. Twice during the night I awoke and saw Dersu sitting alone by the fire.

Next morning they reported that Dersu was not to be seen, but as his things and his rifle were there, I knew he was coming back. While waiting for him I went for a stroll and chanced upon the river. On the bank, near a big boulder, I saw the Gold. He was sitting motionless, staring into the water. I called to him. He turned his face towards me. I could see he had spent a sleepless night.

" Come, Dersu ! " I called to him.

" I live here one time ; one time my hut here and store ; burnt long time ; father, mother, too, all live here one time. . . ."

He did not complete his phrase. He stood up, waved his arm, and silently came back to camp. There everything was ready for the road, and the men were only awaiting our return.

Early in the afternoon we came to the hut of the Iolaiza which we knew well. When we passed the natives' huts, Dersu went up to them. In the evening he came running in a terrified state with the shocking news that but two days ago a Chinaman and a young native had been buried alive, according to a verdict under Chinese law. This cruel punishment was for murdering their creditor out of revenge. The execution had taken place less than a mile from the last cabins. Dersu and I went to see the place and found two low hummocks of earth. On top of each was a board with the name of the victim painted on in Chinese ink. The dead men no longer needed our help, and besides, what could we four do against the numerous and well-armed Chinese population ?

I had intended stopping a couple of days at Iolaiza, but now the spot had become repulsive to me, so we decided to go on farther and stop for a day somewhere in the forest.

After discussion with Dersu, I worked out a route. We decided to go from the valley of the Fudzin to the Noto, follow it up to its source, cross the Sihoté-Alin, and come out by the Vangou back to the Tadusha. Dersu knew the district well, so there would be no need to keep asking chance Chinese about the road.

We left that dreadful place in the morning of 8 August, the

place where they buried men alive. From the hut of the Iolaiza we first turned towards the hills of Siayen Laza and then due north by a brook called Pougou, which means Goat Valley. An elderly native came with us some of the way. He walked along with Dersu all the time, chatting with him in an undertone. I afterwards learnt that they were old acquaintances, and the native was secretly making up his mind to move from Fudzin to the coast. When we parted, Dersu gave him as a token of friendship that old rum-bottle that I had thrown away at Li-Fudzin. It was worth seeing the expression of delight on the face of the old native as he accepted the gift.

After midday Dersu found a path leading us to the pass, covered with thick forest. Here there were numbers of badgers' earths, one old, but several quite fresh. In some foxes had taken up their abode, as we could easily see from their tracks in the sand.

The caravan lagged behind, while Dersu and I went on ahead, talking. Suddenly I caught sight of something moving in the grass about thirty paces ahead. It was the badger, a local race, *Meles amurensis*, closely related to the Japanese and distributed throughout the country. The Chinese do not go out after badger, but  shoot if they happen to come within gunshot. The skin, covered with stiff bristles, is used by them for gun-covers and the edges of bags.

The badger I had noticed stood up on his hind legs and tried to reach something, but I could not see what. He was so absorbed in his own affairs that he never noticed us. We watched him for a long time, until I had had enough and started forward. Startled at the sound, the badger sprang aside and quickly vanished. When we came to the place where he had been, I examined the ground, and then suddenly heard Dersu calling.

He was waving his arms and signing to me to hurry back. At the same moment I felt a sharp pain in the shoulder. Grabbing the sore place with my hand, I picked up a large insect, which at once stung me on the hand. Then I noticed for the first time a big nest of hornets. I bolted, swearing like a trooper, but some of the brutes chased me.

" Wait, captain," said Dersu, taking his axe out of his bag. Then, choosing a slender sapling, he cut it down and trimmed off the twigs, and then tied a piece of bark at the end. When the hornets had settled down again, he lit the piece of bark and held it under the nest. It blazed up like paper. As he burnt them out, Dersu addressed them :

" What, you would sting our captain."

When he had done with the hornets, he went into the wood again, picked some herb, and, after rubbing it on the blade of his axe, applied it to the painful spot, bandaging it on with strips of bark and a bit of rag. In about ten minutes the pain began to subside. I asked him to show me the herb, so he went into the wood again and brought me back a piece of what turned out to be *Clematis manshurica*. Dersu told me it was also good for snake-bite and that even dogs eat it too as a cure. It induces abundant salivation, and when they lick the wound, it has a beneficial effect and counteracts the venom.

When he had done tying me up, we walked on. Conversation now revolved round hornets and wasps. Dersu called them ' very bad man,' saying :

" Him always sting me ; now me all time burn them."

A couple of days later we came to the watershed. Both ascent and descent were steep. On the far side we came on to a path at once, which brought us to the cabin of a Chinese sable-trapper. After a look at it, Dersu said that the owner had lived here several days on end and left only yesterday. I expressed doubt, suggesting that it might not be the owner, but some chance wayfarer. In place of reply, Dersu pointed out the old things flung out of the cabin and replaced by new ones. Only the actual owner would do that. Which was unanswerable.

CHAPTER XII: A HATEFUL SPOT

TOWARDS evening that day we managed to reach the Noto.

The upper reaches of the Noto are regarded as the most remote and wildest parts of Ussuria. The Chinese hovels scattered about the *taigá* here cannot be described as trappers' cabins, or as farms. The only Chinese that turn up in this district are the unstable element, the ne'er-do-wells that eke out a living somehow, ready for robbery or murder.

We found some abandoned native wigwams and tumbledown old huts. Dersu told me that once there lived here some aborigines, Udehé, four men, two women, and three children, but the Chinese drove them away. At present there are only Chinese on the Noto, shooting and trapping sable.

When we were marching Dersu kept his eyes fixed upon the ground. He was not looking for anything special, but did this from sheer habit. Once he bent down and picked up a little stick. On it were the marks of a native knife, the cut long since turned black.

The remains of wigwams, the blazes on the trees, the stumps on which their store-sheds had stood, and this piece of whittled stick all showed that the Udehé had been here a year previously.

At dusk we pitched camp on the beach by the river-side, in the hope that the mosquitoes would leave us in peace.

The roe had long since been consumed and we were in need of meat. We talked it over with Dersu and started out to bag something, I following up-stream, while he worked up a small brook into the hills.

In Ussuria the *taigá* awakens twice in the twenty-four hours, in the morning before sunrise and in the evening at sunset.

SECOND EXPEDITION

 When we left camp the sun was already low upon the horizon, its golden beams breaking through between the trunks of the trees and irradiating the most shady corners of the *taigá*. In that light the forest was wonderfully beautiful. The magnificent cedars seem to be trying to shelter the young growth with their spreading shade. Immense poplars, veterans perhaps of three centuries, seemed to be disputing the might and power of the venerable oaks. In company with them stood enormous limes and lofty elms, behind which we could detect the stout trunk of an aspen, and then a black birch or two, firs, hornbeam, yellow maple, and many others. Beyond them nothing more was visible, everything masked by the thickets of elder and bird cherry.

Time went by. The working day was over. In the forest it grew dark, and now the sun's rays shone only on the peaks of the hills and the sky. The light reflected from them lit up the earth a moment longer, and then gradually faded away.

Life in the feathered world died down, but another life awoke, the life of the big animals.

A rustle came to my ears. I soon detected its cause, a racoon-dog, *Nyctereutes procyonoides*. It is a strange animal, a sort of link between the racoon and the dog, about 2 ft. 6 in. in length, with short legs and rather long greyish fur, with vague, dark, and pale markings, and a long tail. It is common enough in Ussuria, especially in the west and south. It is shy and wary, nocturnal in habits, and omnivorous, but its favourite dainties are fish and mice. It gets food enough in summer, but spends the winter hibernating. I watched it fade away, and walked on.

In half an hour the light in the sky had moved still farther westward. From white it had turned to green, then yellow, orange, and last dark red. Slowly the earth completed its revolution and left the sun to greet the night.

Presently I heard the crack of a broken twig. I froze, as two dark forms gradually appeared out of the blackness. I saw they were boar, making their way to the river. From their leisurely pace I knew that they had not winded me. One was huge, the other a good deal smaller. I chose the latter and raised my rifle to my shoulder, when suddenly the big one uttered a loud snort and at the same moment I fired. The report re-echoed through the forest and the big boar sprang aside. I thought I had missed, and was just starting on my way  again when I saw the wounded beast struggling to rise from the ground. I gave him a second shot. The brute thrust his muzzle into the ground, and again made an effort to rise. I then let him have a third, which brought him down finally. I approached cautiously. It was a middle-sized pig, turning about 270 lb., I should say, not more.

To prevent the meat being spoiled, I cleaned it, and was turning to rejoin my party when again I heard a rustle in the wood. I was at once on the alert again, when I saw the figure of Dersu. He had come on hearing my shots. To my surprise he asked whom I had killed. I might well have missed.

" No," he said with a smile. " Me know well, you hit, you kill."

I asked him to explain how he knew that I had had a kill. He explained that he knew from the intervals between the shots. An animal is not often killed by the first shot. If he had heard only one, he would have taken it that I had missed. Three shots in rapid succession would have meant that the animal had bolted and that I was firing wildly after it. But three shots at uneven and rather long intervals showed him that the animal had been wounded and I was finishing him off.

We decided to leave the carcass there, taking only the liver, heart, and kidneys. Then we lit a fire round it and walked back to camp.

When we got there it was quite dark, and the light of the fire threw a broad bright band across the river. This band seemed to move, to be broken, and re-appear on the far bank. From the camp we could hear the sound of axes, talking, and laughter. The mosquito-curtains, spread on the ground with lights inside, looked like gigantic lanterns. The men had heard the shots and were waiting to see the game. The titbits we had brought were converted into supper forthwith, after which we drank our fill of tea and turned in to sleep. I set one watch, as the horses were loose.

On the 11th we continued our journey down the stream Danantse. Here there were great numbers of cedars. As one approaches the Sihoté-Alin the good timber forest gives way to mixed growth, until on the tops itself there are only mossy, thin firs, Siberian larch, and spruce. The roots do not penetrate deep into the ground, but spread over the surface, and in fact they are only just covered by moss alone. This makes them short-lived and shaky. A man can easily push over a sapling of twenty-five years' growth. They die from the top. Sometimes a dead tree may stand a long time on its roots until you touch it, when it crumbles into powder.

In climbing steep places, especially when carrying a load, one must be very careful, and have a good look at every tree one grasps. There is not only the danger of losing one's balance if it gives way, but also of getting a nasty hit on the head from a falling branch. In birch the wood decays quicker than the bark ; the touchwood is scattered, and the hollow sheath of bark is left upon the ground.

Such parts of the forest are lifeless. There are neither spoor of game nor sound of bird, nor even the buzz of insects. The trunks of the trees have in mass a monotonous brownish-grey tint. There is no undergrowth, not even ferns or rushes. Whichever side you look, there is nothing to see but moss, under one's feet, on the rocks, and on the trees. Forest like that has a depressing effect. In it is always a deathly stillness, broken only by the soughing of the wind in the tops of the dead trees. In that sound there is something sinister, ill-omened. The Udehé say places like that are haunted by evil spirits.

Towards evening we stopped to camp at the foot of the Sihoté-Alin. That day I sent the Cossacks out on reconnaissance and stayed in camp with Dersu. We quickly had the tent pitched, the fire alight, the kettle sizzing merrily over it, while we sat and waited for the men. Dersu silently smoked his pipe while I made entries in my diary.

In the passage from day to night there is to me always something mysterious. In the forest that hour is mournful and sad. Around reigns an oppressive silence. Then the ear just catches some barely audible sound, as though a distant sigh. Whence does it come? It seems as though the *taigá* itself were sighing. I dropped my notebook and gave myself up to the influence of my surroundings. Dersu's voice brought me out of my pensiveness.

" Bad sleep here," he was saying, as though to himself.

" Why? " I asked him.

He pointed to a wisp of mist appearing on the hills, drifting across the forest.

" You no understand, captain. Him too just same man."

I gathered from his words that such wisps of mist had once been men who had lost their way among the hills and died of hunger, and now their souls were wandering restlessly about the *taigá* in places where living men seldom come. Suddenly he pricked up his ears.

" Hark ! " he said softly.

I listened. On the side in the opposite direction from the Cossacks I picked up strange sounds, as though someone were felling a tree. Then silence. Ten minutes went by, and then the sounds began again, as though someone were chinking metal, but very far away. Suddenly a loud noise resounded through the forest. It must be a tree had crashed.

" That him ! That him ! " muttered Dersu in fear, and I realized that he meant the soul of the man who had died in the forest. Then he sprang to his feet and began to shout something in his own tongue into the forest in an angry voice. I asked him what he was doing.

" My swear him just little," he answered. " Me tell him we sleep here only one night, to-morrow go away."

At that moment the Cossacks arrived and brought a little liveliness into the picture. No more mysterious noises were heard and the night passed peacefully.

Next morning I awoke before the sun and at once aroused the sleeping Cossacks. Sunrise found us already on the road.

The pass itself was a fairly deep hollow, covered with conifers, at a height of 2855 ft. I named it Forgotten.

In the Sihoté-Alin the highest peaks are always alongside such mountain valleys. So it was in this case. On our left there rose a peak with a flat top, which the Chinese call Tudinza.

Leaving the Cossacks to wait for us, Dersu and I climbed the peak. Towards the top the climb became very steep. It is beyond question the highest peak in the district, reaching an altitude of 3800 ft. The top itself was flat, covered with grass, with some stunted alders and birch at the edges.

It gave us a splendid view all round. The country at our feet looked like the sea, the hills the crests of the waves. The nearest peaks had fantastic forms, and behind them massed the others, their contours veiled in bluish mist.

We brewed tea and returned to the Cossacks below.

I do not know which was more fatiguing, the climb up or the climb down. It is true that wind plays an important part in climbing up, but the position of the body is more natural, because in climbing down one is struggling all the time against the weight of one's own body. Everybody knows how much easier it is to climb up a scree than to go down one. All the time you must keep placing your foot upon a stone, a fallen trunk, the roots of a shrub, a tuft of grass. There is no danger in this going up, but coming down one must always be on one's guard. It is so easy to twist an ankle or take a bad fall head first.

The climb up Mt. Tudinza had taken us all day, and when we rejoined the men it was late. In the pass itself there was a joss-house, where the Cossacks found some Chinese candy. They sat down to tea and enjoyed themselves.

Before dark I took my rifle and went for a look round. I walked slowly, often stopping to listen. Suddenly my ear caught some strange sound, a kind of sing-song croaking. I crept forward and soon saw a raven. This bird is very much bigger than an ordinary  crow. It utters various noises, which are not unpleasant to listen to. He was sitting on a branch and seemed to be talking to himself, and in his voice I counted nine notes. Catching sight of me, he took fright, rose lightly into the air, and flew

 off. A little farther on I came across the nest of a tree-creeper in a gap between the bark and trunk of an old tree, and a moment later the little owner herself. The bright little bird was nimbly running up the trunk, scanning the bark for insects with its long, thin beak. At times it ran under a branch back downwards, clinging to the bark with its claws. Near it were a couple of nuthatches, quietly piping and attentively examining every fold in the bark, tapping with their sharp, conical beaks just like a chisel, not striking straight, but first from one side, then from the other.

On the way back I bagged a brace and a half of hazel-hen, which provided an excellent supper for us.

At dawn—it was 12 August—Dersu awoke me. The Cossacks were still asleep. I took my aneroid and we climbed up the Sihoté-Alin, as I wanted to compare the altitude with that on the other side of the little valley. On one flank there is only moss and pine needles, on the other rich and varied forest full of life.

When we returned to the hut the men were ready to start. They had had breakfast, brewed tea, and were waiting for our return. After a snack I told them to load up and started off ahead with Dersu.

When we came to the mouth of a burn, we stopped to let the caravan overtake us. Dersu sat on the bank to change his moccasins, and I strolled on.

The path here made a big bend. When I had gone a little way I glanced back and saw him still sitting on the bank. He waved me on.

Just as I came out to the edge of the wood I stumbled on some boar, but was not quick enough to shoot. Seeing which way they were moving, I dashed ahead to cut them off, and actually overtook them in a few minutes. I saw something flicker through the bush. Choosing a moment when the black spot stopped, I fired.

At that instant I heard a human cry, followed by a groan of pain. A wave of horror overwhelmed me as I realized I had shot a man, and I dashed forward to the fatal spot. What I saw struck me like a thunderbolt. On the ground lay . . . Dersu !

"Dersu ! Dersu !" I cried, and my strangled voice did not sound like my own.

He was leaning on his left arm, supporting himself on his elbow, while with his right he was covering his eyes.

Hurriedly, desperately, frantically, I asked him where he was hit.

"Back hurt," he answered.

As quickly as I could I took off his jacket and shirt. Both were torn. At last I succeeded in stripping him, and a sigh of relief escaped me. There was no bullet wound, but a bruise and extravasation of blood about as big as a halfpenny. Only then

I noticed how my hands were trembling, as though in a fever. I told Dersu what the wound was like. He was relieved. Seeing my emotion, he started calming me.

" No matter, captain, not your fault. Me come behind. As you know, me go front."

I raised him and made him comfortable, and then asked how it happened that he was between me and the boar. It seemed that we had both caught sight of them at once. This aroused his hunter's passion, and he sprang up after them. He soon overtook me. The colour of his jacket was extraordinarily close to that of a boar. I had caught a glimpse of it just when he was stooping to peer through the shrubs. I had taken him for the boar, and fired.

The bullet had cut through his jacket and bruised his back, and the shock had knocked him off his legs.

In about ten minutes the horses arrived. The first thing I did was to paint his bruise with tincture of iodine and then to take the load of one of the horses and distribute it over the others, to put Dersu on the horse thus released, and so we left that accursed spot.

In the afternoon we came to a place where three streams joined the Vangou, and there was a trapper's cabin. It was impossible to go any farther. Dersu's head was aching badly and his back hurting him, so I decided to stop for the night. We carried the wounded man inside and gently laid him on the k'ang, while I did my best to nurse him as tenderly as possible. The first thing I did was to put a hot compress on the injured spot, which I made from a piece torn off a mosquito-curtain.

Towards the evening Dersu felt a little easier, but I could not forgive myself. The thought that I had shot the man to whom I owed my life was a torment. I cursed the day, cursed the boar and the shooting. If I had shot but a fraction to the left, if my hand had trembled the slightest, I might have killed him ! That livelong night I could not sleep. I could see nothing, hear nothing, and think of nothing but the trees, the boars, my shot, the bush where Dersu crouched, and his cry of pain. I could bear it no longer, sprang up from the *k'ang*, and went out into the air. I tried to console myself by the thought that Dersu was, after all, alive and still with me, but it was of no avail. Then I lit the fire again and tried to read. But I quickly saw that before my eyes was not the print, but another picture. . . .

CHAPTER XIII : THE GINSENG-HUNTER

AT length the orderly for the day awoke and began to prepare breakfast. I helped him.

That morning Dersu felt a little better. The pain in the back had quite gone. He tried to walk a little, but complained all the time of weakness and headache. Again I detailed a horse for him, and by nine we left the camp.

The lower reaches of the Vangou are rather swampy. There are some patches of fertile land, covered with hazel-scrub, reeds, and mugwort. About four miles from its mouth, on the left bank, a brook falls into the Vangou called by the Chinese the Valley of the Big Rock. There is a big rock there, which has weathered down to a white, friable mass like clay. According to the natives, during the summer quantities of wapiti come here, when their antlers are in velvet, greedy to lick this white stuff. And when I examined it I saw in fact many marks of their teeth, and on one side they had gnawed away a hole a couple of feet deep.

Not far from the rock there is a big pitfall. This is in the form of a stout fence to keep animals away from their watering-place, built up partly of fallen logs and partly of growing trees. Big stakes had been driven in to hold it firmly and prevent the animals from trampling it down. In a few places openings were left with pits dug underneath them, hidden by grass and dry twigs spread over the top. When the deer come down to the water at night, they come up against the fence, and in trying to find a way round, come to the holes and fall into the pits. There are fences like that stretching over a distance of thirty miles and more, with a couple of hundred pitfalls.

This pitfall on the Vangou had been abandoned, and it was

131

clear that the Chinese had not inspected it for a long time. In one of the pits we found a wapiti hind which, evidently, had fallen in two or three days previously, poor brute. We stopped to discuss how to get it out. One of the riflemen wanted to let himself down into the pit, but Dersu advised him not to, as the animal might struggle desperately and even break one of his legs. Then we decided to haul it out with lassos. We dropped two down the pit, and the deer caught its feet in them, which we tightened, and then dropped a third over its head and hauled with all our might. I thought the poor brute would be strangled. Directly we took the nooses off, it began rolling its eyes and, after regaining its breath, it struggled to its feet, and stumbled off a little way, but before going into the forest it caught sight of the brook and at once, without paying the slightest attention to us, started thirstily drinking.

Dersu abused the Chinese terribly for abandoning the pits without filling them in.

In about an hour we came to the hunter's cabin. Dersu was now fit again, and wanted to go at once himself and break down the fence round the pits, but I advised him to wait and rest till the next day. After our dinner I suggested to the Chinese that they should get busy on it, and ordered the Cossacks to see that the pits were filled in properly.

After five in the evening the weather turned ; a fog came in from the sea, and the sky clouded over. At dusk the men came back and reported that they had found two more wapiti in the pits dead, and one live roe.

We stayed at that spot all the next day. The weather was changeable, but for the most part showery and overcast. The men washed their linen, repaired their clothing, and cleaned their rifles. Dersu was by now quite fit and well again, to my immense relief.

In the afternoon we heard shots. It was my assistants, G. I. Granatman and A. I. Merzliakoff, announcing their arrival. We were delighted to meet again and at once started comparing our adventures and exchanging yarns till late into the night.

On 14 August we were ready to continue our travels. I now proposed going up the Dinzahé and down into the basin of the Tiutihé, while Granatman and Merzliakoff undertook to make a reconnaissance of another route down the Vandagou which falls into the Tiutihé not far from its mouth. The next morning our parties started, each in its allotted direction.

The dense mist lying till then in the valleys suddenly began to rise. First the feet of the hills were exposed, then the flanks, and finally the crests. On reaching the tops, it spread out little table-cloths, and remained there. It looked like rain, but favourable weather prevailed, and although it was cloudy, no rain fell.

For the first seven miles or so up the Dinzahé there is open country, studded with clumps of woodland, and then begins the actual forest, as exuberant as in the valley of the Li-Fudzin. Here for the first time I noticed the Japanese birch, *Betula japonica*, with triangular leaves ; then another  kind of spindlewood, *Euonymus pauciflora*, with fringed branches and pale leaves ; the Manchurian apricot, *Prunus manshurica*, with small fruit, and Maximovich's cherry, always growing alone, bearing a tasteless black fruit. At one place I saw a creeping willow, *Salix vagans*, and the ashy willow, *Salix cinera*, growing sometimes as a bush, sometimes into a tree. Here and there were some bushes of Maximovich's currant, which one can always tell by its pretty foliage and small berries, and occasionally an *Atragene, A. ochotensis*.

I was struck by the dimensions of some of the trees. A cedar measured 9 ft. 6 in. in girth at the height of a man's chest, a spruce gave 4 ft. 7 in., a fir 9 ft. 1 in., a birch was 7 ft. 8 in., and a huge poplar 11 ft. 6 in.

The Dinzahé is a very winding stream in the valley, and in places very shallow, the water running over the gravel, with many little cascades, but in places there are deep holes. The water is of a reddish opal tint.

Every day the flies were becoming fewer, which was an immense relief, and made work much easier. But the mosquitoes were yellow, cold, and fierce.

We did not go far that day, and stopped to bivouac in the thick forest near an abandoned hut.

When it was dark fog was wafted up again from the sea, and the condensation was so strong that the damp settled on the ground like a heavy dew, and the fog so thick that a man was invisible at a couple of paces, and the shadows stood out as though on a screen, grew into giants, and flickered from one place to another. In damp like that one does not want to sit long by the fire, so directly after supper, as though by mutual understanding, we rolled ourselves up inside our mosquito curtains and went to sleep.

When the sun came up it scattered the fog. As usual, Dersu and I did not wait for the others, but started off ahead.

The farther we went the denser became the forest. In this virgin *taigá* there was something which impelled us into its heart, yet at the same time something that struck with the awe of the unknown. In the quiet display of the forces of nature there grew here representatives of all the trees of the Manchurian flora. These silent monsters could have told many a strange tale of the sights they had seen during the two and three centuries of their life on earth.

Few reach the very heart of the *taigá*. It is too vast. The wayfarer is ever struggling with the force of vegetation. Many secrets does the *taigá* conceal in her breast, hiding them jealously from prying eyes of man. She seems morose and grim. That is the first impression. But the man who grows to know her better soon becomes accustomed to her, and pines if taken away from the forest if he does not see forest for long. It is only outwardly that the *taigá* seems dead ; in truth she is full of life.

Dersu and I walked on unhurriedly, watching the birds. In the clumps of undergrowth here and there flitted a brisk little rustic bunting, and I caught an occasional glimpse of the little Ussurian woodpeckers. Most interesting of these was the green one with the golden crest. It hammered away busily at the trees, paying no attention to the approach of men. A few dusky thrushes flew across, some jays flew off, and once we startled a merlin, which flew low and soon was lost among the trees.

Dragon-flies appeared over the water. A wagtail gave chase, but the insect was too quick for it.

Suddenly behind me a nutcracker uttered his cry of alarm. Dersu signed to me to stop.

" Wait, captain," he said. " Him come here."

And in fact the sound approached. There was no doubt that this timid bird was escorting something through the wood. I was right. In five minutes a man appeared among the thickets. He stopped dead, as though petrified, and his face showed great alarm.

I knew him at once for a ginseng-seeker. He was dressed in the usual shirt and breeches of blue *daba*, skin moccasins, and a birch-bark hat upon his head. In front hung an oiled apron to protect his trousers from the dew and to his belt behind there hung a badger skin, so that he could sit on a log without wetting them. From his girdle hung a knife, a piece of bone for digging up ginseng roots, and a bag with flint and steel. In his hands he carried a long staff for scraping away grass and leaves on the ground.

Dersu told him not to be afraid, and he came nearer. He was a man of about fifty-five, already turning grey. His hands and face were burnt to a uniform greenish red. He was unarmed.

When the Chinaman realized that we meant him no harm, he sat on a log, pulled a rag out of his shirt, and wiped his face. The old man's expression showed extreme exhaustion.

So this was a hunter for ginseng ! In his way he was a sort of hermit, who buried himself in the mountains and entrusted himself to the protection of the spirits of the forest.

In answer to our inquiry, he told us that he had a cabin on the upper waters of the Dinzahé, but in his search for the wonder-working root he sometimes wandered so far from home that it took him weeks to make his way back. He told us how to find the way to his cabin, and invited us to stop there. After a little rest the old fellow bid us farewell, picked up his staff, and went on his lonely way. Long I followed him with my eyes. Once he stopped, picked up a handful of moss, and put it on a tree. Farther on he tied a knot in a twig of a bird cherry. Those are signals to show others who might come that way that he had worked it for ginseng and drawn blank. There is true philosophy in that, to prevent the seekers walking over the same ground and wasting time. In a few minutes the old man disappeared from view, and we continued our road.

By midday we were half-way between the Tadusha and the pass, and in the evening we came to the Udagou, the highest feeder of the Dinzahé. Here we came across a little cabin, like a native *yurtá*, or portable hut, with a ridge-pole roof, resting on the ground at each side. The two windows, one each side of the door, were covered with paper, torn and patched. Here was none of the hunter's or trapper's kit, but spades, rakes, shovels, birch-bark boxes of different sizes, and digging-sticks, for digging out the ginseng roots.

Fifty yards from the cabin was a little joss-house, with the following inscription :

' Chem shan lin van si zhi Khan chao go sian Tzin tzo zhen
tsian fu lu men.'

That is to say :
' To the Lord Tiger who dwelleth in the Forest and the Mountains. In ancient days, in the time of the Khan dynasty, He saved the state. To-day his Spirit brings happiness to man.'

CHAPTER XIV: DOWN TO THE COAST

OVER the pass we followed the course of the streams towards the east and stopped to bivouac at the junction of two of them in thick forest.

The river was teeming with *malma*, the local race of Alpine char, *Salvelinus alpinus malma*. We simply caught them in our hands, and we had them for lunch and for supper. This fish is widely distributed through the Trans-Ussurian country. The natives say that on the west of the Sihoté-Alin it is replaced by the *lenok*, another member of the salmon tribe, *Brachymystax lenok*, a well-known Siberian char, which is never found in the Maritime Province.

The soldiers amused themselves fishing with rod and line, but I took my gun and went to have a look round the hills. I walked till dusk without finding anything, and came to the bank of a river. Then suddenly I heard a sound of splashing coming out of a hole in the bank. I carefully crept up to the edge and peeped over. It was a couple of racoon-dogs, so busy catching fish that they did not notice my presence. They were standing in the water, snapping at the fish as they shot by. I watched them for a long time. Sometimes they suddenly turned round and busily started digging for shrews in the bank. Then one of them raised its head, caught sight of me, uttered a yelp, and the pair of them vanished into the grass.

When I returned everybody was already back in camp. After some supper we were all busy on our own various jobs, drank some tea, and turned in, each in the spot he fancied.

The next day we continued down the Lazagou. The valley narrows about the middle and broadens out again lower down. On the hills on the right bank, which are steep and rocky, the

Chinese have found some veins of silver-lead, which have given the valley its name. The valley is free from forest, but as the soil is rocky it is not suitable for agriculture and so there are no Chinese settlers in it above the mouths.

In several places I noticed that the ground had been trampled and rooted up. I thought it was due to pig, but Dersu pointed out a small tree stripped of leaves and bark, and said :

" Him soon begin cry out."

He explained that when a young wapiti stag feels its antlers getting strong, it tries to rub off the velvet against a tree. Another stag, hearing the noise, knows what this means. He grows jealous and excited, paws the ground, and hits the other with his antlers.

A mile or two from the mouth the river becomes swampy. At one place there is a long pool, about a mile from the coast, probably representing the deepest part of the old bay now silted up. It was heavily overgrown with reeds.

There were a lot of duck swimming on it. I stayed behind with Dersu to have a shot at them, while the party went ahead. There is no sense in shooting swimming duck unless one has a boat, so we kept an eye open for the flying ones. I used the shotgun, but Dersu shot from his rifle and he seldom missed. As I saw that, I involuntarily exclaimed a compliment at his marvellous shooting.

" Me one time shoot well," he answered. " Never missed then. Now little-little get bad."

At that moment a duck came over high. Dersu raised his rifle to the shoulder and fired. The bird toppled over in the air, came down like a stone, and bounced on the ground. I looked at him in astonishment and then at the duck. Dersu was delighted. He asked me to throw up a stone as big as an egg. I threw up ten, and he shattered eight of them. The old fellow was immensely pleased, not from any sense of vanity or in boasting, but simple because he could still earn his living by his shooting.

We stopped by the river shooting for a long time, and the evening crept on imperceptibly. When the whole valley was gilded by the rays of the dying sun, I knew the day was over. After the hard day's work, all nature prepares for rest. Hardly had the sun gone down below the horizon, when on the other side the night arose out of the sea.

A broad belt of sand stretched before us for a couple of miles. Far ahead, like a caravan in the desert, we could see our party. We picked up our birds and went after it.

The party stopped by the shore, and in a few minutes a column of white smoke rose to the sky. In half an hour we were with them.

The soldiers turned in alongside a small hut made of drift-wood, where there lived a couple of Chinamen engaged in collecting edible shell-fish at low tide. A more hearty welcome and hospitality I never met.

This last day's tramp had left us tired out. I had the misfortune to have rubbed my heel badly. We all were in need of a good rest, so I decided to stop there a day and wait for my assistants.

That night the pain in my heel kept me awake all the time and I could not shut my eyes. It was an immense relief to see the light of dawn. I sat round the fire and watched the return to life of nature.

The first to awaken were the cormorants. They slowly and unhurriedly flew across the water to an unknown destination, probably to their feeding-grounds. On the reed-covered lake there were great flocks of duck. Over both sea and land reigned a perfect calm.

Dersu was up before the others and started brewing tea. Then the sun appeared. Like a living thing, one edge peeped across the waters, and then his whole form emerged from the horizon and he started his daily climb into the heavens.

" How beautiful it is ! " I could not help exclaiming.

" Him most important man," said Dersu, answering to my exclamation. " If he go, all other things go."

After a pause he went on :

" Earth too . . . man. Him head there," and he pointed to the

139

north-east, " him feet there," and he pointed to the south-west. Fire and water also strong man. If fire and water go, then all thing go. That . . . end all thing."

In those simple words there was pure animism, but also profound philosophy.

Our conversation awoke the others. I sat there all that day. The soldiers were glad to have a day's rest too, and all they did was to keep an eye on the horses to see that they did not stray.

We employed ourselves in improvising a steam bath. We pitched a tent, heated some big stones in the fire, and boiled water in two kerosene tins borrowed from the Chinamen. When everything was ready we drenched the tent with the water and put the hot stones inside. The tent was at once filled with steam, and it made not at all a bad steam bath. There was not much room inside, and we had to take it in turns to soap down, but while one of us was washing the others were busy heating stones.

There was a lot of laughter about it, but we all had a good wash, and even washed our things.

The next three days we spent mending our footwear.

I was very anxious to get through provisions to N. A. Palchevski, who was collecting plants round Terney Bay. Luckily, at the mouth of the Tiutihé we came across a big sailing-boat bound for the north. Dersu persuaded the owner, a Manchu by name Hei Batou, to put in there and deliver letters and a case of supplies to Palchevski.

About this time the weather became changeable. Keen winds blew from the west, and the nights became cool. Autumn was approaching.

My foot was soon well again and I was able to continue our march.

A little to the south of the mouth of the Tiutihé the coast ends in cliffs about a hundred feet high, with a narrow belt of alluvium on which the tide has thrown up piles of seaweed.

Such piles of seaweed are always the haunt of wading birds of many kinds. First of all I noticed numbers of the eastern

Siberian broad-billed sandpiper, running swiftly along a sand-bank. They waded out into the water, and seemed to pay no attention at all to the surf. With them were redshanks, peaceful birds, in little flocks, hunting for grubs and worms in the weeds. When anyone came near they timidly rose into the air with

mournful cries and flew off, first a little way out to sea, and then, suddenly turning sharply, settled again on the shore as though at the word of command. Where there were belts of weed alternating with sand I could see Ussurian sand-pipers, jolly little chaps, all the time busily hunting under bits of wood, stones, and shells for their dinners; they often waded out into the sea, and when there came a bigger wave than usual they simply fluttered up into the air until it had subsided. Not far from them a couple of oyster-catchers stalked along with dignity, poking about for something. Near the cape there floated on the water diving sea ducks with grey backs, and variegated harlequin ducks that kept diving for food. Coming up to the surface again, they would have a look round, wag their tails, and get ready for another dive. Farther out to sea were the Pacific cormorants. These dived very deep and came up again a long way off from the spot where they had gone under. Many gulls were soaring over the waters, especially the East Siberian laughing gulls. Every now and then they alighted on the water and then raised a wild shriek, really not unlike a human laugh. The gulls kept dropping to the water, and criss-crossing each other in the air, and again settling on the surface, trying to jab each other with their beaks or to snatch their prey. On the far side, over the mouth of the river itself, soared a pair of white-tailed eagles, eagerly scanning the country for food. Suddenly, by mutual assent, they dropped to the beach. The crows, gulls, and waders unresistingly yielded place.

The last two days had been thundery. There had been a very violent storm on the evening of the 23rd. We could see nature getting ready for it even in the morning. It was oppressively hot all day and the air filled with mist. This became thicker and thicker, until in the afternoon it was so dense that even the outlines of the hills near by became vague and cloudy. The sky became whitish. The sun could be faced with the naked eye, and a yellow corona surrounded it.

" Will be *agdy*," commented Dersu. " Him all time begin like that."

About two that afternoon we heard the rumble of distant thunder, and at once all the birds vanished. It became murky, as though someone had drawn a dusky shroud across the heavens, and then began to fall heavy drops of rain. Suddenly a tremendous roar shook the air, and violent lightning flashed, first here, then there, in such rapid succession that they were no sooner out in one spot than they were flashing in another. The hills picked up the thunder and reverberated its rolls ' through the wide, white world.' Then on top of the rain came a whirl-wind, smashing off small branches, tearing off leaves from the trees, and lifting it all high into the air. Then started a terrific downpour. The storm lasted until eight in the evening.

The next day there were three thunderstorms in succession. I noticed that as they approached the sea they quieted down, and over the water lightning flashed only in the upper layers of the atmosphere, among the clouds. As was to be expected, the cloud-burst turned into a steady, fine rain that lasted all night and all the next two days and nights without stopping.

On 26 August the rain eased off and the weather cleared up a little. In the morning the sun came out in all his resplendent beauty, but the earth still retained the traces of the storm. Water streamed from every side, and brooks were converted into torrents.

That day Granatman and Merzliakoff arrived at Tiutihé. The

Chinese had laid out the coast trail very cleverly; it followed the valleys running along the shore, took the lowest passes, and chose the flattest slopes. At the point where the Inza Lazagou flows into the Tiutihé there are some Chinese living and some natives. I counted forty-four cabins, of which half a dozen belonged to the natives, who were somewhat different from those we had seen near Olga Bay, even in the shape of their faces. Owing to the pressure of the Chinese and alcohol they were in terrible poverty. They had adopted a certain amount of the Chinese culture, which had only increased their demands, but without substantially altering their method of life, with the result of a rapid fall in their prosperity. The old men could still remember the days when they were a numerous people, before the Chinese appeared on the scene. It was the arrival of the latter, with disease in their train, which had wiped out most of the natives. There was not a single family without its opium-pipe. The women in particular were addicted to this fatal vice.

Among them I found one old woman who still remembered her native language. I persuaded her to allow me to partake of her knowledge. At first, only with difficulty, she recalled eleven words. I wrote them down, and they struck me as being of the Udehé tongue. Fifty years ago, when she had been a girl of twenty, she had not known a single word of Chinese, but now she had completely lost her sense of nationality, even her own mother-tongue.

We had reached the Tiutihé at the moment of the run of the dog salmon, *Salmo keta*, up the river to spawn. Imagine thousands of thousands of fishes, running from seven to a dozen pounds in weight, swarming into the river and fighting their way up-stream. Some irresistible force drives them to struggle against the current and overcome all obstacles. It is this *keta* that supplies the coarse-grained, scarlet caviare.

At this time it takes no food, nourishing itself solely on the stores of vitality acquired during its sojourn in the sea. From the terraces, looking down at the scene, we could see what was taking place in the water. There were such quantities of fish that in places they completely hid the bottom. It was most interesting to see them across the rapids. They swam in zigzags, turning over from side to side, leaping and turning somersaults, but all the time forging ahead. When they came to a waterfall they sprang out of the water and tried to hook themselves on to a rock. Worn out and battered, they eventually arrive in the upper reaches, where they drop their spawn and die.

At first we flung ourselves upon all this fresh fish greedily, but it quickly palled.

After the good rest on the coast, both men and horses felt invigorated and ready to start again.

The distant hills were clad in the bluish haze of the evening mist. Dusk was approaching. I noticed that as darkness drew on the valley was filled with vague, indistinct sounds. I could pick out human cries and the chink of metal. Some of the sounds seemed far away, some quite near.

" Dersu," I asked. " What is it ? "

" Chinee drive pigs," he answered.

I did not understand him, and thought he meant the Chinese were driving their own pigs home, but Dersu explained that they did not let their pigs out before the maize was all collected and all the vegetables.

" Chinee drive pigs," he repeated.

Still I did not understand him.

At last we turned the cliff and came out on to the flat. Now the noises were much clearer. A Chinaman was shouting, and every now and then hitting a copper pot with a stick. Hearing the sound of the approaching caravan, he shouted louder than ever, and started lighting a pile of firewood standing beside the path.

" Stop, captain ! " cried Dersu. " Bad go there. Him may shoot. Him think we all same pig," he cried.

Then I began to understand. The Chinaman took us for a herd of wild pig, and might easily have fired at us. Dersu shouted something to him. The Chinaman answered at once

144

and came running to meet us. Evidently he had been afraid too and was relieved at our arrival.

I decided to spend the night there. When the Cossacks were unloading the horses and pitching camp, I went into the cabin to have a talk to the Chinamen. They were bewailing their lot, and said that for three nights running wild pig had come and ruined their gardens and pastures, and in two days destroyed almost all their vegetables, so that there was only the maize left. They had already seen pig near it by day, and there was no doubt that they would come again during the night. The Chinaman implored me to shoot into the air, and said he would pay me for doing so, and then again he ran out of the house and started yelling and beating his pot again. Away in the hills I could hear another, and, farther still, yet a third. These noises came wafting down the valley, dying away in the still night air. After supper we decided to go out and have a shot.

When the glow had faded from the sky the Chinaman went off to his maize-field and lit a fire near it. I took my gun and went off with Dersu for a hunt. The Chinaman came with us and never stopped yelling. I tried to prevent him, but Dersu said it did not matter, as the pig would come just the same. We soon came to the mealie patch, so I sat on a stump and waited on one side, while Dersu went to the other. A column of smoke rose into the air from the fire, and a reddy glow played upon the ground unevenly, lighting up the maize, the grass, the stones, and everything around.

We did not have long to wait. Just opposite the spot where we were sitting we heard a sound. It gradually grew louder. The boars were trampling down the grass and by their snorting expressing their disgust at sensing the neighbourhood of man. Without paying any attention to the yelling or to the fire they went straight to the maize-field, and in a couple of minutes we caught sight of them, and saw the leaders start their work. We fired almost simultaneously.

Dersu laid one low and I another. The herd dashed back, but in a quarter of an hour turned up again at the maize. Again two shots, and again a brace of pig came down. One, with gaping jaws, charged at us, but a shot from Dersu quieted him.

The Chinese dashed at them with blazing brands. Shots rang out again, one after another, but it made no difference. The boars came on as though it were an invasion. I wanted to go up to the dead animals, but Dersu stopped me, saying that it was very dangerous, as some of them might be only wounded. We waited a little and then went back to the cabin, had some tea, and turned in. But sleep was out of the question, for the Chinaman kept up his yelling and hammering the livelong night.

About dawn he was evidently tired, and I fell into a profound slumber. I awoke about nine and asked what was the latest news about the pigs. Dersu told me that during the night we had killed five. After we had gone they still insisted on pressing on, and ruined the rest of the maize crop. The Chinaman was terribly upset. We took only one pig, leaving the rest.

According to the Chinamen the pig used to be far less numerous, but they had increased a great deal in later years, and unless the tigers kept their numbers down they would soon fill the whole *taigá*.

We bade farewell to the Chinaman and proceeded on our way.

The farther we went, the more interesting the valley became, as every turn revealed a fresh panorama. Here an artist would find inexhaustible subjects for his studies. Some of the views were so lovely that even the Cossacks, who as a rule are indifferent to the beauties of nature, could not take their eyes off them and stood there gazing, as though charmed.

The hills encircled us, with their fantastic crests and cliffs, like huge human figures, appointed by someone to guard the place. Other crags were like animals or birds, or simply a long colonnade. The faces of the cliffs, as they faded into the valleys, were clad in garlands and festoons of creeping plants, the foliage of which in their rich autumn hues resembles the porticoes of temples and ancient castles.

During that day we came to a mine of silver-lead. Here was a single cabin in which lived a Korean watchman. He too complained of the pigs and wanted to move down to the coast. The mine had been opened up by the Chinese forty years ago, when they had tried unsuccessfully to extract the silver.

Every day there were fewer mosquitoes and flies, which now came out only at dawn and dusk, probably owing to the heavy dews and lower temperature after sundown.

The nights became much cooler. The best time of the year was approaching. For the horses, however, it was in some respects worse. The grass by the road, which formed the greater part of their food, began to wither. In the absence of oats the Cossacks sometimes managed to buy some local grain, called *buda*, from the Chinese, and give the animals a feed before starting and at camp in the evening.

The cabin of the Korean was so teeming with bugs that even the owner himself was obliged to go outside to sleep, and when it rained he took shelter in a shed built of thin boards. When we heard this we gave that hut a wide berth and pitched camp half a mile away on the bank of a stream.

In the evening after supper we sat around the camp fire and yarned. Suddenly something whitish grey floated by, silently and unhurriedly. The Cossacks said it was a bird, but I thought it was a big bat. A few minutes later the strange thing appeared again. It did not flap its wings, but sailed by in a slightly sloping line. It settled on an aspen and at once started climbing up the trunk. The creature's colour harmonized so completely with the bark that if it had kept still it would have been invisible. When it had climbed about twenty feet it stopped, and seemed to vanish. I took the shot-gun and wanted to shoot it, but Dersu stopped me. He quickly cut off some fine twigs and fastened them in the form of a noose to the end of a long stick, walked up to the tree, and lifted it into the air in such a way as not to shut off the light of the fire. Dazzled by the glare, the creature remained where it was. When the noose was high enough up, Dersu pressed it against the tree and then called to one of the Cossacks to come and hold it. He then climbed on to a neighbouring branch, sat on it, and with the noose caught the animal. The terrified little creature squeaked and tried to escape. It turned out to be a flying squirrel, *Sciuropterus rossicus*, a relative of the common squirrel. The skin of the flanks between the fore- and hind-legs is loose and elastic and can be stretched out something like a bat's wing, which enables the little animal to plane down from one tree to another. The whole body is covered with soft, silky, pale grey fur, with a parting down the tail.

The flying squirrel is common enough in all Ussuria in the mixed woods, where there are birch and aspen. Our specimen was 1 ft. 7½ in. in length and 6½ in. broad across the stretched membrane. The Cossacks and riflemen were very interested in the little captive, especially the queer expression of the head, with its broad whiskers and great big black eyes, to take in the greatest possible amount of light by night. When we had all had a good look at it, Dersu lifted it above his head, said something to it aloud in his own tongue, and let it go. It glided off and vanished in the darkness. I asked the Gold why he had let it go.

"Him no bird, him no mouse," he answered. "No must kill him."

He proceeded to explain that it was the soul of a dead child. It wanders about the earth for some time in the form of a flying squirrel, and only later arrives in the world beyond the tomb, far away on that side where the sun goes down.

I sat long and talked with him about this. He told me about other animals. For him every one had its soul, just like a man. He had even his own system of classification of them. He arranged the big animals in one class, for instance, the little ones in another, and the clever ones he separated from the foolish. The sable he included among the clever ones.

To my question which animal, in his opinion, was the most harmful of all, he considered a minute, and then said :

" Mole."

When I asked why, he answered :

" No one want shoot him ; no one want eat him ; him no good."

By which words Dersu meant that the mole is a perfectly useless creature.

I glanced round and saw that all were asleep. Wishing Dersu good night I rolled myself in my *burka*, lay down near the fire, and fell asleep myself.

THE next day, 30 August, we proceeded on our way. A couple of miles beyond the Korean hut the valley narrows between rocky cliffs and then makes a turn to the north-west. Here was once undisturbed *taigá*, but three forest fires in succession destroyed it completely, and only charred stumps remain to tell of its past woodland glories. Like gigantic fingers, they point to the sky, whence in revenge for the destruction of the forests should pour terrific rains, bringing overwhelming floods in their train. This burnt-out forest stretches far on each side. Extraordinarily depressing and lifeless is the view of such devastation.

At noon we came to dense forest, where we halted for a breather, and I had a look round at the vegetation. I noted the white maple with its smooth green bark and Maak's cherry, distinguished by its birch-like bark ; then there was the rock birch, *Betula ermani*, with dirty yellow bark hanging in tatters ; a special kind of currant, hardly different from the ordinary red currant, and covered with berries although it was in August. Then there was the thornless briar, *Rosa acicularis*, with reddish twigs, small leaves, and large pink flowers, and a *Spiræa, S. chamædrifolia*, with small, pointed, wedge-shaped leaves and white flowers, and the scarlet-berried elder, *Sambucus racemosus*, a shrub with light bark and feathery, oval-lanceolate, slightly dentate leaves and yellow flowers.

After refreshing ourselves with some food, Dersu and I walked on ahead, leaving the horses behind. Now our trail began to rise into the hills. I thought that the Tiutihé flowed through a gorge here, and that was why the path was avoiding an awkward place, but I soon noticed that it was not the track that we had been following. In the first place there were no more marks of horses' hooves, and in the second directly I caught sight of the water I saw that the path was leading up-stream. Then we decided to turn back and make straight for the river in the hope of hitting the trail somewhere. It turned out that the path had led us a long way to one side. We crossed the brook to the left side and came to the foot of a hill.

Age-old oaks, mighty cedars, black birch, maple, *Aralia*, firs, poplars, hornbeam, spruce, larch, and yew all grew together in picturesque profusion. The forest here had some peculiar feature of its own. Below, under the trees, reigned twilight. Dersu walked slowly and, as usual, kept his eye attentively on the ground at his feet. Suddenly he stopped and, without taking his eyes off some object, began to remove his knapsack, lay down his rifle and prop, threw down his axe, and lay full length on the ground, and began praying.

I thought he had gone crazy.

" Dersu," I exclaimed. " What's up ? "

" *Pantsuy !* " he cried. " Ginseng ! "

Here there was a mass of herbage, but which was the ginseng I did not know. Dersu showed it to me. I saw a small, herbaceous plant about fourteen inches high, with four leaves. Each leaf consisted of five divisions, of which the middle was the longest, the outside ones the shortest. It had already flowered, and the fruit appeared. This was in the form of small, rounded cases, arranged like those of umbelliferous plants. The cases had not yet opened or scattered their seed. Dersu cleared the weeds all round it, then picked off all the seed-cases and tied them up in a bit of rag. Then he asked me to hold the plant up with my hand, while he dug up the root. He worked extremely carefully, taking every precaution to avoid tearing the fibres. When he had got it out he took it to the brook and started carefully washing off the soil.

I helped him as best I could. Gradually the earth came away and in a few minutes we could examine the root. It was $4\frac{1}{4}$ inches long and forked, that is to say a male. So that was the famous ginseng, whose magic power is sovereign against all ills of the flesh and restores to the aged the vigour of youth ! Dersu cut

off the plant and packed it, together with the root, in moss in a roll of bark. Then he muttered some prayer, slipped on his knapsack again, picked up his weapon and prop, and exclaimed :

" You lucky, captain ! "

On the road I asked the Gold what he was going to do with his ginseng. He said he wanted to sell it and buy cartridges with the money. Then I decided to buy the ginseng myself, and offered him a better price than the Chinese would give. When I told him of this decision the result was quite unexpected. Dersu thrust his hand inside his jacket, pulled out the roll, and handed it to me, saying that it was a gift. I declined it, but he insisted. I saw that my refusal offended him, and so accepted. It was only afterwards that I learnt that it was the custom to repay gifts by gifts of equal value.

Chatting away like this, we quickly came out on to the river Tiutihé and picked up the lost trail.

Dersu saw at the first glance that our caravan had passed ahead.

It was time to hasten. About a mile and a half farther on the valley suddenly narrowed, where the river flows in a narrow bed. The grinding sound at the foot of the banks showed that the river was full of stones. Foaming cascades broke the surface on every side, alternating with deep pools full of glass-clear water which in mass assumed a splendid emerald tint.

The river was full of big *malma* trout, and Dersu wanted to shoot one, but I persuaded him to save his ammunition. Besides, we wanted to overtake the detachment, especially as they thought Dersu and I were ahead, and would hurry on to catch us up. They might be a long way ahead already.

About five we came to a trapper's cabin, and around it I saw our horses, already unloaded and grazing freely. Inside the cabin, beside the men, were some Chinese. Realizing that Dersu and I had not yet passed that way our men decided to stop and wait for us. The Chinamen had a good stock of venison and fish.

The Chinese employ the following method of catching fish. They build a dam across a stream with stones from one bank to the other, leaving an opening in the middle. The water trickles between the stones, but the fish find their way down the main stream through the opening, where they are caught in an enclosure built of osiers. The Chinese visit it two or three times a day and like that catch plenty of fish.

From the owner of the cabin we learnt that we were at the foot of the Sihoté-Alin, and the Tiutihé flows along it. They told us, too, that beyond his cabin there are two trails, one to the north straight to the water-shed, the other to the west along the Tiutihé. It was about eight miles farther to the source of the river.

That evening after supper we had a conference, at which we decided that the next day Dersu and I and a Chinese hunter would go up the Tiutihé, cross the ridge, and make our way back by the Lian Chi Heze. That trip would take us three days. The Cossacks and riflemen would stop at the hut and await our return.

So the next morning, early, we three slung on our knapsacks, took our rifles, and started.

The farther we went, the worse became the path. The valley narrowed into a gorge, so we were obliged to crawl over cliffs and cling to the roots of trees. It was such hard going that the soles of my feet began to ache.

We tried to go round the rocky screes and walk on moss or soft, friable clay, but it was not much use.

From this side the Sihoté-Alin looked grim and inaccessible. As a result of denudation, or perhaps from some other cause, there were formed deep and narrow gulches, like cañons. It looked as though fissures had been formed in the mountains, and that they had widened. At the bottom of these gullies streams were running; we could not see them, but through the mist could hear the murmur of the cascades. Lower down the flow was quieter, and then we could catch a more cheerful note in the roar of the waters.

How forlorn a man seemed among these rocky mountains, all bare of vegetation! Not long before dusk we reached the pass, at an altitude of 3985 ft. I named it the Rocky Pass; Viewed from up here, everything seemed to be on a tiny scale, even the age-old *taigá* down below in the valley looked merely like a mass of bristles, and the firs and pines like needles.

We bivouacked on the far side, on the edge of the forest. The night was damp and cold, and we scarcely slept. I kept rolling myself up tighter in my blanket, but could not get warm. Towards the morning the sky became covered with clouds, and it began to drizzle.

This was our first autumn day, overcast and windy. We quickly collected our kit and started down the basin of the Iman. The slope was easy and gentle this side as it had been steep upon the other. At first, in fact, I thought we were walking on a plateau and it was only when I saw the flow of water that I realized we were really going downhill.

The forest on the western flanks of the Sihoté-Alin was old, mossy, stunted, and consisted mainly of larch, fir, spruce, with some alder and birch.

Some old blazes brought us to a trapper's cabin. Judging from the stores accumulated, it looked as though the Iman trappers were ready to start out after sable.

The Chinese guide did not take us far along the Iman, but turned eastwards, where he missed the way and spent a long time hunting for the trail.

About midday the weather became very bad. Clouds scudded from the south-east and enveloped the tops of the mountains. I kept my eye on the compass, and wondered how our guide was able to keep so straight a direction.

By one brook we came across a mass of dead alders. Although it was early, I knew from experience that that meant a good supply of firewood at a difficult moment, and so advised a halt for the night. But my fears were groundless, for no rain fell that night, though next morning there was a thick fog.

The Chinaman hurried us on. He wanted to reach another cabin which, according to him, was another eight miles farther on. We reached it about midday. It was an empty cabin. I asked our guide to whom it belonged. He said that in the upper reaches of the Iman there were engaged in sable-trapping Chinese who lived on the coast, and that farther down there would be the huts of Chinese from the Iodzihé, and farther on still for a considerable distance there was a no-man's-land, which livened up again near the Kulumbé.

After a short rest we came again to the Sihoté-Alin. The nearer we approached, the flatter was the slope, and for over an hour it was like walking along a plateau. Suddenly I noticed a shrine beside the trail, a sign that we had reached the pass, and from here began the steep drop down to the Tiutihé.

The track brought us to the cabin where we found our men and horses waiting for us. The Cossacks were rather bored and delighted to see us again. During our absence they had shot a wapiti and caught a lot of fish.

Early in the evening the sky suddenly cleared and the clouds, which had been lying like a shroud over us, broke up. They became ragged, torn, scudding in different direction, meeting each other and scattering, and then suddenly there burst upon us a wind so violent that even the century-old trees bowed before it like reeds. Grass, leaves torn from the trees, and small branches were whirled about in the air. A bird tried to measure its strength with the wind, but was quickly exhausted, carried off, and fell rather than alighted on the ground. Suddenly a cedar growing not far from the cabin began to crack and slowly to fall. Then with a rending crash it fell upon the ground, bringing down a neighbouring sapling with it.

The hurricane raged for about an hour and then dropped as suddenly as it had arisen. Once again stillness reigned in the forest.

I dressed, took my rifle, whistled to the dog, and walked down the river. When a little distance from the hut I sat on a stone and listened. The monotonous murmur of the stream, which one does not notice in the daytime, seems at dusk quite loud. Down below the bank a fish splashed, and from the forest on the far side I heard the hooting of an eagle owl ; far away in the hills the wapiti were belling, and near me I heard the mournful bark of the musk-deer. I was so absorbed in the observation of the wild that I did not notice how time passed. My clothes were wet from dew.

I returned to the cabin, rolled myself up on the nice warm *k'ang*, and slept like a top.

The next two days, 3 and 4 September, we spent on the march from the Sihoté-Alin to the mouth of the Gorbusha. I intended at first to cross by it to the pass, and then drop down the river Aohobé to the sea.

The river Gorbusha is only five miles in length. At a point where a brook runs into it there are some big caves which the deep pools, the galleries, and columns of stalactites make very interesting. The latter stand out like bas-reliefs on the wall, and alongside them are glistening druses of quartz and huge crystals of Iceland spar. In a smaller cave there was a deposit of cave earth, with bones lying about, and the fresh pug-marks of a tiger.

We explored the caves, and continued our road.

In the afternoon Dersu and I again marched on ahead. Beyond the river the road rose a little along the flanks of the hills, and here we stopped for a breather. I began to change my clothes, while Dersu was filling his pipe. He was just putting it to his lips when he stopped suddenly and gazed fixedly into the forest. After a minute he smiled, and said :

" Aha ! Clever man ! Him know something."

He pointed silently. I started, but could see nothing.

" What is it ? " I asked.

Dersu told me not to look on the ground, but into the trees. Then I noticed that one of the trees was shaking, then still for a moment, then shaking again. We stood up and crept towards it. I quickly saw what it was. Up the tree was sitting a bear, having a feast of acorns.

It was the white-breasted Tibetan bear, *Ursus torquatus*, a good deal smaller than his brown brother.
His maximum length is 5 ft. 7 in., and his
height 27½ in. at the shoulder, and his
weight does not exceed 330 lb. His
colour is shining black, with a big white
spot on the chest and throat. Very
rarely one comes across specimens with
white belly, and even paws. Round
his big ears there is a mane of long
hairs, just like a ruffle.

They make their winter quarters in hollow poplars, and so their distribution is limited to the region of the Manchurian flora, the northern limit being a line drawn approximately from the mouth of the Ussuri to the sources of the Iman and from there along the coast to Cape Olympiad. In the spring his chief food consists of roots and leaves, in the summer of berries and acorns, and in the autumn nuts and crab-apples. He hibernates early. Higher up, on the trunk of his tree, he gnaws through an air-hole, round which the rime collects, which is a sign to hunters that there is a bear in the tree.

We crept up to within a hundred paces of the bear and watched him. Bruin had climbed up to the very top of the tree and built himself a sort of platform, a kind of *machan*. There were plenty of acorns left on the branches out of his reach, so then he started shaking the tree, and looking down to see how many fell to the ground. He was, of course, quite right. The acorns were ripe but not quite ripe enough to fall of their own accord. After a short time the intelligent beast climbed down and started nosing for his fruit in the grass.

" Who you want ? " called out Dersu.

The bear spun round, pricked up his ears, and started vigorously sniffing the air. We did not stir and the animal, reassured, was about to resume his dinner when Dersu whistled. The bear rose on his hind-legs, hid behind the tree, and peeped at us with one eye. At the time the breeze was blowing from him to us. He grunted, flattened his ears, and took to his heels. A moment later the Cossacks came up with the horses.

The end of August and beginning of September is the most interesting season in the *taigá*. It is the time of the rutting of the wapiti and the battles of the stags for the hinds. To entice the stags within shot, a birch-bark horn is made. This is a strip of bark about 4 in. wide, which is rolled into a spiral until it forms a kind of horn 22 or 23 in. long, and the sound is produced by inhaling the air into it.

There is no difficulty in shooting a wapiti stag at this season. The stags, blinded by their passion, are regardless of danger and come quite close to the hunter when he calls them with the horn. This ensured us a good supply of meat, so I did not let the Cossacks do any shooting, but went out myself to see this kind of sport.

Dersu and I took a horn each, and walked about a mile into the forest in different directions. When I came to a place where the growth was a little clear, I sat on a stump and waited.

As it grew dusk the forest became stiller and stiller.

There is something majestic in the passage from day to night in the forest. The fading daylight impresses the soul with a pang of regret and feeling of sadness. Solitude engenders meditation and memories. I became so plunged in introspection that I was oblivious to my surroundings and why I had come into the ghostly twilight.

Suddenly away to the south I heard the roar of a stag. The challenge rang through the forest, and at once provoked an answer, quite near me. That, I thought, must be an old one. He began on quite a low note, and gradually rose the complete octave. I replied on my horn. Within a minute I heard a crackle behind me, and turned to see the splendid picture of a stag. He was advancing with a graceful, confident step, shaking his head as his antlers caught in the branches. I stood frozen on the spot. The wapiti stopped, stretched out his head, and sniffed the air, trying to catch the wind of his rival. His eyes were blazing, his nostrils distended, and his ears pricked forwards. For a couple of minutes we stood thus, while I drank in the beauty of this splendid beast. I  could not bring myself to deprive him of his life. Sensing the presence of an enemy, he became excited. He began tearing the earth with his antlers, then raised his head and emitted another mighty bellow. A wisp of vapour shot out of his throat. Before the echo could fling back his voice his challenge was taken up from the direction of the Sinantsa. The stag stiffened and gave a grunt which passed into a roar and a bellow, but short and savage. At that moment in his wrath he looked simply splendid. Suddenly from one side I heard a sound. I looked round and saw a hind, but by the time I turned my head the two stags had met. They charged with the utmost ferocity. I heard the crash as their antlers met, the heavy, laboured breathing, forced out of their lungs with deep grunts. Their hind-legs were stretched, but the front doubled back under

 their bellies. By a violent effort one of the stags broke off the top tine from his rival's antler, and thus released himself from the clutch. The duel lasted for about ten minutes, and then I could see that one of them was beginning to yield. He was breathing heavily, and slightly giving ground. Seeing this, the other redoubled his onslaught, but then the two fighting monsters disappeared from my sight.

I turned to look at the hind. She was standing in the same place, apathetically watching her two suitors locked in mortal combat. The noise of the fight resounded through the forest.

Evidently one was driving the other from the field. The hind followed at a respectful distance.

Suddenly I heard a distant shot. That was evidently Dersu. And then I noticed for the first time that the duel I had witnessed was not the only one. The bellowing resounded on every side.

It was now growing rapidly dark, as the last flicker of light struggled with the blackness approaching from the east. I turned back to camp, and within half an hour was there, to find Dersu had arrived before me. He was sitting by the fire cleaning his rifle. He could have killed several wapiti, but contented himself with a single hazel-hen.

Long we sat and listened to the belling of the stags. They kept us awake the whole night, and through my drowsy slumbers I could hear grunting and roaring, which kept arousing me. The Cossacks were sitting round the fire swearing. The sparks rose like fireworks, twirled a moment in the air, and vanished. At length came the signs of dawn and the wapiti began to quiet down, though one or two unsatisfied⁻ stags continued their uproar. They were wandering about the shady slopes and roaring, but none answered. Then out came the sun and the *taigá* lapsed again into silence.

Leaving the men in camp, Dersu and I walked up to the Sihoté-Alin. The rise was gentle at first, but soon became steep, and we were obliged to force our way through pathless thickets, all encumbered with fallen and charred trunks.

Autumn was approaching, and the foliage had already begun to fall. By day it crackled under one's feet, but at night the dew made it soft again, which is a help to stalking.

By midday we were on the crest, where I saw a now familiar scene, forest to the west and to the east all burnt-out ground. Dersu found the spoor of elk which, he said, in this district are found only as far as the river Noto, below which they do not pass.

About six in the evening we were back in camp. It was still quite light when the most eager stags began their belling again, at first on the hills, and then in the dales.

The duel of the stag had made a great impression on me, and I decided to go out into the *taigá* again to watch another, and invited Dersu. We crossed the stream and dropped into the forest, now wrapped in the mystery of darkness. We stopped about a mile and a half from camp and listened. As soon as the sun disappeared and twilight fell, the darker it became in the forest, the more violent the bellowing of the stags. Before long their masculine music reverberated  throughout the forest. We tried to stalk close to them, but without success. Twice we caught sight of them, but vaguely, getting a glimpse only of the head and horns, or of the stern and hindlegs. At one spot we came upon a fine, handsome stag with three hinds in attendance, not standing, but moving slowly forward. We followed in their tracks, but without the help of Dersu I should have quickly lost them. The stag led the way. He was well aware of his great strength, and so picked up every challenge that came ringing through the air. Suddenly Dersu stopped and listened.

He turned round and stood motionless.

There came to my ear the roar of an old stag, but the note was somehow different.

" Hm," muttered Dersu. " Understand what man him ? "

I replied that I supposed it was a wapiti, only an old one.

" Him Amba ! " he whispered to me. " Him very clever man. Him all time trap wapiti like that. Wapiti now not understand, not know what man call. Amba soon catch hind."

And as in confirmation of his words, at that moment the deep voice of a stag answered the tiger, which at once replied. He made a very fair imitation of the roar of the stag, but at the end broke off in a sort of deep purr.

The great cat was coming nearer, and would soon probably pass quite close to us. Dersu seemed excited, and my own heart was thumping. Suddenly Dersu cried out :

" A-ta-ta ! ta-ta-ta ! Ta-ta-ta ! "

He then fired a shot into the air, dashed up to a birch, hastily ripped off a strip of bark, and set fire to it with a match. The dry bark burst into a bright flame, which made the darkness around seem blacker than ever. The wapiti, startled by the shot, bolted in every direction, and then all was still. Dersu fastened the burning bark to a stick, and we started back to camp by torchlight. Crossing the stream, we came on to the footpath, and so returned to camp.

CHAPTER XVI : A BEAR HUNT

THE next day, 7 September, we continued our journey. I decided to make our way down to the coast by the river Aohobé, which is a corruption of the Udehé name Ehé, meaning Devil.

Our trail took us first towards the south, for a mile or two along the highest feeder of the Sinantsa till we came to the watershed, where the forest all around had been destroyed by fire. Only in the valleys had it escaped, where patches remained like islands. After a breather on the pass we started down the Duntsa, following the narrow, winding valley, overgrown with birch and poplar. Presently we came up against a fence. It turned out to be one of those hunter's fences, a *ludeva*. It cut across the valley of the Aohobé, and followed one of its feeders for a distance of eight or nine miles.

Near the fence was a cabin with a door, surrounded by a high palisade. It was here that the Chinese hunters performed their operation of sawing off the velvety horns of young living wapiti. Behind the hut were some cages like stalls, where the Chinese kept their deer until the antlers reached the best condition. On the right was a shed, standing on piles, in which were stored wapiti hides, dried horns, and about 350 lb. of tendons drawn from their hind-legs. Boiled horns and dried wapiti tails hung in rows from the ridgepole close under the roof.

In the cabin we found four Chinamen. At first they were alarmed, but when they saw we did not intend them any harm, their servility gave way to civility.

In the evening three more arrived. They started relating something and swore terribly, which made Dersu laugh. It was a long time before I understood what was the matter. It turned out that a bear had fallen into one of their pits. He had, of course, made his way out at once, and started smashing down the fence and scattering the branches which had been laid across it to mask the hole, which would involve them in a great deal of work to repair the damage.

The cabin was small and the Chinamen numerous, so I decided to walk on another mile or two and bivouac in the open.

The middle of the valley of the Aohobé is free from forest but unsuited for agriculture, as the thin film of soil barely covers the barren, stony ground, and is easily washed away by the heavy rains. On the shady side there is a thin growth of woodland, with cedar, lime, oak, poplar, birch, walnut. In the sunny places, clumps of hazel, *Lespedeza*, meadow-sweet, and Viburnum. By the brook, where there was more moisture, there were thickets of thin-stemmed alder and sallow.

In the lower reaches there were many Chinese living. They made their way here about twenty years previously, with the result that the native Udehé had vanished, died out, or moved elsewhere.

Seen from the sea, the river looks very short, but it is an interesting stream, as about four miles from the coast it disappears and flows under the stones. Only in rainy weather does it appear above ground, and then it is very turbulent.

In the afternoon we missed the path and found ourselves in a game track, which took us a long way out of our way. As we crossed a spur of the hills, covered with scree and bare of vegetation, we stumbled unexpectedly on to a small stream, the bed of which was littered with fallen trunks of trees. The quantity and size of these gave us a good idea of the magnitude of the floods here. It was obvious that here they were of short duration but very violent while they last, owing to the proximity of the sea and the steepness of the slopes. The stream is a feeder of the river Mutuhé, which is one of the best districts for game in the region. As we walked through the thickets of *Lespedeza* and walnut trees, we disturbed deer, roe, and wild pig. The Cossacks yelled and became very excited, and I had some difficulty in preventing them from shooting, which would have been useless waste of life. At three in the afternoon I gave the signal to pitch camp.

I was very anxious to kill a bear. Other men kill them by the dozen, so why should not I ? Vanity fanned my hunter's ardour, and I resolved to try my luck.

Many sportsmen tell how they have killed their bears without any feeling of fear, and relate only the humorous side of the hunt. According to some, bears run away at the shot. Others say that they stand up on their hind-legs and charge the hunter, and that is the moment to fire. Dersu did not agree. When he had heard stories like that he became quite angry and spat, but never argued.

When he heard that I was anxious to kill a bear, he advised me to be very cautious and offered to come and help. This inflamed my ardour still more, and I firmly resolved to go and have a shot at Bruin single-handed, whatever it cost.

Before I had gone half a mile from the camp I had moved a roe and a boar. There was such an abundance of game here that it seemed like a game park, where animals had been collected and allowed to move about freely.

Crossing a brook, I stopped in an open clearing and waited. Within a few minutes I saw a wapiti, and among the nuts near by I could hear the grunting of pig and the squeaks of the piglings.

Suddenly ahead I heard the cracking of branches and immediately after that I heard steps. Someone was moving with a regular, heavy tread. I was alarmed at first and wanted to retreat, but pulled myself together and held my ground. A moment later in the bush I caught sight of a dark mass. It was a huge bear. He kept stopping, had a dig, or rolled over a log and attentively examined the ground beneath. Waiting till the brute was not more than about forty paces from me, I aimed carefully and pulled the trigger. Through the smoke of the shot I could see the bear spin round with a hoarse roar and bite at the spot where the bullet had hit him. What happened next I do not remember very clearly, as it was all so swift that I cannot remember the order of events. Immediately after the shot the bear charged me with all his might. I felt a violent blow and at the same moment fired again. When and how I had been able to reload I could never understand. I seemed to have fallen on my left side. The bear crashed head over heels and rolled down the slope. How I recovered my feet and did not drop my rifle I do not remember. I ran down the valley and heard the brute chasing me. He was following my tracks, but already with reduced speed, and each leap was accompanied by heavy panting and grunts. Remembering that my rifle was now not loaded, I stopped.

"I must give him another! A straight shot to save my life!" flashed through my mind.

I raised the weapon to my shoulder, but could not see the sights. All I could see was a huge brown head, with gaping maw and savage eyes. If anyone could have caught sight of me at that moment he would have seen, I dare say, my expression of terror.

I never believe those hunters who say they shoot at a charging brute at close quarters as calmly as at an empty bottle. It is all lies! Lies, because the instinct of self-preservation is innate in every man. The sight of an enraged monster out for blood cannot but excite the hunter and will certainly affect the steadiness of his aim.

When the brute was quite near me I fired at him again point-blank. He crashed over, and I started running again. When I turned round to have a look, I saw the bear rolling on the ground. At that moment I heard a sound on the right. I glanced round instinctively, and was rooted to the spot, to see . . . another bear!

I could see its head, but the rest of the body was concealed by the bushes. As quietly as possible I crept off and bolted, till I came to the river.

For twenty minutes I walked about until I had calmed down. I was ashamed to return to the camp empty-handed. And if I had killed the bear it was a pity to leave him there, but there was the second bear there, unwounded too. What was the best thing to do ? I walked about trying to make up my mind till the sun went down. Then I decided to creep back and have a look at the bears. My nerves were strained to the utmost. Every sound, every rustle started me on the run. The whole place seemed alive with bears, hard upon my tracks. I kept stopping to listen. At last I caught sight of the tree beside which the bear had collapsed. It had a menacing look in my eyes. I decided to walk round it and have a look at it from the higher ground. I threw stones.

Suddenly I noticed something moving in the scrub.

" A bear ! " I thought at once, and started back.

But this time I heard a human voice. It was Dersu. I was immensely relieved and dashed to meet him. As soon as he caught sight of me the Gold sat down on a log and lit his pipe. I went up and asked him why he had turned up. He answered that from the camp he had heard my shots and came to help me. By my tracks he had found the place where I fired and where the bear had charged. Then he showed me the place where I had fallen, and, in fact, he told me the whole story as he read it from our tracks.

" The brute must have gone off," I said.

" He has stopped here," answered Dersu, pointing to a large heap of earth.

I understood. I had heard the tales of hunters that bears, when they come across a dead animal, bury it and dig it up as a dainty when it is high. But I had never heard that a bear will bury a bear. That was new even to Dersu.

In a few minutes we had exhumed the bear. Not only had it been covered with earth, but a lot of stones and even logs had been laid on top of it.

I started lighting a fire, while Dersu cleaned the carcass. It was a great, big, dark brute, a true brown bear, *Ursus arctos*.

The body was 6 ft. 8 in. long and weighed over 690 lb. Bears are distributed over all Ussuria, but they are darker in the south and lighter in colour towards the north. They are good-natured brutes until touched, when they are highly dangerous, and the males are very savage in the breeding season. They ramble about the *taigá* and attack anything, even birds. Their food is mainly vegetarian, but they are not above enjoying a piece of meat or fish when they get the chance.  Brown bears make their winter quarters under the roots of trees, in clefts in rocks, and even in the ground. They are very fond of taking up their abode in caves, not only in winter, but in the warm weather too. Sometimes they keep moving as late as December. They are not fond of climbing trees. Probably their great weight is an obstacle.

All three of my bullets were in the carcass, one in the flank, the second in the chest, and the third in the head.

By the time Dersu had finished his job it was quite dark. We put moist wood on the fire so that it would last till the morning, and walked slowly back to camp.

The evening was still and cool. The full moon hung in the cloudless sky, and the brighter its rays, the blacker the shadows it threw. On the way we disturbed several more pigs, which crashed off through the scrub in different directions. At last we picked up a light between the trees. It was our camp fire.

After some supper the men turned in early. That day I had been through so much excitement that I could not go to sleep. I arose, sat by the fire, and thought over the events of the afternoon. The red glow of the fire, the black shadows of the trees, and bluish light of the moon blended in one whole. Round the sleeping forest wild beasts were roaming. Some of them came quite close to the fire. The roes were particularly inquisitive.

At last drowsiness overcame me, I lay down alongside the Cossacks, and fell into a heavy slumber.

At daybreak Dersu was first up. Then I and then the rest. The sun was just above the horizon, illuminating the tops of the mountains. Exactly opposite our camp, only a couple of hundred yards away, yet another bear was moving. He was pottering about on one spot all the time, and probably would have stayed there much longer if Murzin had not frightened him. The Cossack picked up his rifle and fired. The bear spun round, glanced in our direction, and swiftly disappeared into the forest.

After a bite we collected our bundles and moved on. By the shore we came upon the camp site of Palchevsky. He had left a letter for me in a bottle tied to a stick, in which he informed me that he had been working at that spot a few days earlier, and then gone northwards.

The river Mutuhé, which runs out here, means in Chinese the Pig River. There were two other streams without Chinese names so I christened them in Russian the Bear and the Wapiti rivers. At the junction of the two was a small cabin. It was empty. Dersu had a look round and reported that it had been used by four Korean sable-hunters, who had lately left for the winter season's hunting.

Here, along the brooks and the seashore, we saw a few migratory birds. But as neither species nor individuals were numerous I decided that the coast does not coincide with an important line of migration. There were a few Amur curlews gracefully stalking about in the grass. When we approached they stopped, stared at us, and then rose into the air with a hoarse protest, flew off a little distance, and settled again, but were more shy the next time. On the other side, near the water, was an eastern white-fronted goose, which looked a much bigger bird than it actually is. Murzin crept round and shot it with a bullet. Of the duck tribe, there were plenty of teal, which kept to the brooks and alder thickets. When I crept up quite close they did not fly away, but merely swam off a little distance, evidently not afraid of man.

A path leads up the Mutuhé from the Korean's cabin. On the left bank there is mixed coniferous and deciduous forest, on the right only broad-leaved trees. This is the nearest point to the sea where the cedar grows. It reaches here a height of over 70 ft., with a girth of 10 to 11 ft. Higher up the stream there are a few clumps of yew, *Taxus cuspidata.* This representative of a relict flora never forms complete thickets in this country, and although it attains an age of three or four centuries does not attain any great dimensions and becomes hollow at an early age.

The trail up the Mutuhé is extremely stony, and progress up it was difficult, as the crevices in the boulders and between them and the network of roots form regular traps, and one must go very carefully to avoid the risk of a broken ankle. It is astonishing how the local unshod Chinese ponies manage to go on such a track, and even carry quite substantial loads.

After following the river up for several miles, we turned back to the sea in an easterly direction.

In the morning I had already noticed that there was something peculiar about the air. There was mist hanging and the sky changed from blue to a whitish tint, while the distant mountains were no longer visible. I pointed this out to Dersu, and asked him what he thought it foretold, and told him all I knew about dry fog.

" Me think it smoke," he replied. " No wind; me no understand."

Directly we mounted to the top I saw at once what was the matter. From behind the hills, from the right of the Mutuhé, columns of white smoke were rising in great billows, and away to the north the hills were smoking too. Obviously, a forest fire had spread over a big area. We watched the impressive scene for a while and then turned back to the sea, and when we struck the cliffs, turned to the left, following deep clefts and high capes.

It was interesting to note how the passage of sound-waves was affected by obstacles in their path. As soon as we passed some high ground the sound of rain died away, but when we came down to the ravines it was audible again. Then suddenly some unfamiliar sounds caught my ears, rather like a hoarse, prolonged bark, wafted up from below by the breeze. I quietly went to the edge of the cliff and looked over. It was an extraordinary sight that met my eyes.

A huge herd of sea-lions, great and small, lay upon the shore. It was *Arctocephalus stelleri*, Steller's sea-lion, one of the eared seals. They are huge creatures, running to over 12 ft. in length, and in weight running to 1700 lb. In the Maritime Province they occur all along the shores of the Sea of Japan,  where the natives hunt them, chiefly for their hides, which they use for moccasins and harness for dog-teams.

They were evidently thoroughly happy, playing about on the rocks washed by the foam of the breakers. They stretched themselves, threw their heads backwards, lifted their hind flappers as high as they could into the air, rolled over on to their backs, belly upwards, and then quite unexpectedly rolled off their rock into the water. The moment a rock was vacated, up popped another head, and a second sea-lion hurried to take possession of it. The cows were lying along the shore with their calves, while on one side, near some caverns washed by the spray, the big bulls were drowsing. The old ones were light brown in colour, the younger ones much darker. These carried themselves with dignity. Raising their heads, they slowly turned to gaze from side to side, and in spite of their clumsy frames it is impossible to deny them grace. From the manner in which they carry themselves, from their size and their swiftness of movement, they fully deserve the title of sea-lions as much as their congeners of the Californian coast.

Like a typical Cossack hunter, Murzin promptly raised his rifle and started to aim at the nearest monster, but Dersu stopped him, and gently deflected the barrel.

" No need shoot," he said. " No can take body ; shoot all same wrong."

Only then did we notice that the place was inaccessible. On the right and left the water lapped cliffs projecting out to the sea, and from the mainland side the vertical cliff was a good 150 ft. or more high. The only possible approach to the animals would have been by boat. It would have been impossible to have taken away the body if we had shot one, and we could only have abandoned it where it lay.

But I was struck by Dersu's words. To shoot for nothing was wrong ! How true and simple a thought ! Why is it that we Europeans so often abuse our power and our weapons, and take the life of animals thoughtlessly, as it were for mere amusement ?

We watched the sea-lions for about twenty minutes, for I could not tear my eyes away from them. Suddenly I felt someone touch me on the shoulder.

" Captain, time we go," said Dersu.

It is always easier to follow the crest of a range than the flank, because the outstanding peaks can be passed on the contour.

By the time we came back to our trail night had already descended upon the earth.

We had now to climb a lofty hill and then drop into a valley. The height of the pass was about 2400 ft.

When we reached the top the scene that met my eyes made me ejaculate a cry of astonishment. The forest fire was creeping along, the line of fire engirdling the mountain like an illumination, a majestic but mournful picture. The flames sprang up and died down, and then again burst out into a blaze. They had already passed the valley and were descending into the ravine. The highest peaks were not yet victims of the flames, which were climbing up in an enveloping ring, like a veritable assault. Against the sky were two distinct glows, one on the west, the other on the east. One was motionless, the other quivered. The moon began to emerge, its edge protruding above the horizon. Slowly, undecidedly, it swam up out from the waters, higher and higher, big, mournful, purple. . . .

" Captain, must go ! " whispered Dersu to me again.

We dropped down to the valley, and as soon as we had found water, halted in some open woodland among the oaks. Dersu advised us to pull up grass for our bivouac and start an opposition fire. The dry grass and fallen foliage sprang into flame like gunpowder, and the fire spread rapidly down-wind and sideways. Now the forest had a fairy-like, fabulous kind of appearance. I started to follow the fire. Through the foliage, its progress was rather slow, but directly it gripped the grass it sprang forward. The heat picked up bits of dried leaves and twigs and whirled it into the air, where it caught fire and was carried off, thus spreading the conflagration ever farther. At last it reached the scrub, and then with a roar a huge flame leapt into the air. Here was growing a yellow birch with ragged bark, and in a flash it was converted into a blazing torch, but only for a moment. The bark burnt off and the flame went out. Old trees with dried hearts burnt standing upon their roots. Behind the fire hung here and there wisps of pale smoke. Half-burnt brands lay smouldering on the ground.

Animals and birds fled in terror. A hare dashed past me. A little chipmunk scurried from a log just beginning to burn. A chequered woodpecker flew from tree to tree, uttering hoarse screams of fear.

I followed the fire farther and farther, without thought of the danger of losing my way. I went on walking until my stomach reminded me that it was time to return to camp. I was counting on our camp fire showing me the way, but when I looked round I saw a dozen fires. I approached one. It was a burning log. How could I tell which was ours ? One seemed bigger than the others, but when I came up to it it was a blazing stump. I went to another. The same thing. Then I walked systematically from fire to fire, but no sign of our camp. Then I started shouting, and the answer came from exactly the opposite direction.

I turned back and quickly rejoined my party. They all chaffed me, and I myself could not help laughing.

Dersu's fears were justified. In the second half of the night the fire began to move in our direction, but not finding anything left to feed it, passed to the side. Contrary to our expectations, the night was warm, in spite of the cloudless sky. As in all cases where I could not understand anything, I turned to Dersu for an explanation, and was never disappointed.

" No can frost," he said. " Look-see round . . . much smoke."

And then I remembered how fruit-growers protect their fruit against the morning frosts by lighting smoke fires.

During the day we saw a wapiti grazing near a smoking log. It calmly stepped across it and began to browse on a shrub. The frequent fires have evidently accustomed wild life to them, so that they have ceased to fear them.

Sunrise found us on the road. After coming down from the pass the path for a time follows a pile of shingle, so that we had on the right the sea, on the left a marsh, which shows that there was once a lagoon here. On the other side were huge boulders of gneiss. No waves could have thrown them so high, and their presence there must be due to ice, which in winter is wind-driven, and churns up the shore. Besides the boulders there were masses of bones of a whale, ribs, paddles, vertebræ, and pieces of skull. Beasts and birds had carried off what they could, and only the bones were left.

After a rest we continued our road, and in an hour the trail brought us to some lakes. There were three of them, the biggest a couple of miles long. Here the trail forked, one branch leading up to the hills, the other following the shore, which brought us to a small but deep stream, which connected the longest lake with the sea.

There was nothing to do but camp there. Luckily there was no shortage of firewood, as the sun had dried a mass of jetsam thrown up by the sea. The only disagreeable thing was the salt taste and unpleasant smell of the water. I noticed some waders by the shore, sand-pipers with a large greenshank among them.

While the men were pitching camp and collecting firewood, I slipped off for a bit of shooting, and came back with four sand-pipers for supper.

Our bivouac was not particularly comfortable. A sharp breeze from the west blew up the valley all night, as though up a pipe. The only thing to do was to take refuge on the sea side of the pile of shingle. Inside the tent it was smoky ; outside it was cold. After supper we turned in in a hurry, but I simply could not fall asleep. I lay listening to the murmur of the waves, wondering at the fate that had brought me to this wild shore of the distant ocean.

On 20 September the weather remained warm and dry all day. I decided to survey the river Seohobé. The first thing to do was to cross the lake, which, in the absence of a boat, was not easy. We could either make a raft or try to ford it. I decided on the ford as being quicker, and the experiment was justified. The lake was shallow, the deepest places barely reaching 20 ft. The shallows, though, were winding, and we kept plunging in deeper water up to our waists. We could feel the water growing colder the nearer we came to the river.

Directly we emerged on the far bank we hit a trail.

It was noticeable how birds were becoming fewer and fewer every day. The only ones I had noticed during the last few days had been the long-tailed Ussurian owl, that is so brave by night but so timid by day. On bright, sunny days it buries itself in the thickest pine forest not so much for food as for the dim light that there reigns ever. Then there was the Ussurian white-backed wood-pecker, the largest of the *Picidæ*, a bird that haunts the mixed woodlands, where there is plenty of rotten timber ; then there was the wedge-tailed shrike, a greedy and lively bird of prey, not afraid to attack even birds bigger than itself; there was a green pipit in the edge of the forest, and some black-headed buntings, handsome little birds with yellow bellies and black caps on their heads. They prefer open ground to shady places, and collect in a small flock.

The trail brought us to a game-barrier fifteen miles long, with seventy-four pitfalls. Never had I seen such slaughter as here. Alongside the cabin stood a shed on piles crammed full of wapiti tendons tied in bundles. Judging by the weight of one bundle, there must have been here something like 1500 lb. of tendons. The Chinamen told us that they dispatch the tendons to Vladivostok twice a year, whence they are sent on to Chifu. On the walls of the hut there hung hundreds of hides of sea-lions, all taken from young animals.

There was no doubt that the Chinese knew all about the rookery of the sea-lions near the mouth of the Mutuhé, and did as much slaughter there as on the Seohobé.

" All round soon all game end," commented Dersu. " Me think ten years, no more wapiti, no more sable, no more squirrel, all gone."

It was impossible to disagree with him. In their own country the Chinese have long since exterminated the game, almost every living thing. All that is left with them are crows, dogs, and rats. Even in their seas they have exterminated the trepangs, the crabs, the various shell-fish, and all the seaweed. The Pri-Amur country, so rich in forest and wild life, awaits the same fate, if energetic measures be not taken soon to prevent the wholesale slaughter by the Chinese.

Near the sea, about half a mile from the lake, there is another of these *ludevas*, or game-fences, only a couple of miles long, with seven pitfalls.

CHAPTER XVII : BRIGANDS

ON the path that day Dersu came across human tracks. He started examining them attentively. Once he picked up a cigarette-end and a piece of blue material. In his opinion two men had passed that way. They were not working men, as working men do not throw away a new piece of *daba* merely because it is patched, but go on wearing it till it falls to pieces.

Besides, working men smoke pipes; they cannot afford cigarettes. Carrying on his investigations, he came to a place where the two men had stopped to rest, and one had changed his shoes. An empty cartridge-case showed that they were carrying rifles.

The farther we went the more information he picked up. Suddenly Dersu stopped.

" Two more men go," he said. " Now four men ; me think bad men."

We discussed the situation and decided to abandon the track and cut straight through the forest. As soon as we came to a hill we climbed it and had a look round. Ahead, three miles or so away, we could see Gulf Plastun. On the left, a lofty ridge, beyond which was, probably, the Sinantsa ; behind, the long lake ; to the left, a row of rounded hills, and beyond them the sea. Without having noticed anything suspicious, we proposed to return to the trail, but the Gold advised us to drop down to the brook flowing towards the north and follow it as far as the Tetibé.

In about an hour we came to the edge of the wood, and here Dersu told us to stop and await his return, as he went out on a reconnaissance.

It grew dusk. The swamp assumed a general yellowish-brown colour, and now had a lonesome, lifeless look. The hills faded into the blue haze of evening and looked full of gloom. The darker it grew, the brighter seemed the glow of the forest fire against the sky. An hour passed. Then another, and still no Dersu. I began to feel uneasy.

Suddenly in the distance a cry rang out, followed by four shots, again a cry, and then another shot. I started running in that direction, but pulled up at the thought that like that we should miss each other.

Twenty minutes later the Gold arrived. He looked exceed-

ingly alarmed. As far as he could, he hurriedly told us what had happened. Following the tracks of the four men, he had come to Gulf Plastun, and here he saw a tent. In it were sitting about twenty Chinese, all armed. Convinced that they were brigands, he crept back, taking cover behind the bushes, but a dog winded him and gave tongue. Three Chinamen picked up their rifles and ran out after him. In fleeing, he ran into a quagmire. The brigands called out to him to stop, and then began shooting. Dersu aimed from a kneeling position and shot one of his pursuers. He clearly saw him fall. Two of them stopped beside the fallen man, but Dersu ran on farther. So as to throw the brigands off the scent, he ran in the opposite direction from our camp, and then circled round to come back.

" Hunhuz him make hole in my shirt," said Dersu, concluding his story, and showed his jacket with a bullet-hole through it. " We must go soon, go quickly, go right away," and he started picking up his knapsack.

We started forward as quietly as possible. The Gold led us along screes and the dry bed of a brook, avoiding the trails. About nine in the evening we reached the river Iodzyhé. We did not go to the cabin, but bivouacked under the open sky.

That night I was chilled to the bone ; I rolled myself up in the tent, but the damp penetrated everywhere. No one closed an eye, and we impatiently awaited the dawn. But time, as though on purpose, lagged desperately slowly.

At the first touch of light we started ahead. We wanted to meet Granatman and Merzliakov as soon as possible. Dersu suggested that it would be better to abandon the path and go by the mountains, and that is what we did. Fording a brook, we came out on to a path, and just as we were stepping into the grass there appeared out of the bushes a native with a rifle in his hand.

At first he was frightened and in his turn gave us a good fright, but, seeing our riflemen and Cossacks, thrust his hand into his shirt and pulled out a packet. It was a letter from Palchevski informing me that a party of hunters, under the leadership of the Chinese head-man, Chan Bao, was in the Sanhobé on the trail of the brigands. While I was reading the letter Dersu interrogated the man, who in his turn asked Dersu a mass of questions. It appeared that Chan Bao, with some thirty men, had bivouacked not far from us, and was probably already quite near.

And so it turned out. About twenty minutes later we met him.

Chan Bao was a tall man of about forty-five years. He was wearing the same kind of blue costume as ordinary Chinamen, only rather cleaner and better than usual. On his mobile face I read the impression of much privation endured. He had the usual drooping black moustache of the Chinese, already touched with grey. Through his black eyes shone the light of intelligence, and a faint smile hovered constantly upon his lips, though not for one moment did his expression lose its seriousness. Before speaking he always considered his answer, and spoke quietly, unhurriedly. I had not before had occasion to meet a man in whom were so perfectly blended seriousness, good nature, energy, judgment, firmness, and diplomatic talent. From the personality of Chan Bao, from his movements and gestures, from his whole poise, there radiated intelligence. His wisdom, his self-respect, and his power of dominating the crowd, all showed that he was no ordinary John Chinaman. Most probably he was a political offender who had escaped from China.

Chan Bao's band consisted of Chinese and natives. They were all young, active, and strong men, well armed. I noticed at once that he held them under a firm discipline. All his orders were carried out instantly, and not once did he have occasion to repeat one.

Throughout the district, from Kusun to the Olga Bay, Chan Bao was regarded as the most influential personage. Chinese and aborigines alike turned to him for counsel, and if there were ever need for reconciling two irreconcilable enemies the Chinese always referred to him. He often took the side of the oppressed, and on this ground had many enemies. He had a particular hatred for all brigands, and by his action against them he inspired them with such respect that they never ventured beyond the Iodzyhé.

The gang into which we had stumbled had arrived in Gulf Plastun in boats with the object of plundering the junks that put in there during bad weather.

Chan Bao received me politely but with dignity. When he learnt that Dersu had been attacked by them during the night, he questioned him closely about details, where it had happened, and with a stick sketched a plan in the sand.

When he was satisfied with his information he said he must hurry on, and that he would return to the Sanhobé two or three days later. He then said good-bye to me, and set off with his men.

As we now had no longer any need to avoid the Chinese, we called at once at the nearest cabin and lay down to sleep. At midday we arose, drank some tea, and set off up the valley of the Dungu. Vegetation here was scanty. The few scattered oaks, black birch, larch, and lime could hardly be dignified with the name of forest. Saplings there were none. They are all burnt off systematically twice a year by the forest fires. The southern flanks of the hills are covered with bush, chiefly *Spiræa*, *Viburnum*, and *Lespendeȝa*. All the rest of the country is grass or bog.

During the second half of the day we succeeded only in reaching the pass. Noticing that the water in the river bed began to fade away, we turned to one side and pitched camp not far from the water-shed. Merrily crackled the dry wood in our fire. We warmed ourselves round it, and talked over our adventures of the night.

I noticed that Dersu wanted to ask me something but evidently hesitated. I helped him out with it.

" Me hear Russian brigands too. Can be or not ? " he eventually blurted out shyly.

" It is true," I answered, " but they usually work singly, or at the most in pairs, and never form bands like the Chinese," I answered. " The Russian Government would never let that happen."

I thought my reply had satisfied the Gold, but still I noticed that his thoughts were directed in another direction.

" How that ? " he worked it out aloud. " There is Tsar, there is many captains, and there is brigands. Chinese, too, have Tsar and brigands. How we live ? We Golds no Tsar, no captains, no brigands."

At first that struck me as a rather odd association, Tsar and brigands, but when I turned it over in my mind I understood his line of reasoning. Once he started sorting out people into a kind of classification, there had to be rich and poor, idle and workers. Then when he came to honest and dishonest, the criminal class is sorted out, and forms a kind of a caste by itself, which the Chinese call ' *hunhuȝ*.'

We did not sit yarning long. The rest we had had in the morning had not been enough, and our tired frames were hungry for more sleep. We piled up some old wood on the fire so that it would go on burning, lay down on the grass, and fell sound asleep.

When I awoke the next morning the sun was already high.

We drank some tea, picked up our bundles, and continued our trail to the pass. Here the track followed the crest, bending with its contours, first to one side, then to the other, so that we received the impression that we were constantly climbing and dropping and cutting several spurs of the range.

In the pass itself, at about 500 ft., I gazed at a rather interesting picture. On the left was a lofty hill shaped like a truncated cone. Seen from the sea it looks as though it had a double hump, and so on the navy charts it is called the Camel. To our east there were hills covered with thin forest, and before us stretched a broad, boggy valley, covered with yellow-brown grass.

The bog is fed by the burns flowing down the mountain-sides. The journey from the Mulumbé to the Kaimbé is only about four and a half miles, but the trail through that quagmire was so difficult that it took us the whole of the day, and it was dusk before we were across. Ahead, near the Kaimbé, we saw a cabin and made straight for it.

In it we found two Chinamen, but there was neither garden nor pasture near it. Dersu's keen eye, however, noticed a saw, long-handled axes, baskets plaited of bast, and far longer *k'angs* than necessary for the inhabitants of the cabin. It appeared that the Chinamen were collectors of fungi and lichens off rocks. They specially hunted for fungi of the family *Tremellinaceæ*, which grow only on oaks. They have a peculiar aroma, and contain as much as 98 per cent of water. In order to grow them the Chinese fell a number of big oaks. When these begin to rot the fungus *Tremella lutescens* appears on them, looking rather like white coral. They collect and dry them, first in the sun and then in the cabin on very hot *k'angs*.

The lichen they collect is *Parmelia centrifuga*, a dark, olive-green growth on rocks that turns black on drying. They collect them off limestones and shales and dispatch them to Vladivostok, where they are sold as a dainty.

It is really impossible to refrain from admiring the enterprise of the Chinese. Some of them hunt wapiti, others ransack the forest for ginseng, others hunt sables, others musk from the musk-deer ; others collect seaweed, crabs, lobsters, trepang, and others again cultivate poppies for the opium. At every new cabin you come to you find a new trade : pearling, hunting for some sort of vegetable oil and roots, till you lose count. Everywhere they seem to find some source of wealth. The question of labour is to them of secondary importance, if only the supply be inexhaustible.

We were so tired after our day that we did not go any farther but stopped there the night. Inside, the cabin was clean and tidy. The hospitable Chinese gave up their seats to us and tried to make us comfortable in every way they could. Outside was dark and cold, and the sound of the waves reached us from the sea, but within was warm and snug.

In the evening they gave us some of their ' stone's skin,' as they call the lichen *Parmelia*. The dark brown, glutinous stuff was crisp like *vyaʒiga*, the dried backbone of the sturgeon, but insipid and could satisfy the palate only of a Chinaman.

They told us it was only one day's march to the Sanhobé, and as we wished to reach there before dark we started very early the next morning.

The trail took us down to the sea and over the top of five headlands. It was hard going, both for horses and men. The Chinese had informed us correctly, and it was only in the evening that we reached the Sanhobé. The path brought us straight to a Chinese settlement. A fire was burning in one of the cabins, and through the thin paper I heard the voice of Palchevski and saw his profile. He had not expected me to arrive at so late an hour. Granatman and Merzliakov were in an adjoining cabin, but came hurrying along directly they heard of our arrival.

Then began a regular cross-examination. I told them of all our adventures on the road, and they talked of their work on the Sanhobé. The conversation was extremely interesting, but fatigue claimed its own. Palchevski noticed that and arranged a bed for me on the *k'ang*, on which I turned in and fell asleep at once.

All the next day we spent exchanging yarns. The river

Sanhobé was the end point of our expedition up the coast. From here we were to make our way to the Sihoté-Alin and farther on to Iman. On consultation we decided to stay on the Sanhobé long enough to give us a good rest and to make preparations for the winter expedition.

In view of the approaching winter the supply of fodder for the horses raised a question of great difficulty, so I sent back Merzliakov with all the horses and several of the men to Olga Bay. In consequence of the disappearance of the vegetation Palchevski also wanted to return to Vladivostok. He decided to take advantage of the arrival of the schooner *Gliasser*, which was due to sail in a couple of days.

The result was that for the winter trail across the Sihoté-Alin there were left with me only Granatman, Dersu, and a couple of Cossacks, Murzin and Kozhevnikov, and Rifleman Bochkarev.

On 25 September we parted company with Palchevski and the next day Merzliakov also left us.

CHAPTER XVIII : FIRE !

SEPTEMBER 27 was given up to a reconnaissance of the Bay of Terney, discovered by the famous La Perouse on 23 July 1767, who then and there gave it its name. What was once a much deeper bay has been largely filled up by the sea and the tide has turned the gulf into a lagoon, and later dunes have been formed.

Such lagoons are always rich in bird life. Some were on the shore, others preferred the creeks. Among the former I noticed the Pacific dunlin, which, judging from the time of year, must be a resident here. Gulls were flying to and fro, often settling on the surface of the sea, and then taking to the wing again. In the deeper creeks were plenty of cormorants, which kept continuously diving but never could satisfy their greedy bellies.

The vegetation in the lower part of the valley of the Sanhobé is straggly and stunted. On the right bank, by the marsh, were some Siberian larches in small groups.

The population consists of a mixture of Chinese and aborigines, the former on the coast, the latter farther inland. There were thirty-eight Chinese cabins, with a population of 233 souls. The local Chinese are all firmly persuaded that the land belongs to them and look upon the Russians as outsiders. There were only fourteen native huts, with a couple of hundred souls.

The position of the natives here is very bad, and they all have an abandoned and down-trodden appearance. I wanted to interrogate them, but they were terrified, muttered something among themselves and crept away. Evidently they were afraid of the Chinese. If any one of them were to venture to complain to the Russian authorities or report what goes on in the valley of the Sanhobé, their punishment would be a cruel one, at least drowning in the river, or even being buried alive.

The aborigines of the Sanhobé are in no way different from those of the Tadusha. They are dressed in the same way, talk Chinese in the same way, and also are engaged in agriculture. Near each cabin is a shed on piles where they keep various implements and utensils. These sheds are characteristic native constructions. Besides these, I noticed that the older men carried peculiar curved knives, in the use of which they are very skilful. For them they serve as awl, auger, chisel, and plane.

According to their stories, thirty years ago there was a violent outbreak of smallpox in the Sanhobé, and not one cabin was spared. The Chinese were afraid to bury the dead, and cremated them instead, hauling the bodies out of the huts with grappling-hooks. Often enough they hauled out among the dead and burnt men yet living, in an unconscious condition.

That evening Chan Bao returned. He told that he had not found the brigands in the Gulf of Plastun. After the attempt on Dersu they had evidently taken to their boats and sailed away to the south.

The next three days, 28–30 September, I was busy in camp working out our routes, entering records and notes, and writing up my diary and letters. The Cossacks shot a wapiti and dried the meat, while Bochkarev prepared our winter footwear. I did not want to distract them from their work, and did not call any of them off to come with me for my strolls round the district.

The Sanhobé really consists of two rivers, the Sitsa and the Duntsa. My route to Iman lay up the Duntsa, so I decided to have a look at the Sitsi before leaving. For this reconnaissance I allotted seven days.

On 1 October Dersu and I slung our packs on our shoulders and started off from my local headquarters.

The view up the valley of the Sitsa from the sea is fine. The lofty hills with their sharp and capricious peaks look magnificent. I several times saw them afterwards, and they always produced on me an impression of a peculiar wild beauty.

Half-way up from the sea, at the junction of the two streams, there is a rock on the left bank, called Da Laza. They say that once upon a time an old Chinaman found near it an unusually large ginseng. When the root was brought into the cabin an earthquake took place, and they all heard the rock Da Laza groaning during the night. The Chinese maintain that the mouth of the Sanhobé is the northern limit of distribution of the ginseng.

The valley of the Sitsi is covered with a fine mixed forest. In the lower part the forest is magnificent, with many fine cedars. Near the river much of it has been felled by the concession-holder Hromansky, but only a quarter has been removed and all the rest left on the ground. In their crash the giants of the forest brought down with them a host of smaller trees, which were not yet ready for the axe. In general, more timber has been spoilt than living. It is hard to make one's way through forest like that. Once we tried to break away from the track and force our way direct, but we quickly came into such a windfall of tangled logs and trunks, smashed down by the storms, that we could hardly make our way back. The area of felled forest covers about ten square miles. The track goes almost through the middle of the forest. To have cleared it no doubt would have involved heavy labour and the spoiling of many an axe and saw.

The next day we mounted farther up the Sitsi. The farther we went, the denser became the forest. The all-devouring hand of the timber merchant had not yet touched this virgin forest. Besides cedar, poplar, fir, cork, oak, spruce, and walnut, there grows here the Chinese ash, *Fraxinus rhynchiphylla*, a handsome tree with grey bark and sharp-pointed oval leaves ; *Deutzia parvifolia*, a small tree with little black berries ; the osier, *Salix viminalis*, very widely distributed throughout Ussuria, usually growing on gravel spits near rivers. The vegetation near the streams consisted mainly of alder, a species of hawthorn, *Cratægus pinnatifidia*, with grey bark, wedge-shaped leaves, and small thorns ; a kind of mountain ash, *Sorbus sambucifolia*, with dark green leaves and big, dark red, edible berries ; the edible honeysuckle, which can be recognized by the brown bark, small leaves, and elongate berries of dark blue colour with a dull sheen, and, lastly, the hanging trailers of the creeper *Menispermum dauricum.*

The farther we went from the traces of human activity, the more numerous the wild life. Tigers, lynxes, bears, wolverines, wapiti, deer, roe, pig, all are resident in this rich *taigá.*

Dersu strode on in silence, serenely seeing everything. I was revelling in the view, but he looked at a twig broken off at the height of a man's arm, and from the way it was hanging knew the direction in which the man had been going. From the freshness of the fracture he judged the time that had elapsed. Whenever I failed to see a point, to draw a conclusion, or express doubt, he said reproachfully:

" How you go many years in *taigá* don't understand ? "

What to me seemed incomprehensible was to him clear and simple. Sometimes he would pick up a spoor where with the best intention in the world I could see nothing. Yet he could tell that an old wapiti hind had passed that way with her fawn. They had browsed on the *Spiræa* as they passed and then been suddenly startled at something and bolted.

This was not all done for the sake of impressing me. We knew each other too well for that. It was simply done from lifelong habit, never to overlook details, and to be attentive to everything, and always observant. If he had not learnt from childhood to understand the art of tracking, he would have soon died of hunger. Whenever I passed by a particularly obvious track, Dersu would chuckle, wag his head, and say:

" H'm ! Just like small boy. Go walk, wag head; have eyes, no-can look-see, no-can understand. True, that sort man live in towns. No need go hunt wapiti. Want eat . . . go buy meat. No-can live all-alone in *taigá*, soon go-lost."

He was quite right. A thousand risks await the solitary wayfarer in the *taigá*, and only he who can read the signs can count upon reaching the end of his journey in safety.

As we went I trod upon a thorn. The sharp spike penetrated through my boot and entered into my foot. I at once pulled my boot off and picked out the thorn, but, apparently, not completely, for the tip must have remained in the wound which the next day began to be painful. I asked Dersu to have another look at it, and it was already inflamed round the edges. That day I managed to limp along, but at night it hurt severely, and I could not close my eyes till it was light. In the morning a big sore was formed.

For want of provisions we were compelled to push on. We had already run out of bread and for food been dependent upon what we could shoot. Antiseptics and bandages had been left in camp; bad weather might set in, and there was no knowing how long we might be held up, so I decided to push on at all costs, in spite of my pain. I could put only the one sound foot firmly to the ground, and dragged the wounded one as best I could. Dersu took my knapsack and rifle, and when we had to climb down difficult places he supported my weight and did all in his power to ease my suffering. That day, with the greatest difficulty, we managed to travel five miles, but there were another fifteen to the camp.

At night it hurt desperately. The suppuration spread over the whole sole. I wondered if I should ever get through, even to the nearest Chinese hut, and I could see the same fear was troubling Dersu. He often glanced at the sky. I thought he was looking for signs of rain, but his anxieties were for something very different. A kind of mist overhung the forest, which grew denser and denser. The moon was just rising. His face was not bright as usual, but grim and reddish, and at times he was obscured from vision. At last beyond the hills appeared a ruddy glow.

" Much big smoke," said my companion.

At the spark of light we were on our legs. Anyhow, I could not sleep, and so long as I could move at all we ought to push on. Never shall I forget that day. I struggled on a hundred yards and then sat down upon the ground. To ease the pressure on my foot I ripped open the stitches of my boot.

Presently we reached the point where the Da Lazagu falls

into the Sitsi. Here we entered the forest, all encumbered with storm-felled trees. All around was enveloped in smoke. Trees were invisible at fifty paces.

"Captain, must hurry!" exclaimed Dersu. "Me little frightened. Grass no burn, but forest him burn."

I collected my last remaining strength and by a desperate effort dragged myself on a little farther. At the slightest slope I crawled on hands and knees. Every root, every pine-needle, every tiny pebble, or twig that touched my wounded foot caused me to cry out with pain, and lie full length upon the ground.

Through that smoke progress became harder and harder. My throat began to dry up. We could see that we should never get through that entangled mass of fallen logs and trunks which, dried by the sun and wind, was now nothing but an enormous bonfire waiting for the spark.

When a big flame blazes out a whirlwind is formed. The roar of this whirlwind caught the trained ear of the Gold. Our only hope of salvation lay in the river. We must cross that at all costs. But to ford the Da Lazagu meant sound limbs, and for me in that condition it was out of the question. What was to be done?

Suddenly Dersu, without saying a word, picked me up in his arms and carried me across the river. He put me down on a broad bank of shingle and hurried back for our weapons. All the time the smoke was whirling round us, nothing was visible . . . and I lost consciousness.

When I came to Dersu was lying on the gravel by my side, both of us covered by a wet canvas. Sparks were flying up. The thick, pungent smoke was suffocating.

For the first time in my life I beheld a raging forest fire at close quarters, a fearful spectacle! Enormous cedars, gripped by the flame, were blazing like colossal torches. Beneath them, on the ground, was a sea of fire. Everything was burning, grass, fallen leaves, trunks, logs, stumps. We could hear living trees groan and burst from the heat. The yellow smoke rolled upwards in enormous billows. Waves of fire raced over the ground. Tongues of flame wound round the stumps and licked the red-hot rocks.

Suddenly the wind changed and the smoke was carried aside. Dersu sat up and propped me up. I tried to crawl to the end of the gravel spit, but quickly realized that it was beyond my strength. I could only lie there and moan.

As in limping along I had thrown extra weight upon my heel, that now ached badly. The other leg was tired and also ached at the knee. Seeing that I was incapable of going any farther, Dersu pitched our little tent, collected some firewood, and told me that he would go to the nearest Chinese for a horse. That was the only hope of getting me out of the *taigá*. Dersu went and I was left alone.

Beyond the stream the fire was still blazing. Across the sky raced clouds of sparks among the smoke. The fire marched forwards, on and on. Some trees burnt through rapidly, some slowly. I saw a wild boar make his way across the river, a big snake swam sinuously over, and a woodpecker flew from tree to tree like a mad thing, while a nutcracker never ceased its raucous chatter. I accompanied it with my groans. At length it grew dusk.

I realized that Dersu could not get back that day. The bad foot was enormously swollen. I stripped it and felt the blister. It had come to a head, but the hardened skin had not yet burst. I thought of my pocket-knife, and started sharpening it on a stone. Then, flinging some wood on the fire and waiting till it burnt up brightly, I opened the abscess. Everything went dark before my eyes from the agony. Black blood and pus squirted from the wound. By dint of a ghastly effort I crawled to the edge of the water, tore off a corner of my shirt-sleeve, and started bathing the wound. Then I bound it up and crawled back to the fire. In about an hour I felt a little easier. The foot was still extremely painful, but not so desperately as a short while previously.

In the direction of the fire's advance could be seen a ruddy glow. Fires were twinkling still in many places as big logs were burning out. I sat there by the hour in my little tent stroking my aching foot. The heat from the camp fire warmed me, and eventually I dropped off to sleep.

When I awoke I saw Dersu and a Chinaman standing by my side. I was covered with a blanket. Tea was brewing over the fire. Near by stood a saddle-horse. The pain in my foot was easier and the swelling had begun to subside. I washed the wound again with warm water, drank some tea, chewed a piece of sour Chinese bread, and pulled my things on. Dersu and the Chinaman helped me on to the saddle and we started.

During the night the fire had passed far away, but the air was still full of smoke.

In the afternoon we reached the Sanhobé. Granatman was not in camp. He had gone on a reconnaissance and would not be back for two or three days.

I had no choice but to stay there till my foot had properly healed. In three days' time I could walk, and in a week was quite well again.

Chan Bao paid me several visits and told me many interesting things. He told me of the wreck of the *Viking* near the Terney Bay some years ago, and the story how the Japanese killed his comrade in 1905 and of his revenge. He told me that in 1906 a party of escaped convicts had landed near Cape Olympiad and left a trail marked by pillage and murder. Chan Bao with his band of hunters had caught them near Lake Blagodat and wiped them out to a man. All his yarns were tales of violence and bloody drama.

I noticed the immense popularity of Chan Bao among the Chinese. His words and sayings were passed from mouth to mouth, and every order he gave was carried out instantly and without discussion. Many came to him for advice, and it seemed that no case was so involved that he could not disentangle it and lay hands upon the culprit. Some were discontented. These were usually men with a criminal past, and Chan Bao knew how to curb their passions.

He had prospectors out the whole time, some up the Iodzyhé,

some along the coast, and others up the northern trail. In the evenings he checked up their reports and told me the results every day. Chan Bao maintained a heavy correspondence. Almost every day a runner brought him dispatches.

During these days Dersu spent his time among the natives. Among them he found an old man who used to live on the Ulahé, whom he had known when a young man. He made friends with everybody, and was a welcome guest everywhere.

A couple of days before my departure, Chan Bao came to say good-bye. Urgent business called for his presence on the river Takemé. He detailed two Chinese to accompany me as far as the Sihoté-Alin, who would return by another route and report to him all that they had seen.

October 15 was our last day of preparation. We baked rolls and dried meat. Everything had been anticipated, and not even hay for our boots been forgotten.

CHAPTER XIX : A WINTER EXPEDITION

WE were not able to start on the 16th as our Chinese guides detained us. They did not put in an appearance until the middle of the next day. Natives kept us company from one cabin to another, inviting us to come and see them, if only for a minute. Dersu was showered with greetings, and the women and children shook him by the hand. He replied in the same way. And so, from cabin to cabin, with constant delays, we came at length to the last native hut, for which, to tell the truth, I was heartily glad. Beyond, the path crossed the river and followed the left bank for a mile or two, and then started rising towards the pass.

That day I was seedy. I had severe pain in the stomach. One of the Chinese guides offered me some of his own medicine, consisting of a mixture of ginseng, opium, deer's horn, and infusion of bear's bone. As I thought the opium would have a soothing effect, I consented to drink a few drops of his decoction, but he begged me to take a whole spoonful. He said there was very little opium in it and more of the other ingredients. Perhaps he measured the dose according to his own capacity, as he was accustomed to opium, but I was not, and a small dose for him was quite a big one for me.

And as a matter of fact, soon after taking the medicine the pain in the stomach did pass off, but in revenge a feeling of lassitude overcame my whole body. I lay down by the fire and dropped into a heavy slumber, almost like a faint. Half an hour later I awoke and wanted to stand up, but could not; I wanted to move, but could not. I wanted to call out, but could not. It was an extraordinary situation. All my sensations were numb. I could see nothing, hear nothing, feel nothing.

I made a superhuman effort to control myself, raised my arm, touched my face, and was frightened. It seemed to me that it was not my hand, but some other hand, and not my own face that I had touched, but a sort of mask. Fear overcame me. After a tremendous internal struggle, I sprang up, leapt to my feet, and at once fell headlong on the ground again. Then I was violently sick. Luckily, Dersu was not yet asleep. He brought me some water, which I managed to sip, and then felt a little better. My head swam so severely that I could not concentrate my eyes upon any object. I realized that I had been poisoned. Two or three times I swallowed substantial quantities of water and several times artificially induced vomiting, which saved me. Like that I struggled on till morning. When it was light Dersu went off into the forest and brought me back some herb, which he advised me to chew and swallow the juice.

At length I began to feel a little better; the vertigo and headache ceased, but I felt desperately weak, with a consuming thirst.

The herb was the amphibious Persicaria, *Polygonum amphibium*, a well-known simple, which the natives also take for dysentery.

After that attack I could not walk fast, and was obliged to stop often to sit down and rest.

We came eventually to the pass, which is covered with dense pine wood. A couple of miles or so from the Duntsa we came across a Chinese hunter's cabin, but the owners were away.

Towards the evening I felt well again, but could not eat anything, from a feeling of nausea. So I decided to turn in early and hoped to sleep it off and awake perfectly fit again the next morning.

About midnight I awoke. By the fire a Chinaman was sitting, guarding the camp. The night was still and moonlit. I looked up at the sky, which had a strange appearance, as though it were flattened and falling down on to the earth. Round the moon was a dull spot and a large halo. The stars were also surrounded with spots like that.

' There's going to be a hard frost,' I thought to myself, rolled over in my blanket, and fell asleep again.

In the morning it was rain that aroused me, fine and steady. My sickness had passed and I felt quite fit again. Without any delay we picked up our bundles and started. After midday the rain increased, and we were obliged to pitch camp early. As there was plenty of daylight left, Dersu and I took our rifles and went to have a look round.

In the autumn, the time of bad weather, the forest always has a mournful look. The bare trunks of the trees, lightly wrapped in cold mist, the yellow grass, the fallen leaves, and the sodden, blackened ferns, all point to the twilight of the year. Winter was approaching.

Suddenly our ears caught a strange sound on one side. We left the path and went to the bank of the river, where an unusual sight met our eyes. The stream was literally crammed with fish, the dog salmon or *keta*. In places there were whole piles of dead ones. Thousands of them were stranded in the creeks and shallows. It was a repulsive sight, their fins torn off, their bodies gashed and bleeding. The greater part were dead, but some were still exerting their remaining strength to struggle on up-stream, counting on finding there release from their sufferings.

For clearing up these swarms of fish nature sent sanitary officials in the form of bears, pig, foxes, badgers, racoon dogs, crows, rollers, and jays. The dead fish were taken by the birds as a rule, while the mammals tried to catch the living ones. Along the bank they had trampled regular paths. At one place we saw a bear ; he was sitting on a bank of gravel, hooking fishes out with his paws.

The brown bear and his cousin of Kamchatka eat the heads of fishes, and throw the body away. The white-breasted bear, on the other hand, eats the meat and throws the head away.

At another spot two boars were enjoying a fish dinner. These ate only the tails of the fish. A little farther on I saw a fox. He jumped out of the thicket, grabbed one of the fish, but was too cautious to eat it on the spot, and dragged it off into the scrub.

But the birds were most numerous. Eagles sat near the water and slowly, without haste, as though aware of their own superiority, pecked at what was left of the bear's dinner. Most of all were the crows, their jet-black plumage standing out prominently against the pale stony background. They advanced with hops, and showed a marked preference for the fish which had already begun to decompose. On the bushes round the

jays were poking about, squabbling with all the other birds and never ceasing their piercing shrieks.

In the shallows the water was already starting to freeze in places. A fish caught in the ice would be a prisoner for the whole of the winter. Only in the spring, when the sunshine warms the earth, will it be carried down-stream with the lumps of ice into the sea, there to be the object of attack of all marine creatures.

What a chain of nature! How wise it all is! Nothing is wasted! Even in the depths of the remotest *taigá* there are scanvengers to collect the carrion.

" One man eat other man," said Dersu, expressing his thoughts aloud. " Fish him eat something, then boar eat fish, now we must eat boar."

As he said this he aimed and fired at one of the pigs. With a roar the mortally wounded creature sprang into the air as

though to plunge into the forest, but its muzzle stuck into the ground instead, and it kicked convulsively. Startled by the shot, the birds rose screaming into the air and in their turn frightened the fishes, which began to dash up and down stream like mad things.

At dusk we returned to camp. The rain had stopped, the sky cleared, and the moon came out. On its pale face I could clearly see the dark and pale patches. That meant that the air was clean and transparent.

We turned in early and were up early next morning, and by the time the sun had gilded the peaks we had left the camp a mile or two behind. Here the river Duntsa makes a sharp bend to the west, but soon resumes its northerly course, and just at the bend, on the left side, there stands out a high rock, crowned with a sharp, jagged crest.

Our Chinese guides told us that some misfortune always happens to men at this spot, that either somebody dies, or at least breaks a leg, and in confirmation of their words pointed to two graves of unfortunate men whom the evil fate had overtaken at this spot. With us, however, nothing happened, and we passed the Accursed Rock in safety.

Farther on we came into a belt of dense, mixed forest, with a lot of the prickly devil thorn, *Eleutherococcus*, which in winter turns brittle, and if anyone catches hold of it he is sure to get a number of splinters into his hand. The trouble is that they go vertically into the skin and break off when pulled out.

At midday we came to a small hunter's cabin, situated at the junction of three brooks. Our path lay along the middle one.

All this time we had been enjoying calm, pleasant weather. It was so warm that we walked in our summer shirts, and only put on warmer things in the evening. I revelled in the fine weather but Dersu disagreed with me.

" Look-see, captain," he explained, " how quick all birds eat. Him know well will be bad."

The barometer stood high. I began to chaff the Gold, but he only answered :

" Birds him know now ; me know later."

From the little cabin to the pass over the Sihoté-Alin was about five miles. In spite of the weight of our bundles, we stepped out bravely and made good going, with few breathers. About four in the afternoon we reached the Sihoté-Alin, and only had to reach the crest. I wanted to push on, but Dersu detained me by the sleeve.

" Wait, captain," he said. " Me think better camp here."

" Why ? " I asked.

" Morning, all birds eat quickly ; now, look-see, no-can see bird."

And in fact, although birds are usually very lively just before sunset, now in the forest there was a deathly stillness. As though at the word of command, all the birds had hidden themselves.

Dersu advised us to pitch camp and fix the tents particularly firmly and to lay in a good big stock of firewood, not only enough for the night, but for the next day too. I did not argue with him any more, but set out to pick up firewood. A couple of hours later it grew dark. The soldiers had piled up a good lot of firewood, a good deal more than apparently necessary, but they never stopped, and I heard what he said to the Chinamen.

" Lotsa him no know ; us must work too."

' Lotsa ' is what the Manchurian natives call the Russians.

Again he set to work, so I sent a couple of Cossacks to help him, and it was not till the last glimmer of daylight had faded from the sky that we stopped working.

The moon came out. A clear, calm night looked down on the earth from the sky. The moonlight penetrated deep into the forest, in long pale bands across the dry grass. On the ground, in the sky, and all around, everything was still, and there was no sign of bad weather. Sitting round the fire we drank hot tea and chaffed the Gold.

" You've made a mistake this time, old man," said the Cossacks.

Dersu did not reply, but silently continued strengthening

his little tent. He tucked himself under a rock on one side, and on the other rolled up a great big stump and packed it round with stones, filling the holes between them with moss. Over the top he stretched his piece of canvas, and in front he lit a fire. He looked so snug, tucked in like that, that I at once joined him with my things.

Time passed, and all around was as still as before. I too began to think that the Gold had made a mistake, when suddenly round the moon appeared a big dull circle, tinged at the edges with the colours of the rainbow. Then, little by little, the disc of the moon darkened, and its outline became vague and indistinct. The dull circle expanded and enveloped the outer ring. A kind of fog soon veiled the sky, but when it came and whither it was travelling we could not say.

I thought it would end in a shower, and lulled by the thought, fell asleep. How long I slept I do not know, but I was aroused by one of the men. I opened my eyes and saw Murzin standing by me.

"It is snowing," he reported.

I flung off my blanket. All around was pitch dark. The moon had disappeared and a fine snow was falling. The fire was burning brightly and lit up the tents, the sleeping men, and the pile of wood. I roused Dersu. He awoke with a start, looked round in a half-sleepy way, glanced at the sky, and lit his pipe.

Around all was still, but in this very stillness I could now sense a feeling of menace. A few minutes later the snow became thicker, and fell on the ground with a peculiar rustling sound. The rest of the party awoke and began collecting their things.

Suddenly the snow started whirling.

"Now begin," said Dersu.

And as though in answer to his words, in the mountains a distant roar could be heard, and then there fell upon us a violent gust of wind from the side whence least expected. The burning timbers blazed up. Then came a second gust, then a third, followed by a fourth, fifth, and more and more, each more violent and more prolonged than the preceding one. It was a good thing that the tents were firmly pegged down or they would have been carried away.

I glanced at Dersu. He was calmly smoking his pipe, serenely gazing into the fire. The opening of the blizzard did not disturb him. He had in his time seen so many that it had no novelty for him. He seemed to divine my thoughts and said :

" Got much wood ; tents well fixed ; nothing fear."

In an hour it began to grow light.

The blizzard was what we call a *purga*, during which the temperature can drop well below zero, with the gale so violent that it will lift roofs off houses and uproot trees. Walking during a *purga* is out of the question, and the only hope of safety is to stay where one is. As a rule every blizzard is accompanied by loss of life.

Around us the scene was unbelievable. The wind raged with the utmost violence, smashing off branches of trees, lifting them into the air like feathers. Huge cedars rocked from side to side like saplings. Nothing was visible, neither mountains, nor sky, nor earth, everything enveloped in the roaring whirlwind of snow. For a moment I seemed almost to detect the outline of the nearest tree, just visible through the blinding snow, but only for an instant. Another gust and the misty picture vanished.

We shrank back in our tents and sat in silent awe. Dersu looked round at the sky and muttered something to himself. I reminded him of the blizzard that had caught us on Lake Hanka in 1902.

" Me very much afraid then," he answered. " No firewood ; soon all finish."

In the afternoon the storm gave vent to all its fury. Although we were protected by cliffs and the tenting, it was still a wretched shelter. When the wind blew the fire our way, it was hot and smoky as in a house on fire, and when it blew the flame away it was cold.

We had given up going for water and filled the teapot with snow. Luckily there was no lack of that. Towards dusk the blizzard reached the very limit of its violence, and the darker it grew the more terrible it seemed.

We slept little that night. Our attentions were concentrated on keeping warm.

The 21st we spent still sheltering from the storm. Now the wind changed, veering round to the north-east, and the gusts were fiercer than ever. Nothing was visible, even quite near our shelter.

" Why him angry ? " said Dersu, in an upset and anxious voice. " When we hurt him ? "

" Whom ? " asked the Cossacks.

" Me not know how say Russky," answered the Gold. " Him little god, little man, hill all alive, can blow wind, break tree. Us say : Kangu."

' The spirit of the forest or mountain,' I thought.

We had great difficulty in keeping the fire alight. The trouble was that every gust blew the burning brands about and covered them with snow piled up in great drifts, and in the afternoon whirlwinds of the utmost violence broke upon us. They raised clouds of snow high into the air and spread a white pall over everything, and then burst out afresh, howling through the forest. Each whirlwind like that left its track marked by a row of fallen trees. Every now and then would come a short pause, and then it would redouble its efforts with intensified ferocity.

Later that afternoon the heavens began to clear slightly, but at the same time the temperature began to fall. Through the thick curtain of snow-cloud a vague, pale glow showed the position of the sun.

It was time to think of more firewood. We crept out and began to amass the fallen timber lying within easiest reach. We worked hard till Dersu said we had enough.

There was no need to try to persuade anybody. We hurried back at once and dived into our tents to warm our benumbed hands by the fire. Thus we passed through yet another night.

Next morning there was a slight improvement. The wind was cutting and fitful. After consultation we decided to make the effort to cross the Sihoté-Alin in the hope that it would be easier on the lee of the west flank. The casting vote was given by Dersu.

" Me think him soon finish," he said, and set the example for starting on the road.

It did not take us long. In twenty minutes we had humped our packs and were off once more.

From our camp the ground rose steeply. During those two days a great deal of snow had fallen, and in places it was over a yard in depth. At the top we stopped for a breather. The barometer showed us an altitude of 3000 ft. We called it Patience Pass.

It was a doleful picture we gazed upon on the Sihoté-Alin. Here the gale had swept down whole avenues of trees. We were obliged to make a long detour. I have explained earlier in the book how in the mountains the roots do not strike deep, but spread near the surface, and are often held in position only by a carpet of moss. Many of these had been torn bodily out. The trees rocked and strained and dragged their roots. Black crevices opened and shut in the snowy carpet like great jaws. Kozhevnikov thought he would like to have a swing in one of these, but at that very moment a violent gust burst on us, the tree leant right over, and the Cossack barely had time to jump clear when it crashed to the ground, scattering all round a shower of frozen earth.

CHAPTER XX : THE IMAN

THE descent from the Sihoté-Alin towards the west is gentle, littered with boulders, and covered in a mantle of dense forest. We followed the course of a burn, which brought us to the river Nantse, with a broad, boggy valley, covered with thick, coniferous forest.

On the way we came upon a hovel of cedar bark, thrown over a ridge-pole. Worn out by the two preceding nights we stopped there to bivouac and, the moment we had had something to eat, turned in to sleep.

As on the 23rd we continued our road down the Nantse; the spoor of game showed up clearly in the freshly fallen snow. We could see the hoof-marks of elk, of musk-deer, the tracks of sable, polecat, and other animals. Dersu walked ahead, attentively examining the ground. Suddenly he stopped, looked round, and asked :

" Who she afraid ? "

" Who ? " I asked.

" The musk-deer."

I glanced down at the tracks, and could see nothing distinctive, just the numerous little impressions.

Dersu was astonishingly attentive to details of tracks. He could even tell the nervous state of the animal that made them. A slight irregularity in their spacing showed him that the creature had been startled.

I asked him to explain the grounds on which he judged that the musk-deer had been frightened. It was so clear and simple, he exclaimed. The animal had been walking along at an even pace and then pulled up and walked on more slowly, then suddenly sprang aside and bounded off. On the fresh snow that all stood out as clear as on the palm of your hand. I wanted to walk on, but Dersu restrained me.

" Wait, captain, wait-see what man frightened musk-deer."

A minute later he called to me that the musk-deer had been frightened by a sable. I went up to him. On a big, prone tree, buried in snow, there were the tracks, clearly enough. It was evident that the little hunter had quietly lay hidden behind a branch, and then suddenly flung itself upon the deer. Then Dersu found the place where the deer had come down. Specks of blood showed where the sable had bitten it near the nape, but further tracks showed that the little deer had succeeded in throwing its assailant off. It had galloped on, but the sable, after starting to pursue it, had stopped and climbed up a tree.

I feel that if I had been able to stay longer in the bush with Dersu and he had been a little more communicative, I should probably have learnt to read tracks, if not as well as he, at least a good deal better than most other hunters.

Dersu saw a lot that he did not talk about. He kept silent because he did not want to waste time on what to him seemed trifles. Only in rare cases, where something struck him as being particularly interesting, did he talk about it aloud to himself.

Presently we came to the river Kulumbé, which was to take us to the Iman. It ran through a swampy valley running from east to west. The forest on the surrounding hills consists entirely of conifers, with a high percentage of cedars.

In the afternoon the wind dropped finally. There was not a speck of cloud in the sky, and the bright rays of the sun were reflected by the snow, which made the day seem even brighter. The pines were in their winter garb, their branches weighed to the ground with snow. Around all was still and silence reigned. It seemed as though nature were drowsing, to recover from the strain of yesterday's agitation.

Of the feathered world I noticed long-beaked crows, red-headed and speckled woodpeckers, and nuthatches. Twice we flushed mergansers, with black caps and red beaks. We noticed them only when quite close alongside us.

There was another little bird, a charming little fellow, that I must mention, whose cheerful habits have earned it the name of *veselushka* among the Cossacks, that is ' cheery fellow.' I mean the dipper. It is as big as a thrush and always found near water. I stopped to watch one. It was alert, kept turning round and uttering a sprightly warble, flirting its tail in unison, and then

 suddenly plunging into the water. The natives say that it walks freely along the bottom regardless of the strength of the current. Popping up at the surface again, and catching sight of men, it flew off with a whistle to another ice-hole, and then on to a third. I followed it until the river disappeared round a bend.

At another spot we flushed a snipe. It stayed by ice-free water where there was no snow. I thought it was a straggler from the migration, but it seemed strong and cheerful. Afterwards we often flushed them from the banks of unfrozen streams, so I came to the conclusion that in Ussuria they stay till the middle of the winter and fly off to the south only after December.

That day we made eight miles, and stopped at a cabin called Siu-Fu, inhabited by Chinese engaged in catching wapiti in pitfalls.

In the morning the Chinese were up early, to be off hunting, and we for the road. Our supply of provisions that we had brought with us was running low, and it was necessary to replenish. In these localities flour and millet are very dear owing to the cost of transport. Flour worked out at about 2s. 3d. a pound and millet about 1s. 9d.

During the night the frost was so hard that we were able to walk on the ice on the Kulumbé, which made progress much easier for us. The high wind had swept the ice free of snow, and it grew stronger every day, although there remained several thawed-out spots. A thick mist was always rising from them.

After two or three more miles we came to a couple of Korean cabins. Their owners, two old and two young Koreans, were engaged in hunting and trapping. Their cabins were new and clean, and looked so inviting that I decided to stay there for a day's rest.

In the afternoon two of them started off to the forest to inspect a fence put up for musk-deer, so I went with them to have a look.

The fence was not far from the cabins, about a yard and a half high, built of fallen timber, reinforced with stout stakes. Fences of that sort are always put up in the mountains on the paths of the musk-deer. Here and there they leave openings in the fence, in which they set nooses. The wretched animal thrusts its head into the noose, and the more it struggles the tighter it strangles itself.

In the fence we inspected there were twenty-two nooses, in four of which we found game, three bucks and a doe. The Koreans pulled the doe out and flung it aside for the crows. When I asked why they threw away the doe they had captured, they answered that it was only the buck that gave the valuable musk glands for which the Chinese pay as much as a rouble apiece. As for the meat, a single buck was enough for them, and they would get as many again to-morrow. According to them, during the winter season they kill as many as one hundred and twenty-five musk deer, of which three-quarters are does.

This excursion left a mournful impression. On every side one sees nothing but robbery and exploitation. In the not-distant future this land of Ussuria, so rich in animal life and forest, will be turned into a desert.

The next day we set out early on purpose to make up for the time lost the previous day. With us we took the carcass of one of the musk does abandoned by the Koreans.

We now left the thick forest of conifers, which began to be replaced by poplars, elms, birch, aspen, oak, maple, and so on.

In the mountains the firs and spruce gave way to magnificent cedars.

That day we managed to march about nine miles. At dusk the riflemen noticed a solitary hut on the side of the stream, where the smoke issuing from a hole in the roof betrayed the presence of men. On frames nearby rows of fish were drying. The hut was of cedar bark, thatched with dried grass. On the bank lay a couple of upturned boats. One was rather big, with a curious prow, shaped something like a ladle, the other light, pointed fore and aft.

As we approached a couple of dogs raised a din. Out of the hovel came a creature resembling a human, which at first I took for a boy, but a ring in the nose showed that it was a woman. She was very short, like a twelve-year-old child, dressed in a skin tunic down to the knees, breeches of wapiti skin, and gaiters decorated with coloured embroidery, moccasins of the same pattern, and handsome flowered false sleeves. On her head was a white scarf like a turban.

The brown eyes, placed horizontally, were half-concealed by the marked Mongolian fold of the eyelids, the prominent cheekbones, broad, flattened nose, and thin lips, all combined to give her face a very exotic expression. It seemed flat and pentagonal, and it was really broader than the skull.

The woman stared at us in astonishment, and then suddenly an expression of alarm dawned over her face. What could Russians be wanting here? Respectable ones would never come

all the way here . . . we must be *choldoni*, as the Udehé call brigands, she evidently thought, and bolted back into her hovel.

To allay her anxieties, Dersu talked to her in her native tongue, and introduced me as leader of the expedition. Then she was reassured. Etiquette forbad a woman to express her curiosity aloud. She was reserved, and glanced at us slyly, when unobserved.

The hut, small without, was yet smaller within. Inside, in fact, there was room only to sit or lie down. I told the men to pitch the tents.

The difference between the Chinesified aborigines on the coast and these forest-dwellers who had retained so much of their primitive customs was very marked.

The woman set to work silently to get supper ready. She hung a kettle over the fire, filled it with water, and put in a couple of good-sized fish ; then she took her pipe, filled it with tobacco, and lit it, every now and then addressing a question in an undertone to Dersu.

When supper was ready the owner arrived. He was a man of about thirty, thin, of middle height. He, too, was wearing a long tunic, tied round the waist by a girdle, which gave him a waist. All along the right edge of the tunic, round the neck and skirt ran a broad strip of embroidery. On his legs were breeches and gaiters, and moccasins of fish skin. He had a white scarf round his head, and on top of it a cap of goat-skin, with a squirrel's tail sticking up. His ruddy, sunburnt face, the variegated costume, the squirrel's tail on his cap, the ring and bangles on his hand and wrists, all gave this savage the appearance of an American Redskin. The impression was still stronger when he sat by the fire and silently smoked his pipe, paying scarcely any attention to our presence.

Etiquette demanded that guests should break the silence. Dersu was aware of this and so asked him about the road and the depth of the snow on the trail. Conversation sprang up. When he learnt who we were and whence we had come, the Udehé told us that he knew that we intended going down the Iman, as he had heard from his tribesmen living lower down the valley, and that down there they had been expecting us for some time. This information surprised me considerably.

In the evening his wife had a look through our clothing, darned it where necessary, and gave us new moccasins in place of our outworn ones. Our host gave me a bearskin to sleep on, I rolled myself in my blanket, and quickly dropped off.

During the night I awoke from the biting cold. Throwing off the blanket, I saw that there was no fire in the hut, but only a few cinders glowing in the grate. Through the opening in the roof I could see the dark sky spangled with stars. From the other side of the hut I heard a snore. Evidently, on turning in, the Udehé put out the fire, to prevent accidents. I tried wrapping myself tighter in my blanket, but it did not help, as the cold crept in through every fold. I struck a match and looked at the thermometer. It showed thirty-six degrees of frost. Then I tore off a piece of the bark carpet, put it on the fire, and blew

it into flame. Collecting the embers on the fire, I dressed and went out.

Under cover of a tent my soldiers were asleep and near them the fire was still burning. I warmed myself and was thinking of going back into the hut, when on the side near the river I caught the glow of another fire. There, under the bank, I found Dersu. The water had eaten away the bank, and a large lump of turf was overhanging, so as to form a sort of niche. In this he had made himself a bed and lit his fire. His pipe hung from his mouth and his rifle lay by his side. I awakened him. The Gold at once sprang up and grabbed his weapon and bundle, thinking he had overslept.

When he saw it was I he made room for me by his side, and I found it warmer and snugger there than inside the hut on a bearskin, and slept far better.

I did not awake till all were afoot. Bochkarev was roasting a steak of musk-deer. When we were ready to start the Udehé came out, put on his wraps, and said that he would go with us as far as Sidatun.

While we were drinking our morning tea, Granatman and Kozhevnikov had an argument, which way the wind had been blowing during the night. Granatman pointed to the south, Kozhevnikov to the east, while I thought it had come from the north. We could not agree, so referred the problem to Dersu. The Gold said instantly that it had blown from the west, and pointed out a reed. The wind had dropped at sunrise, and the reed remained bent in the direction the wind had left it.

We did not go far that day. Our bundles were lightened in proportion to our consumption of stores, but more troublesome to carry. The straps rubbed the shoulders badly, and I was not the only one to notice it.

The cold wind made the snow dry and powdery, which handicapped movement. It was particularly difficult going up-hill, and the men oftentimes slipped, and rolled down-hill. Our strength was no longer the same; vigour was much reduced and fatigue was telling on us all. We all needed more rest than a mere day.

By the river we found another empty hut. The Cossacks and Bochkarev made themselves at home in it, and the Chinamen were left to sleep outside by the fire. Dersu at first wanted to sleep with them, but seeing that they collected all kinds of firewood indiscriminately, he decided to sleep separately.

" Him no know," he explained. " Me no want burn shirt; must get good wood."

The empty hut had evidently often served to give a night's shelter to wandering hunters. Around it all the dry wood had long since been cut down and burnt. This did not worry Dersu. He went a little deeper into the forest and dragged up a dry ash. Right up till dusk he collected wood, and I helped him to the best of my ability. Thanks to that, we slept well that night, without anxiety for our clothes or tent.

A purple glow in the evening and mist on the skyline before daylight were sure signs of a hard frost for the next day. And so it was. The sun came out dull and misshapen. It gave light, but no heat. From its face there radiated bright beams above and below, but at the sides were bright circles of prismatic colours, which Polar explorers call the sun's ears.

The Udehé who accompanied us knew the locality well. He knew the short cuts. A couple of miles from the mouth of the Kulumbé the track turned into the forest, through which we walked for about an hour. Suddenly the forest came to an end and the path broke off. Before us was the river Iman.

It was not yet frozen, but merely fringed with ice. On the far bank, exactly opposite us, were clustered some little figures. They turned out to be Udehé children. A little farther down in the clumps of willow could be seen a hut and a shed on piles. Dersu called out to the children to bring us a boat. The little boys looked towards us in terror, and ran away. A moment later there came out of the hut a man with a gun in his hand. Dersu and he exchanged a few words, and then he pulled across to our side.

The native boat is a kind of long, flat-bottomed punt, so light that a single man can without difficulty drag it up on to the bank. The fore portion is blunt, but the bottom projects and is curved upwards, so as to form a kind of ladle or shovel-shaped prow, which gives it an ill-proportioned appearance. Owing to this construction it does not cut the water, but rides over it, so to speak, and as the centre of buoyancy is high, it seems to be very unsteady.

When we stepped into it, it rocked so that I instinctively gripped the sides, but directly we had put off from the bank, I realized how steady she really was. The Udehé punted her with a long pole, standing in the middle. With vigorous thrusts he pushed the boat smartly through the water against the stream, which carried him to one side and gradually brought him to the opposite bank.

At last we came to the place where the hut was situated and disembarked on the ice. There came out to meet us a woman and three children, who hid timidly behind their mama. In admitting us, the woman went into the hut too, squatted by the fire, and lit her pipe, while the children stayed outside and busied themselves stowing fish in the shed.

The walls of the hut were a mass of chinks, through which the wind whistled mercilessly. In the middle a fire was burning. From time to time the children came running in to warm their frozen little hands. I was astonished to see how lightly clad they were, with bare chests, no sleeves, or anything on their heads, yet they worked on, apparently not suffering from the cold at all. When one of them sat a bit too long by the fire his father called him sharply to order and sent him packing.

" The little chap is frozen," I said to Dersu, and asked him to translate my words to our host.

" He'll have to get used to it," replied the father, " for if he doesn't he'll soon die of hunger."

It was impossible to disagree with him. He who has dealings with nature and wishes to enjoy her gifts in the raw must learn to commune with her even when she is not in a caressing mood.

The upper reaches of the Iman are covered with dense mixed forest. It would be hard to imagine a wilder and more desolate region. Only in the beginning of winter is there some sign of human life, when some Chinamen wander up here from the coast after sable, but they do not stay long. They are afraid of being entrapped by the deep snows and soon return home.

At Sitadun we stopped for three days, during which time I had a look round the settlement and met all the residents. Most of them were criminals of various types, escaped prisoners, fugitives from justice, and adventurers whose passions knew no bounds. They did nothing but smoke opium, drink vodka, gamble, quarrel, and blaspheme. The inhabitants of each cabin fell into three groups : owners, workers, and idlers, who lived on the means they earned by robbery and murder. I thought of Chan Bao. He had warned me not to trust the Chinese of Sitadun.

As everywhere, the native tribes were in a state of complete slavery. Without a notion of letters, the Udehé had no idea to what extent they were in debt to the Chinese, who outnumbered them some twenty times or more. Here was to be seen real slavery, in the literal sense of the word. For instance, an Udehé who failed to deliver the prescribed number of sable skins by a certain date was so savagely beaten with clubs that he was crippled for the rest of his life. They took his wife and children from him and sold him for 400 roubles to another Chinaman as an unpaid labourer.

All this made me aflame with indignation. But what could we do, but half a dozen against a whole company of armed, desperate men? I promised the Udehé to do what I could to help them and improve their position when I returned to Khabarovsk.

On 31 October the frost was intensified, and blocks of ice came floating down the river. In spite of this, the Udehé decided to take us by boat as far as possible.

CHAPTER XXI : A NASTY SITUATION

ON 1 November we left Sitadun and started down the Iman by boat.

The Chinese learn from childhood how to handle boats on mountain streams. You have to keep a look-out far ahead, to know where to hold the boat and where to turn her nose against the water or, on the other hand, to drive her as much as possible and shoot over a dangerous spot. You must appreciate all this and promptly take such action as necessary, as the slightest slip and the boat, caught by the swift current, would be smashed to bits on the rocks in a moment. In the rapids the water is very turbulent, so the boat rocks, and it is harder than ever to maintain the balance.

It was more dangerous than ever for us, as great blocks of ice were being carried down and the navigable part of the stream encroached upon by bank-ice. The floes compelled us to steer not where we wanted to, but where we could. This was particularly noticeable in places where there were rapids in a bend of the river. The broader the bank-ice, the more rapid the stream in the middle.

Near the mouths of a couple of tributaries, we saw some empty Udehé huts. From some they had not taken away the stores of fish, but had left dogs to keep the crows away, and they did their duty very well. Whenever one of those feathered thieves poked his beak into the place, they charged it with a savage bark and drove it away.

In the Iman, as in all mountain rivers, there are many rapids. The one half way between Sitadun and the river Armu is looked upon as the most dangerous. Here the roaring of the water could be heard far away, and in spots the bottom was exposed.

A big rock hung on the far bank, and the foaming water boiled beneath it.

The Udehé stopped the boat and consulted among themselves. Then they let her drift down the stream broadside and then, just at the moment when it seemed that the current was going to dash them against the rock, by a swift and vigorous thrust, they swung her on to a new direction. I could see in their eyes that we were taking a big risk. Most serene was Dersu. I compared impressions with him.

" No matter, captain," he answered calmly. "Udehé all same fish. Very well know work boat on water. Us no can do so-how."

The farther we went, the harder it became. The ice-floes increased, and bank ice became broader than ever.

All this district is covered with conifers mixed with deciduous trees. The latter are dominant on the islands, with cedar, but the banks and shingle spits were overgrown with willows and osiers, which gave the natives an inexhaustible supply of material for their skis, huts, harpoons, and other instruments.

Since the morning the sky had been threatening, and another blizzard seemed to be looming. Our Udehé skilfully manœuvred our craft between the floes. Where the stream Gadala joins the Iman there is a bend, and here there was a mass of floating ice, with a narrow passage through the middle. Whether this was open all the way through or closed at the far end, our men could not say. They turned and asked me whether they should risk it or not. I was so sick of tramping with a pack on my back that I decided to tempt fortune. Dersu began to dissuade me, but I did not agree with him, thinking that even in case of some disaster we should manage to get to the bank. Anyhow we could not stay long in one place.

So we went for it.

We had hardly gone fifty yards before we realized that the channel was closed. Ahead was a wall of solid ice. To approach right up to it was dangerous, as if our heavily laden craft bumped against it it would be sure to fill at once. The only thing to do was to retreat as quickly as possible, but that was easier said than done. To turn the boat in that narrow channel was impossible, so we had to back her. As luck would have it, we were right in mid-stream, and our poles hardly touched bottom. By dint of tremendous effort we managed to get half-way back, when one of the natives gave a cry. From the tone of alarm in his voice I knew that there was some danger and glanced round. A huge block was bearing right down on us, and looked certain to plug the entrance of our channel before we could reach it. The men strained themselves to the utmost of their power, but the berg would not wait. With a crash it landed right against one side of the channel, and then against the other. To make things unexpectedly worse, the shock set the rest of the ice in motion. The channel began to narrow.

" Ice soon break boat ! " cried Dersu in an unnatural voice. " Must go quick ! "

He sprang out of the boat on to the ice, dragging the end of a line with him. Twice he came down and was plunged into the water, but both times he managed to climb out on to the ice again. Luckily the bank was not far off. The Cossacks followed his example. Kozhevnikov and Bochkarev reached the bank safely, but Murzin went through. He started trying to climb up on to a floe, but it rolled over with him, and the harder he climbed the deeper it sunk, and in another moment he would have gone to the bottom.

At that desperate moment Dersu dashed in to save him. For a moment it looked as though both must perish. The Udehé and I were struggling from one block of ice to another, dragging the boat along with us and holding on to it. Luckily, the nose of the boat soon passed close to where Dersu and Murzin were struggling, and that saved them both. She was now again overloaded and almost awash, swung across the stream, and was carried downwards bodily, with the blocks of ice.

We were now near the bank, and started flinging our things ashore and then crawling to dry ground ourselves. A few moments later the boat was dashed against the cliff. Like a living thing it clung there a moment quivering, then suddenly cracked and was rent in two. Another crash, a fragment protruded an instant from the water, and then all disappeared.

We crawled up on to the bank. The first thing to do was to light a fire and dry ourselves. Somebody had the inspiration of brewing tea and having something to eat. We looked round for the bag of supplies, but it was not to be found. One of the rifles also was missing. There was nothing to do but for each to nibble whatever he happened to have in his pocket, and trek on. The natives told us that towards evening we should reach a cabin where we should probably find a store of frozen fish.

Towards dusk we reached the cabin. It was empty, but the Cossacks found a couple of dry fish in the store, and that was the scanty supper with which we were obliged to content ourselves.

From that spot to the place where a big feeder joins the Iman, where there is a small native village, was a three days' journey. That could be shortened by taking a cut across the mountains. That would bring us direct to a place called Sanshi-heza, about thirty miles below the Armu. In view of our shortage of food supplies it was essential to shorten the routes. The Udehé promised to go with us as far as the point where we should turn off from the Iman, as from there we could find the way ourselves.

The next day we came to a couple of springs, one flowing to the north, the other to the west. We ought probably to have taken the right-hand one, but I made a mistake and chose the northerly direction. Directly we came to the pass we stopped to camp as soon as we could find some firewood and more or less even ground.

In the morning of 3 November we ate our last crumb and marched with light loads. Now our only hope lay in hunting, and for that reason we sent Dersu ahead while we followed at a good distance behind so as not to disturb the game. Our road followed a river we did not know, which, so far as we could see, was flowing towards the west.

We all hoped that Dersu would shoot us something to eat,

but in vain. Not a shot did we hear. In the afternoon the valley widened out a little, and we picked up a faint trail. It went to the left in a northerly direction, cutting across a hummocky marsh. The pangs of hunger asserted themselves. We trudged on in silence. Suddenly I caught sight of Dersu. He was walking up and down, stooping and picking up something from the ground. I hailed him. He waved to me.

" What have you found ? " asked Granatman.

" Bear eat fish, throw away head ; me pick up," he replied.

And, in fact, lying on the snow were a number of fish heads. Evidently a bear had been here since the snow had fallen.

In time of need the devil eats flies, or, as our Russian proverb has it, in time of fishlessness a crab is fish, and a starving man will wolf the remains of a bear's dinner. We all flung ourselves upon those relics and in quarter of an hour not a head was left in the snow. We had all stuffed our pockets with them.

Absorbed in our work, we had not noticed that the little valley had brought us out to a fairly big river. This was the Sinantsa. If the Udehé were right, the next day would bring us to the Iman.

Crossing the brook, we camped in a thick pine forest. How delicious those fish heads seemed to us ! Some had quite good-sized lumps of meat still attached to them, and those were regarded as a very lucky find. We divided up the whole stock evenly and had a most enjoyable, though not altogether satisfying, supper.

That night the temperature dropped sharply, but as we had plenty of firewood we slept well. We dreamt chiefly of caviare and steak-and-kidney pudding.

On the morning of the 4th we awoke hungry. On empty stomachs we started down the Sinantsa. The snow here was much deeper than it had been on the Kulumbé, and in places was up to our knees, which made it very hard going, and we hardly managed to tramp more than a mile and a half in an hour, at the outside.

We were disappointed in our hunting and in our hope of finding more fish heads. Kozhevnikov caught sight of a musk-deer and fired, but missed.

Judging by the time we had been upon the road, we ought by now to have come to the Iman again, and at every bend in the river I expected to see the mouth of the Sinantsa, but it was perpetual forest, then another bend, and then more unending forest.

At dusk we came to a small hut of cedar bark. I was pleased at this. Dersu, however, pointed out that there were remains of several fires round the hut but a complete absence of any of the utensils of life in the *taigá*, so that it could only have been used as a bivouac for wayfarers. There must be at least another day's march to the Iman.

Hunger was now torturing us. The Cossacks sat gloomily round the fire and hardly spoke. Several times I asked Dersu how we had taken the wrong trail, and were we on the right road. He answered that he had never been in this district before, that he had nothing to go by and, like me, could only guess. Hoping to forget their hunger a little, the men tried to sleep. I lay down too, but could not sleep. Anxiety and doubt tormented me. If we did not manage to kill something to-morrow, or reach the Iman, things would be desperate indeed. In the summer a man can carry on without food for several days, but in the winter hunger kills quickly.

In the morning Dersu was the first awake, and aroused me. Again there was discussion about the way. We must go while we could still walk, insisted Dersu, while we could still move our legs.

But we had barely started when I knew that my strength was no longer the same. My knapsack seemed twice as heavy as it had been yesterday, and every half-mile we were obliged to sit down and rest. I craved to lie down and do nothing, a bad sign.

Like that we dragged on till midday, but covered little ground. Evidently we should not reach the Iman that evening unless we did better than that. As we crawled along we managed to shoot a couple of small birds and bagged three nut-hatches and a woodpecker, but what was that among five starving men?

The weather looked threatening, and the sky again was covered with clouds. A sharp gust of wind raised the snow into the air. The air seemed filled with powdery snow, and whirl-winds spun down the river. In places the wind blew all the snow off the ice and in others piled it up in heaps. That day we were all chilled to the bone. Our clothing was worn out and our rags were little protection against the cold.

On the left bank a rocky hill loomed up, standing with steep cliffs over the river. Here we found a sort of shallow cave and in its shelter lit a fire. Dersu slung a kettle over it and boiled some water. Then he pulled a piece of wapiti hide out of his knapsack, scorched it in the fire, and began to cut it into thin shavers with his knife. When it was all minced fine, he poured it into the kettle and boiled it for a long time. Then he turned and said to us all:

" Every man must eat. Cheat stomach. Add little-little strong. Then go more quick. No-can stop-rest. To-day sun finish, we find Iman."

There was no need for persuasion. We were all only too anxious to swallow anything. Although the piece of hide had been boiled for a long time, it was still so tough that we could not make an impression on it with our teeth. Dersu advised us not to eat much, and to remain hungry, saying:

" No must eat much . . . bad."

In half an hour we moved on. We found in fact that the chewed hide, although it had not satisfied our hunger, had at all events given the stomach some work to do. Whenever anybody stopped for a moment, Dersu began to abuse him.

The day was reaching its close, but we were still crawling on. Each bend raised our hopes, only to show the same perpetual picture. We dragged our legs along like drunken men, and but for Dersu's insistence would have stopped long since to bivouac.

About six that evening we came upon the first traces of humanity, tracks of ski, freshly felled timber, sawn logs, and so on.

" Iman not far," commented Dersu with relief.

We all felt encouraged, and an access of increased buoyancy. As though in answer to his words a distant bark of a dog caught our ears. One more bend in the river, one last bend, and . . . we saw a fire. It was the Chinese village.

In a quarter of an hour we had dragged our steps up to the hamlet. Never in my life have I felt such fatigue as that day. Going up to the first cabin, we walked straight in and dropped on to the *k'ang* without undressing.

I did not want to eat, or drink, or talk, but only to lie down.

Naturally, our arrival provoked a sensation among the Chinese, the owner of the cabin being most excited of all. He sent off his workmen somewhere secretly. After a little time another Chinaman entered the cabin. By his appearance I should say he was a man of about thirty-five. He was of middle height, powerful build, with typical Mongolian features, and better dressed than the others. He carried himself in a very free and easy manner and had a loud voice. He addressed us in Russian and began interrogating us, who were we, and whence did we come. He spoke Russian fluently and correctly, often inter-larding his words with Russian sayings and proverbs. He then tried to persuade us to go to his cabin, introduced himself as Li-tan-kuy, son of Lu-chin-fu. His house, he said, was the best in the place, that the one we had come to belonged to a mere beggar, and so on. He then went out and held a long, whispered conversation with the owner of the cabin we were in, who in his turn came in then and asked us to move to Li-tan-kuy's house. There was nothing we could do, so we were obliged to give way. Some workmen turned up from somewhere and carried our things round. As we were walking down the path, Dersu plucked my sleeve and said in an undertone :

" Him very bad man. Me think him want cheat. To-day me no sleep."

I must say that the glib Chinaman had produced the same impression on myself, and I did not like his inquisitiveness and familiarity.

In five minutes we came to Li-tan-kuy's house. Round it were several workmen's cabins and beyond we could see store-sheds, a forge, barn, stables, and so on. We went in. Our host wanted to put Granatman and me in his own room, but I insisted that the Cossacks and Dersu should share the room with me. After that Li-tan-kuy set to work to entertain us. And how good that tea tasted ! And those rolls fried in bean oil ! For the time we even forgot our suspicions, but when I had satisfied the first cravings my caution was again aroused. Li-tan-kuy fed us well, it is true, but his entertainment was not whole-hearted. Through all his movements I felt I could discern some hidden purpose, and Dersu followed him attentively. I decided also to keep awake, but to overcome my fatigue was beyond my power, and after supper my eyelids were so heavy that they closed of their own weight. Imperceptibly I fell off into a profound slumber.

During the night I was aroused by someone shaking me by the shoulder. I sprang to my feet. Dersu was standing by me. He signed to me not to make a sound, and then told me that Li-tan-kuy had offered him money and asked him to persuade me not to go to the Udehé at Vangubé but to pass their hamlet by, and, to make it easier for me, he offered to supply porters and guides. Dersu had replied that it did not concern him, and then lay down and pretended to go to sleep. Li-tan-kuy waited till he thought the Gold really was sound asleep, then crept out, mounted a horse, and rode away.

" To-morrow must go Vangubé. Me think something there all same bad," he concluded.

At that moment we heard the sound of horse's hooves outside. We dropped back to our places and pretended to be asleep. Li-tan-kuy came in. He stopped in the doorway, listened, and, convinced that we were really asleep, quietly took off his things and lay down on the *k'ang*. Before long I dropped asleep again, and did not awake till the sun was high.

It was a noise that aroused me, and I asked what was happening. The Cossacks told me that several Udehé had come to the cabin. I dressed and went out to see them, and was struck by the hostile expression of their glances.

After drinking some tea I said I was going on. Li-tan-kuy endeavoured to persuade me to stay another day, promising to kill a pig for dinner. Dersu winked at me. Then he began to appoint a guide for me, but I declined his services. Try as he might to deceive us, he was not successful.

The trail follows the right bank of the river along the foot of some high mountains. There were numerous Chinese cabins, and the Chinese population was well armed and prosperous. They scowled at us with a most hostile expression, and whenever I made inquiries about the population, they answered roughly : " Bu dzhi dao " (I don't know), while some of them said right out : " I know but I won't tell."

A little farther on I noticed some Udehé huts a little off the trail. It was Vangubé, with a population of about eighty-five natives. When we approached their huts the whole population came out to meet us. They gave us a by no means cordial welcome and did not even invite us into their cabins.

The first question they put to me was to ask why we had spent the night in the cabin of Li-tan-kuy. In reply I asked them why they regarded us in so unfriendly a fashion. The Udehé replied that they had been expecting us for a long time, but they had just learnt that I had come and where I had spent the night.

The riddle was quickly cleared up. It appeared that there had been a regular tragedy. The Chinaman Li-tan-kuy was *tsaidun*, or head-man, of the valley of the Iman. He exploited the natives mercilessly, and punished them cruelly if they failed to deliver the fixed amount of furs by a given time. Many families he had ruined utterly, raping their women and selling their children for debt. At length two of the Udehé, Masenda and Somo by name, exasperated beyond endurance, had gone to Khabarovsk and lodged a complaint with the Governor-General. He promised them help, and told them that before long I should arrive from the direction of the sea. He had told them to apply to me for help, assuming that on the spot I should be able to deal with the situation easily. The men returned and told their relatives of the result of their mission, and patiently awaited my arrival. Now Li-tan-kuy heard of their visit to Khabarovsk. Then, as an example to the rest, he had Masenda and Somo flogged savagely. One of them died under the beating, and the other survived but remained a cripple for life. Then the dead man's brother Gulunga started for Khabarovsk, but Li-tan-kuy heard of his departure and sent men to catch him and drown him in the river under the ice. Hearing of this, the Udehé decided to defend their comrade by force of arms. A state of siege ensued. For two weeks the natives had stayed at home, refusing to go out shooting and trapping, and, for want of supplies, were seriously in want. Suddenly the news came through that I had arrived and stopped in the house of their enemy. I explained to them that I had not known anything about it all, and that on arrival at the place I was so exhausted and starving that I simply collapsed into the first house available.

That evening all the elder men met in one of the huts and, upon consultation, it was decided that on my return to Khabarovsk I would submit a report about the whole case and request that help and protection be afforded to the natives.

When they had gone to their huts I dressed and went outside. All around was dark, so dark that I could not see anything at two paces distance. I could tell the situation of the huts only by the sparks that flew out of the holes in the roofs.

Suddenly through the still dark air there were wafted to me strange sounds. It was the noise of drums, followed by chanting, a dirge like groans and tears. These mournful sounds were inexpressibly melancholy. Like waves they floated aside and faded away in the cold night air. I called Dersu and asked him what it was. He told me that in the farthest hut a *shaman*, or medicine-man, was curing a sick child. I walked in that direction, but at the entrance to the hut was stopped by an old man. I understood that my presence would break the spell. I went back.

On the side of the Chinese huts I could see lights. I felt chill, returned to my hut, and began to warm myself by the fire.

CHAPTER XXII : GOOD-BYE !

THE next morning, 8 November, we continued our journey.

All the Udehé came to speed us on the road. The crowd of variegated people with their weather-beaten faces and the white tails sticking up on the tops of their heads, in all their queer costumes, produced a very odd effect. In all their movements there was something wild and childlike.

We walked in the middle, the elder men by our side, and the younger ran along outside the party, eagerly scanning the tracks of otters, foxes, and hares. At the end of the flat the old men stopped. One grey-haired man stepped out of the crowd and handed me the claw of a lynx, which he asked me to put in my pocket as a reminder of their petition against Li-tan-kuy. Then we parted, the Udehé returning to their home while we tramped on.

When walking through the forest in the summer the traveller must keep his eyes wide open so as not to lose the trail, but in winter, when the snow is on the ground, it stands out clearly among the bushes. This made my surveying work much easier.

We now felt our fatigue. We wanted to keep stopping to rest. According to the Udehé, some distance ahead lay the Chinese settlement of Kartun. We proposed to spend a day there to rest and restore our strength and, if possible, hire horses. But our hopes were doomed to disappointment.

The day was approaching its close when we came to Kartun. The sun had just dipped below the horizon and its beams were still playing on the clouds, which reflected the glow back to the earth. Some Chinese cabins could be seen on the side by the river. They were nestling in a group of firs, as though to hide themselves from the casual wayfarer. We went up to them. More prosperous Chinese houses than those of Kartun I had not yet seen. They looked more like factories than living houses.

I went into one of them. The Chinese received me scowlingly. They had already heard who we were and why the Udehé had accompanied us. It is very unpleasant being in a house when the owner is hostile, so I went into another. There the reception was even worse, and in all we tried—the third, fourth, fifth, down to the tenth—it was always the same chilly welcome. It is no good kicking against the pricks. I swore, the Cossacks swore, and Dersu swore, but it was of no avail. There was nothing to do but give way. To spend the night near the houses we did not want, so I decided to push on till we found a spot suitable for bivouac.

The evening drew on. The beautiful glow faded from the sky. Here and there in the sky a star struck light.

The Chinese village was by now some distance behind us, and on we trudged. Suddenly Dersu stopped, threw his head back, and began to sniff the air.

" Stop, captain," he said. " Me smell smoke. That mean Udehé," he added after a pause.

" How do you know ? " asked Kozhevnikov. " Perhaps it's another Chinaman."

" No," answered Dersu. " This is Udehé. Chinee house have high chimney. Smoke go high. Out Udehé hut smoke go low. Udehé smoke fish."

So saying, he strode confidently forward. Every now and then he stopped to sniff the air again. Like that we went some fifty paces forward, then a hundred, then two hundred, but the promised huts did not materialize. The tired men began to jeer at the old chap. Dersu was offended.

" You want stop here sleep, good, but me go on ; me want find hut, eat fish," he answered calmly, and went on.

I followed him, and the Cossacks came grumbling behind me. And in another two or three minutes we did, in fact, come to a native settlement. There were only two wigwams, and in them lived nine men, three women, and four children. I went into one and saw a woman roasting a dried fish over the fire. Evidently, Dersu's powers of smell were much more highly developed than ours. He had caught the odour of the smoke and roasting fish at least 250 yds. away, if not more.

In a few moments we were sitting by the fire eating fish and drinking tea. I was so dead beat that evening that I could scarcely make the necessary entries in my journal. I begged the Udehé not to let the fire out all night, and they promised that they would take watches during the night, and went out at once to split some more firewood.

That night was misty and frosty. To tell the truth, if there had been a storm the next morning I should have been immensely relieved. At least we should have had a good rest and slept our sleep out, but hardly was the sun up when the mist scattered. The shrubs and willows along the banks of the stream were picked out in hoar-frost and looked like coral, and the rime spangled the smooth ice with rosettes. The sunlight played upon them, and it looked as though the river were studded with diamonds.

I saw that the Cossacks were anxious to get home, so gave way to their wishes. One of the Udehé volunteered to escort us as far as Miaulin, a big place on the right bank of the Iman, about five miles down-stream below Kartun.

That day the trail seemed heavier than ever.

About two we came to Miaulin. This was one of the oldest settlements in the Iman district. Here there lived sixteen Chinese with one Gold. The owner had settled here fifty years ago while still a young man, and now he reckoned himself about seventy. Somewhat to our surprise, he received us not in a particularly friendly manner. He gave us at least something to eat and allowed us to spend the night in his house. In the evening he got drunk. At first he began to ask me something, but then his voice grew harsher and he began to shout.

" Miaulin was not built yesterday, nor to-day," he cried.

" Miaulin is as old as I am, and you've come to drive me out. I won't give Miaulin up, I tell you. If I'm made to go, I'll burn the place."

Then he cried that he'd set fire to it then and there, went outside, and brought in a great armful of straw.

It ended up by Dersu giving him more drink till he fell unconscious and went to sleep on the straw he had brought in.

Next morning we were off early, leaving the old man still asleep on his straw in his house which he refused to give to us, who had not the slightest intention of taking it away from him.

It is strange, but the nearer we came to the Ussuri the worse we felt. Our knapsacks were almost empty, but seemed heavier on our backs than when we had them cram full. The straps hurt our shoulders so much that it was painful to touch the place. From the strain we had been through our heads were aching, and we all felt terribly weak.

The nearer we came to the railway, the less friendly the attitude of the natives. Our clothing was in rags, our boots worn out, and the peasants looked upon us as tramps.

The soldiers dragged on wearily, frequently stopping to rest. Not long before dusk we came to a farm with the queer name of Parovoz, the origin of which I cannot guess. Here lived the head-man of the Udehé, Sarl Kimunka, with his family. In 1901, with a surveyor named Mihailov, he had been up the Iman to the Sihoté-Alin, and as a reward for his work received a grant of this farm. Sarl Kimunka knew from personal experience all the difficulties and hardships of surveying on the Sihoté-Alin, and so he gave us the warmest welcome and a full dinner.

The next morning we slept late, ate some fish, and resumed our journey. Sarl Kimunka escorted us as far as the place where some Koreans had recently settled near Parovoz. Below that the Iman was not frozen, and we were obliged to cross it in a boat. We called at all the houses, but could not find a single man. The women looked at us in terror, were silent, and hid their children. Seeing that there was nothing to be done there I waved my arm and told the soldiers to go down to the river.

GOOD-BYE!

The Udehé managed to find a flat-bottomed boat hidden among the bushes. In that he ferried us across one by one and then returned home.

On the left bank, at the foot of an isolated hill, were four mud huts, the Russian settlement of Kotelnoye. The colonists had only recently arrived from Russia and were not yet properly organized. We went into one of the huts and asked for a lodging for the night. The hosts met us with a warm welcome, asked us who we were and where we had come from, and began to bemoan their lot.

What a delight it was to eat a piece of good peasant bread! In the evening all the colonists came crowding round us. They told us all about their difficulties in setting up in a strange country, with many a sigh. Evidently their emigration had not been quite a success. But for the salmon they would have died of starvation, and fish was their sole support.

Beyond Kotelnoye the road was marked with mile-posts. Round the little village was one marked '74.' We had no money for the hire of horses, but in any case I was most anxious to complete the survey, which could be done only on foot. Besides, our ragged clothing was so thin that we could keep warm only by constant movement.

We set out early the moment it was light.

The next village was bigger than Kotelnoye, but no better off. Poverty was to be seen in every window, on the men's faces, in the eyes of the women, and rags of the children.

In the afternoon we came to the Korean hamlet of Lukianovka, consisting of about fifty scattered cabins. Here we were able to rest a little, and then continued our journey. Dusk caught us on the road. We were tired out, chilled, and very hungry. Soon it became too dark for me to be able to read the figures on the instrument, but the road was still visible. So I began to work by firelight. That is to say, at a signal from me one of the Cossacks held a burning match to the dial, and in that minute I was able to read the figure, enter it on the plane-table, and walk on. At last we saw a light ahead.

" A village ! " we cried in one voice.

" At night light all-time cheat," warned Dersu.

And, in fact, in the dark a light is visible from a great distance. Sometimes it seems farther than it really is, sometimes nearer, sometimes quite close. We trudged on, but the light seemed to keep receding. I wanted to stop to bivouac, but suddenly the light seemed quite close, and through the darkness we could discern a hut, then a second, a third . . . in all eight. It was the hamlet of Verbovka. Most of the peasants were away from home, having gone to the town to look for work. The terrified women took us for bandits and wanted to slam the doors, so we were obliged to hunt up the head-man. He put up Dersu, Bochkarev, and myself, and found quarters for the others with a neighbour.

That day we had trekked twenty-one miles and were dead-beat. From over-fatigue I could not sleep, and for hours tossed from side to side. Each new position gave at first a sweet relief, but a moment later came back the aching pain in every joint.

There were still twenty-six miles to the railway. After consultation with my comrades I decided to make the effort to do this distance in one day's march. To do that we started very early. For nearly an hour I worked by firelight, but then the sun came out, and by then we had already reached Gogolevka.

It was a frosty morning. The village was bathed in smoke, as a white column rose out of every chimney. It spread in the morning air and assumed a golden-pinkish tint.

I did not want to stop here, but one of the villagers knew who we were, and begged us to go in and have some tea. To bread and salt no man can say nay. Our host was kind indeed. He gave us milk, white bread, with honey and butter. I do not remember his name, but from the bottom of my soul I thank him for his hospitality and kindness. He crowned it all by giving us ample supplies for the road, and tobacco and sweet biscuits for the men.

The good food restored our strength. Heartily thanking our hospitable host, we continued our journey and soon came to the next village. This was only fifteen miles from the railway. But what are fifteen miles after a good breakfast when you know it is the end of the long journey?

The day was bright and sunny, but cold. I was sick to death of surveying, and it was only by stubborn resolution to carry it through to the end that I did not throw it up. At each sight I hurriedly sketched in the figure, and then blew on my fingers to warm them. In an hour we overtook a man. He was taking fish to the station.

" How can you work like that? " he asked. " Aren't you cold? "

I answered that my gloves had worn right out on the road.

" Then take mine," he said. " I have another pair."

As he said that he took a pair of warm knitted gloves and handed them to me. I took them and went on working. We went along a couple of miles together and I sketched in, while the man told me about his life and swore vigorously at everybody and everything. He swore at his comrades, he swore at his neighbour's wife, swore at the schoolmaster and at the pop, or village priest. I grew sick of his swearing. His old nag crawled along at a snail's pace, and I saw that if we went no faster than that, we should never reach Iman by the evening. I pulled the gloves off, handed them back to him, thanked him, wished him luck, and quickened my pace.

" Here, hi! " he called after me. " Aren't you going to pay? "

" What for? " I asked.

" Why, for the gloves! "

" But you've got them back! " I answered.

" What a chap you are! " he replied irritably. " I was sorry for you, and now you aren't going to give me anything! "

" Good kind of sorry! " broke in the Cossacks.

Dersu was angriest of all. He strode on, spat in disgust, and called the fellow all sorts of names.

" Him bad man," he said. " Me no like see such man. Him got no face."

The Gold used ' face ' in the Chinese sense, or rather in the sense of ' conscience.' And I was forced to admit that this man in fact was without conscience.

This incident upset me for the rest of the day.

" How can such man live ? " Dersu could not throw it off.

" Me think him cannot live ; him soon finish."

At midday we came to the river Vaku and halted by the roadside.

There were now not more than a mile and a half to the station in a straight line, but the mile-posts showed four. The reason was that the road made a big detour to avoid a marsh. The breeze wafted down the whistle of engines, and the station buildings were already visible.

Secretly I cherished the thought that this time Dersu would come with me all the way to Khabarovsk. I was very sorry to part with him. I had noticed that during the past few days he had been particularly attentive to me, as though he had been wanting to say something, to ask me something, but could not make up his mind. At last, overcoming his diffidence, he asked me to give him a few cartridges. Then I understood that he had decided to leave us.

" Dersu," I said to him. " Do not go away."

He sighed and said that he was afraid of the town, and there was nothing he could do in it.

Then I proposed to him that he should come as far as the station, where I should be able to fit him up with money and provisions.

" No need, captain," answered the Gold. " Me find sable . . . all same as money."

In vain I tried to persuade him. He would not budge. Dersu said that he would go up the Vaku and at its source would find some sable and then, when the thaw came, he would cross over to the Daubihé. There, near Anuchino, there lived an old Gold he knew. He would go and pass the two spring months with him. We arranged that when I started on a fresh expedition in the early summer I would send a Cossack for him or come myself.

Dersu agreed and promised to wait for me. Then I handed him all the cartridges I had left. We sat and chatted and talked about the one thing only. Three times we had decided all details about our next meeting, and I tried all I could to prolong the time. I hated parting from him.

At last he stood up and pulled on his knapsack.

" Now must go," he said.

" Well, good-bye, Dersu," I said, shaking his hand warmly, " and thank you for all your help. Good-bye. I shall never forget all you have done for me ! "

The big red disc of the sun had only just dipped below the sky-line, leaving a mournful glow over the horizon. The first star out, as always, was Venus, then out came Jupiter, and then the other stars. Dersu wanted to say something, but felt awkward, and began to polish the butt of his rifle with his sleeve. For a moment we stood there in silence, then shook hands once more, and parted. He turned off to the stream to the left, while we strode on down the road. When we had gone a little distance I looked round and saw the Gold. He had walked out on to the bank of shingle, and was examining some tracks in the snow. I called to him and waved my cap. Dersu waved his arm in reply.

' Farewell, Dersu,' I thought to myself, and stepped out. The Cossacks filed behind me.

Before us stretched a valley, covered with dry, brownish-yellow grass and snow-drifts. The wind howled across it and shook the withered stems. Behind the misty mountains on the west still glowed the twilight, while the chill night advanced from the darkening east. In the station there lit up white, red, and green lanterns.

That day we were more worn out than we had yet been on the whole of the expedition. The men straggled behind. There was still over a mile to the line, but that last mile cost more effort than would have twenty at the beginning of the expedition. Summoning the last remains of our strength we dragged ourselves on to the station, but when only a few hundred yards short of it we simply collapsed on to the sleepers and sat there to rest. Some gangers walking by looked surprised to see us resting so near the station. One plate-layer chaffed us.

" It must be a long way to the station," we heard him comment to his comrades.

We were beyond jokes. The gendarmes also looked at us suspiciously, probably taking us for tramps. At last we succeeded in reaching the group of buildings, and simply fell into the first inn. To a townsman, no doubt, it would have seemed dear and filthy, but to us it seemed like paradise. We took a couple of rooms and settled ourselves down to the comfort.

All our trials and hardships were behind us ! At once we took an interest in the newspapers. Yet I kept thinking of Dersu. ' What is he doing now, I wonder ? I expect he has fixed himself up a bivouac somewhere under the bank, collected some wood, lit a fire, and dozed off with his pipe in his mouth.' With that picture before my eyes I too dozed off.

Next morning I awoke early. The first thought which entered my head with relief was that there was no more need to hump my pack. For long I revelled in the bed. Then I dressed and went to report to the officer in command of the Iman detachment of the Ussurian Cossacks. He received me very kindly, and at once supplied me with cash.

In the evening we went to the baths to enjoy a real Russian steam bath. Through our travels I had lived so intimately with the Cossacks that I did not want to part from them, and after the baths we had tea together.

That was the last time. Presently a train came in. We took different seats in the train, and in the evening of 17 November steamed into my headquarters, Khabarovsk.

Third Expedition

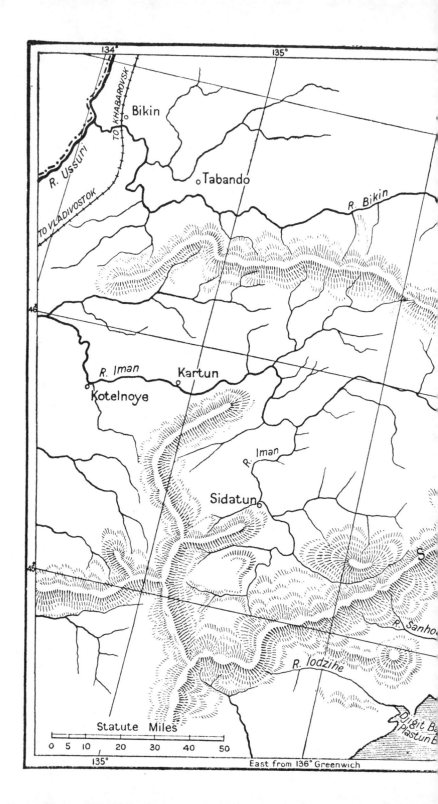

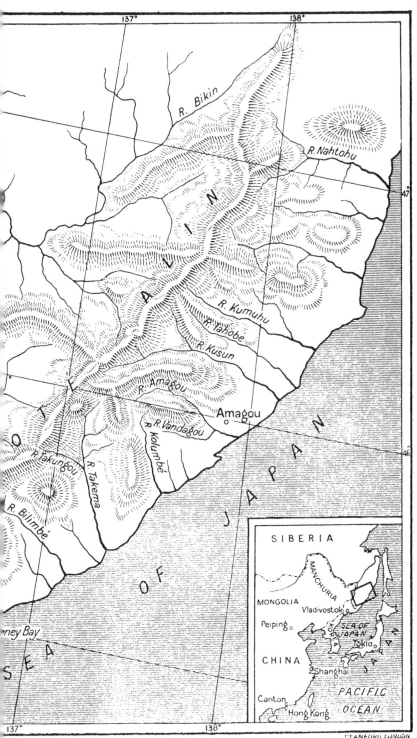

STANFORD, LONDON

CHAPTER XXIII: THE START

FROM January to April 1907 I was busy writing my report on the previous expedition, and it was not until May that I was able to start getting ready for the next.

The district allotted for survey now was the central part of the Sihoté-Alin to the coast, starting from the point where I finished off the previous year.

The organization was on the same lines as the previous expedition, only I took mules instead of horses. They stand the mountain tracks better, as they are harder in the hoof and not so particular about their feed, but are easily bogged in swamps.

My assistant Merzliakov was sent to Vladivostok to buy the mules. It was important to have them unshod, with sound hooves. He was instructed to forward the animals by steamer to Djigit Bay, to leave them there in charge of three riflemen, and go forward himself to establish five supply dumps along the coast.

I sent rifleman Zakharov to Anuchino to find Dersu. He travelled with post-horses, calling in at every native cabin and inquiring of everybody, had they not seen an old Gold of the family Uzala. Before reaching Anuchino in a hut beside the road he happened to meet a native hunter doing up his knapsack and talking to himself.

To the Russian's question whether he knew the Gold, Dersu Uzala, the man answered :

" That me."

Then Zakharov told him why he had come. They spent the night at Anuchino and the next day started back.

I was delighted at Dersu's arrival and spent the whole day chatting to him. He told me how during the winter he had

241

caught a couple of sables, which he had bartered to the Chinese in exchange for clothing, an axe, kettle, and a teapot, and with the rest of the money had bought Chinese material and made himself a new tent. Cartridges he had bought from Russian hunters. Udehé women had made him a new suit of leather jacket and breeches and moccasins. When the snow began to thaw he went over to Anuchino and lived with his old friend and fellow-tribesman. As time went by without news from me he started hunting, and had killed a wapiti in velvet and deposited the antlers with the Chinese on credit.

While in Anuchino he had been robbed. He had made the acquaintance with a trader of some sort, and in his guileless *naïveté* told him of his successful sable-hunting and how profitably he had sold his skins. The trader invited him to the inn to have a drink, and Dersu agreed willingly enough.

Finding his head beginning to whirl, he handed over all his money to his new acquaintance for safe keeping. When he awoke the next day the trader had disappeared. Dersu never could understand that. The people of his tribe always handed each other their valuables for custody, furs and money, and such confidence is never abused.

At that time there was not yet any regular steamer service along the coast of the Sea of Japan. The Immigration Office had as an experiment freighted the steamer *El Dorado* and sent it up to Djigit Bay, but there was no regular sailing list and the office itself did not know when she would return and be ready to sail again.

Our luck was not in. We arrived in Vladivostok two days after she had sailed. I was offered a journey in a torpedo-boat, bound for a cruise to the Shantar Island in the Gulf of Okhotsk. The captain promised to put us ashore at Djigit Bay.

In the open sea we met a school of whales and of dolphins. The whales swam along steadily in one direction, paying little attention to the boats, but the dolphins followed us and, when alongside, began to leap from the water. One of my companions had a shot at one. He missed twice, but the third time a big pool of blood appeared on the surface of the water, and the dolphins disappeared at once.

At dusk we came to America Bay and there stopped for the night.

During the night a strong wind sprang up and the sea became very rough. Next morning, regardless of the weather, she weighed anchor and sailed. I could not sit in my cabin, so went on deck. I was on the *Grozny* and the others followed in our wake, the next behind us being the *Bezshumny*. She kept dropping out of view in the hollows between the waves and then appearing on the tops again, amid their white crests. When the foaming mass of water enveloped the little craft from the bows, it looked as though the sea would swallow her whole at a gulp, but the water was flung off her decks, and she skimmed over the surface and held her line ahead.

When we entered Olga Bay it was already dark.

During the night the sea calmed down a little and the wind dropped and the mist began to disperse. At last the sun came out and lit up the grim, rocky coast.

We reached Djigit Bay towards the evening. The captain said I could sleep on board and go ashore next morning. All that night she rolled on the swell. I awaited the dawn impatiently. What a relief it was to put one's foot again on dry land ! As they started weighing anchor, the breeze wafted us their farewell message through the megaphone : " Good luck to you ! "

Within ten minutes they had disappeared from sight.

We at once pitched our tents and started collecting wood. One of the men went off to hunt for water and came back with the report that the mouth of the river was full of fish.

The soldiers then cast nets and caught so many fish that they could not haul the net ashore. The fish turned out to be the hump-backed salmon, or *gorbusha*.

They were not yet so hideous as they become later in the season, although the jaws had started curving and the hump that gives them their name both in Russian and English was only just beginning to show on the back. I told the men to take only what we could eat and throw the rest back. We all fell on them greedily, but the meat soon began to pall, and after that nobody paid any more attention to them.

At Djigit Bay we were obliged to sit and wait for the mules, as without pack-animals it was impossible to start. I spent the time surveying Djigit and Rynda bays.

After a long delay our mules arrived on board the *El Dorado*. This was splendid news, as it released us from inactivity and allowed us to start on our expedition.

The steamer lay to about 400 yds. off the mouth of the river. The mules were let down straight into the water. They found their way at once and swam ashore, where the men were waiting to receive them.

We spent a couple of days fitting the saddles to the mules and arranging the loads, and then at last we started.

When near a group of cabins Dersu came up to me and asked permission to stay there one night with some natives, promising to overtake us the next day. I told him to take care not to miss us. The Gold roared with laughter and said :

" You not needle ; you not bird, no-can fly. You go on ground, make tracks, leave spoor. My eye see."

To that I had no reply. I knew his talent in tracking and agreed. We went on, but he stayed behind. He caught us up early next morning. By our tracks he had deciphered everything we had done, where we had halted, where we had stopped sometime, and specially, at a place where the trail broke off, he saw where I had sent out scouts to cast for the track. Here one of the men had changed his boots. As he picked up a bit of blood-stained rag he concluded that someone had hurt his foot. I was used to all this, but to the men it was a revelation, and they looked on the Gold with surprise and curiosity.

One of the mules was perpetually giving trouble, and some of the men were obliged to keep dropping behind, with the result that Dersu and I were constantly having to stop and wait for them. So at one of the halts we agreed to leave a sign at every fork in the trail to show which way we had gone. The men could stop behind to re-arrange the packs, while we could go on.

Suddenly the trail forked, one branch following up the stream, the other turning off to the right, so here we had to leave a patteran. Dersu took a stick, pointed the end, and stuck it in the ground. Alongside it he stuck in a small branch and broke it, setting it so that the broken end pointed in the direction we had followed. Having left this signal, we went on confidently that the men would pick it up and come on after us. When we had gone more than a mile we stopped and waited for the men for some time, but as they did not appear we went back to meet them. In twenty minutes we came to the place where the trail forked. At first glance we could see that they had taken the wrong fork.

Dersu began to swear.

" What sort man ! " he exclaimed. " Walk so, head up, no see, all same child. Got eyes, no-can see. That sort man no-can live in *taigá;* soon finish."

He was not so surprised that they had made a mistake, that did not so much matter, but how could they possibly have gone on stolidly on a trail where there were no footmarks ? What was more, they had actually walked on to the patteran we had left them. He could see that it was a man's foot, not a hoof, that had knocked it over.

But talking cures no ills. I took my rifle and fired two shots into the air. In a minute I heard an answering shot from far ahead. Then I fired two more rounds. After that we lit a fire and waited. In half an hour the men returned. They justified themselves by saying that Dersu had left so small a sign that it was easy to overlook. The Gold did not argue, or even answer. He realized that what was clear as crystal to him was invisible to others.

So we drank some tea and went on.

As we started I told the men to keep a sharp look-out, and have their eyes on the ground, so as not to make such a blunder again.

A couple of hours later we came to another place where the trail forked.

Dersu started dragging up logs.

" What are you doing that for, Dersu ? " I asked him. " It's too early to camp."

" Me no get firewood ; me shut trail," he answered quite seriously.

Then I understood him. The soldiers had thrown the blame on him for leaving so small a signal that they passed it by. This time he was resolved to give them such a barrier that it would give them something to think about. I was immensely amused.

Dersu piled up fallen logs across the track, cut off branches, bent across the trees near by, and lashed them all together. In a word, he built up a regular formidable barricade. This time it acted all right.

The name of the river, Iodzyhé, means in the native tongue the river of roedeer, and it is appropriate, as nowhere have I seen so many roe.

In summer the roe is dark reddish, in winter brownish grey with a white spot on the rump, which hunters call the mirror. When a roe is bolting, it lifts its hind quarters very noticeably. The protective coloration of its skin mingles with the surroundings, but the bright white mirror flashes.

The country the roe prefers is boggy, broad-leaved forest, and only in spring does it venture out into the open to graze. Even here, in the absolute stillness and calm of the deep *taigá*, the timid creature is constantly looking round and on the alert. When startled it bolts, making enormous leaps over bushes, fallen logs, and other obstacles.

It is a curious thing that the roe cannot stand the wapiti. If they are put together in menageries, the roe dies. This is specially noticeable in the saltings. If the roe come upon them first, they visit the spot regularly until the big deer appear.

We often caught sight of roe bolting out of the grass, but they were so quick and vanished so rapidly that we never succeeded in shooting one.

Soon after the junction of the two rivers Sinantsa and Iodzyhé we entered the real *taigá*. Overhead the branches of the trees were so interlaced that they completely cut off the view of the sky. I was particularly struck by the dimensions of the poplars and cedars. Beneath their shade a forty-year sapling looked like a last year's shoot. The lilac, which usually grows like a shrub, here grows into a regular tree from 30 to 40 ft. in height and $1\frac{1}{2}$ yd. in girth. An old trunk, all moss-clad, had a very decorative appearance, harmonizing perfectly with the exuberant vegetation surrounding it. The dense undergrowth, consisting of devil's thorns, wild vines, and lianas, make passage exceedingly difficult.

Our detachment advanced slowly. We were obliged to keep stopping and look round to see where the fallen trunks were fewest, to lead the mules around.

The farther we went the more the ground was obstructed with logs, and the trail quite unsuitable for pack-animals. To save time I sent a fatigue party ahead under Zakharov to clear the trail and if necessary mark out detours. Sometimes a fallen tree would be held upright by others. In that case we hacked off only the lower branches, cutting a gateway through;

when a great trunk was lying prone, we hacked off the branches to prevent the mules hurting their feet on them or their bellies.

Near the mouth of the Sinantsa we met the family of a hump-backed Udehé. They were on a shingle spit in the river, busy fishing. Not far from them lay an upturned canoe. The freshness of the wood and whiteness of the cuts on the sides showed that it was brand-new, only just dug out, and not yet christened by the water. The humpback explained to us that he did not know how to make a canoe, and so had asked his nephew, Chan Lin, to come from the Takemé to make one for him. We invited Chan Lin to come with us, and as the canoe was finished he accepted.

Next day we were off early. We had a long day in front of us, and wanted to reach the river Sanhobé as soon as possible as, properly speaking, my real work would not begin till then. Dersu and I usually walked on ahead while the others followed with the animals. After a time I sat down to rest while Dersu changed his moccasins.

Suddenly my ear caught some strange sounds, something like a roar, not quite a whistle, nor yet a growl. Dersu plucked my sleeve, listened, and whispered :

" Bear."

We crept quietly ahead and soon caught sight of the producer of the noise. A good-sized bear was fussing round a big lime. The tree was growing almost flush against a rock. On the front of it was a blaze made by an axe, showing that someone had been here previously and found a swarm of bees before either the bear or ourselves.

I understood the situation at once. The bear was after the honey. He was standing on his hind legs, struggling for something. The stones prevented him thrusting his paw into the hole in the tree. He was not a patient bear, and was shaking the tree with all his might and growling with irritation. A cloud of bees was humming round him, stinging him on the head. He kept rubbing his head with his paws, uttering a high-pitched little scream, rolling on the ground, and going back once more to his work. His antics were most comical. At last he was tired. He squatted on the ground in an almost human manner, opened his mouth, and stared at the tree, evidently thinking it out. He sat like that for a couple of minutes. Then he suddenly sat up, ran up to the tree, and climbed it to the top. Then he squeezed himself in between the tree and the rock and, pressing with all four paws against the rock, began to push with his back against the tree with all his might. The tree yielded little. But evidently it rather hurt his back. Then he altered his position and, putting his back against the rock, began to push the tree with his paws with all his might. Presently the tree gave a rending sound, split, and crashed to the ground.

That was just what the bear wanted. All he had to do now was to clear open the nest and collect the honey.

" Him very clever man," whispered Dersu. " Must drive him off and soon eat all honey," and as he said that he called out :

" What man you ? Why climb steal other man honey ? "

The animal looked round. Seeing us, it shambled off and quickly disappeared.

" Must give him fear," said Dersu, and fired a shot into the air.

Meanwhile our caravan came up. Hearing the shot, Merzliakov made it halt and came to hear what had happened. We decided to detail a couple of men to collect the honey.

The first thing was to let the bees quiet down, and then suffocate them with smoke and collect the combs. If we did not do it the bear would soon be back and help himself. In five minutes' time we were on the road again.

The rest of our journey as far as the Sanhobé was without incident. We came to Terney Bay at four in the afternoon, and an hour later the two men arrived with 25 lb. of first-class honey in the comb.

At the Sanhobé we again met Chan Bao with his band of hunters and spent a day with him. We found that a great deal that had happened to us on the Iman the previous year was well known to him.

I was delighted when I heard he proposed to come with us to the north, partly because he knew the country well, but also because his influence with the natives and authority over the Chinese made my work very much easier.

It rained. We came downhill and, as soon as we found water in the river, stopped to camp.

The men started unloading the mules, while Dersu and I went for our usual look round. I went up-stream, he went down.

Rain in the forest is rain twice over. Every shrub and every tree drenches the wayfarer with a shower-bath at the slightest provocation. Within five minutes I was as wet as though I had taken a header into the river.

I wanted to turn back, but at that moment caught sight of an unfamiliar animal descending from a tree. I aimed and fired, and the creature fell and lay writhing on the ground, when a second shot put it out of its misery. It turned out to be a wild cat. I was astonished at its dimensions, and thought at first it was a lynx, but the absence of a tuft on the ears and the longer tail showed me that it was a true wild cat. It was 3 ft. 3 in. in length. It differs from the domestic cat in its larger size, long whiskers, and thick fur.

The wild cat lives a solitary life, in the thickest, dark forest, where there are rocky cliffs and hollow trees. It is an exceedingly wary and cowardly creature, though capable of the most savage attack in self-defence. Hunters have often tried to bring up the kittens but never successfully, and the Udehé agree that the kittens, even if captured when quite tiny, never become tame. Nobody hunts it specially, and it is killed only by chance, as in this instance. The local Chinese make collars and cuffs out of its skin.

Picking up my trophy, I returned to camp. Everybody was in, the tents pitched, the fire blazing merrily, and supper being cooked.

THE START

At eight the rain stopped, but the sky remained as dull and overcast.

Suddenly a kind of loud buzz surrounded us. Something hit me violently in the face, and at the same moment I felt some object on my neck. I hastily raised my hand and grabbed something hard and prickly and, startled, flung it on the ground. It was an enormous beetle, like a stag beetle, but without the huge mandibles. I then noticed that there was another on my arm and three more on my shirt, and two on my blanket. There were lots of them. They were crawling round the fire and falling into the flames. Those that flew straight at me and tried to settle on my head were terrible-looking fellows. I sprang out of bed and ran outside. The men were tearing the creatures off themselves and swearing.

The beetles kept falling on to our blankets, on our coats, or into a bag, or into one's cap. Dersu stood up and said :

" Me before not seen such man such lots ; one-two find every year. Where so many come ? "

I caught one of them. It turned out to be a very rare representative of the fauna, a relict from the Tertiary period.[1] It was of a brown colour with down on the back, with powerful mandibles turned upwards, and was like the big wood-borers, only the antennæ were shorter. The length was about $3\frac{3}{4}$ in. and a little over 1 in. broad.

The beetles kept us busy a long time, and peace did not reign in camp till midnight.

[1] This remarkable beetle was afterwards described as *Callipogon relictus*, Semenov. Not only is it one of the largest insects, but is of particular interest in that all the other members of the genus *Callipogon* live in tropical America. No doubt in early Tertiary times it extended round the world in the rich forest which then extended across Asia and Europe. Subsequent earth movements and changes of climate have destroyed that ancient forest over vast areas, but a few links have survived. Thus, there are many plants which are common to certain districts in southern China and to the south-eastern United States, and, in the same way, this beetle survives in the *taigá* of Ussuria as a living witness of the former ancient connection with tropical America.—Trans.

WE continued our journey northwards along the crest, and from Mt. Ostraya dropped into one of the gullies which brought us to the river Bilimbé.

Here we let the mules graze, and then proceeded up the Bilimbé, a river about fifty miles long, rising in the Sihoté-Alin. The forest is so dense on both banks that the river seems to be flowing down a corridor, and in many places the trees bend over it and interlace their branches to form living arches.

The weather remained gloomy ; it was cold and damp. The trees seemed to be weeping, as big drops of water kept falling to the ground. Even the trunks were wet.

The higher we went the narrower became the valley, and we passed several empty cabins, obviously visited by Chinese sable-hunters only in winter.

At the last cabin we stopped a little time, and about midday reached the upper waters of the river. The trail had long since faded out and we were going through the rough, often crossing from bank to bank.

I wanted to cross the main ridge and drop down by the Kulumbé, but Dersu and Chan Bao warned us to expect heavy rain. Chan Bao advised us to try to reach the hunters' cabins before it came. His advice was sound, so we turned back. Already fog had been asserting itself on the pass, and now heavy clouds were creeping over it. Dersu and Chan Bao went ahead, and I noticed that they kept looking at the sky and saying something to each other. From experience I knew that Dersu seldom made a mistake, and if he were uneasy it meant there were serious grounds for it.

About four in the afternoon we reached the first cabin.

Suddenly thick fog dropped on to us, so dense that it seemed as though one could not even walk through it.

We quickened our pace, and by dusk reached the second cabin, which was bigger and more comfortable.

In a few minutes it presented an inhabitable appearance. The litter was collected into one corner, the floor swept, and the stove lit. Perhaps because of the fog, or perhaps because it had not been lit for a long time, the chimney would not draw and the room was filled with smoke. We heated up the stove with burning wood, but it was not till it was quite dark that draught was established and the *k'angs* began to warm up. The men lit a big bonfire outside, brewed tea, and chaffed and laughed among themselves. Dersu and Chan Bao sat by another fire, both smoking in silence. After consultation with them I decided that if there were no more rain the next day, we would go on. It was necessary at all costs to get through the narrows, as otherwise, if the water rose in the channel, we should be compelled to make a long and exhausting detour across the stony hill called Onku Chugdyni, which in the Udehé language means the Devil's Home.

The night passed smoothly.

It was still dark when Chan Bao awoke us all. This man somehow could tell the time instinctively even without a watch.

We hurriedly drank some tea and started on the road without waiting for the sun to come up. When, judging by the time, the sun was well up, the sky was still grey and overcast. The peaks were capped with a damp shroud, not quite fog, or yet fine rain. Presently it began to drizzle, and then suddenly to the sound of falling rain was added yet another sound.

" Now begin," exclaimed Dersu, pointing to the sky.

And, in fact, through the rending curtain of fog we could quite clearly discern the movement of the clouds. They were scudding towards the north-west. In a few moments we were drenched to the skin. Now we were indifferent, and the rain was no longer an obstacle. For fear of missing the cliffs we dropped down to the river and walked along the banks of gravel.

Everybody was in a splendid humour, the men laughing and pushing each other into the water. At last, at three in the afternoon, we passed the narrows. The dangerous part was behind us.

When we were in the forest we did not mind the wind, but whenever we came out into the channel of the river we felt chilled. At five in the afternoon we came to the fourth cabin, built on the left bank of a small feeder. We forded the river and settled there for the night. While the men were busy Chan Bao and I climbed to the top of a neighbouring hill, whence we commanded a good view and could see what was going on in the valley of the Bilimbé.

A strong, gusty wind drove the fog in billows up from the sea. Like huge waves they rolled onwards over the ground and mingled with the heavy rain-clouds in the hills.

At dusk we returned. The fire was already burning in the hut. I lay down on the *k'ang*, but for long could not fall asleep. The rain rattled on the windows. Overhead on the roof the bark flapped and the wind howled, and one could not tell which was the noise of the rain and which the groaning of the chilled shrubs and trees. The storm raged all night.

In the morning of 10 August I was aroused by a tremendous din. There was no need to go outside to see what was the matter. The rain was pouring down in bucketfuls, while violent gusts of wind shook the cabin till it quivered on its foundations.

I hurriedly dressed and went out. The wild scene was almost unbelievable. The downpour, the fog, the clouds, all blended into one. Enormous cedars swaying from side to side, and groaning as though to bemoan their fate.

I noticed Dersu on the bank of the river. He was walking up and down, scanning the water.

" What are you doing ? " I called to him.

" Look-see rock ; water grow," he answered, and started abusing the Chinaman who had built his cabin so close to the water.

Then I noticed for the first time that the cabin was

standing on the lower bank and, in the event of flood, would be overwhelmed.

About midday Dersu and Chan Bao, after exchanging a few words, went off into the forest. Flinging on a storm-coat, I followed them, and saw them near the hill which I had climbed the previous day. They were collecting firewood and piling it into a heap. I was surprised that they were collecting it so far from the cabin, but did not interfere. I climbed up the hill, but was mistaken in thinking I could look into the valley of the Bilimbé. I could see nothing, nothing but rain and fog. Sheets of rain, like great waves, raced through the air and forced their way through the forest. There would be a moment's lull, and then it would seem that the storm was making up for lost time and raged more savagely than ever.

Drenched and chilled, I returned to the cabin and sent the men to Dersu for wood. They returned and reported that Dersu and Chan Bao refused to let them have any. Knowing that Dersu never did anything without good reason, I went with the men to collect some wood higher up the stream. A couple of hours later Dersu and Chan Bao returned. They had not a dry thread between them. They undressed and dried themselves by the fire.

Before dark I went to have another look at the river. It was rising slowly, and there seemed no reason to believe it would flood its bank before morning. All the same, I gave orders to pack all kit and saddle the mules. Dersu approved this measure of precaution. In the evening, when it was dark, a more fearful downpour than ever roared upon us. It was miserable indeed.

Suddenly within the cabin for an instant it was bright as day, as a dazzling flash of lightning blinded us, followed by a deafening crash of thunder, rolling with dull echo through the heavens. The mules began to strain at their halters and the dogs started howling.

Dersu was listening attentively to what was passing outside. Chan Bao sat by the door and from time to time exchanged a brief remark with him. I said something, but Chan Bao signed to me to keep silent. Holding my breath, I too began to listen. My ear caught a faint sound through the walls of the hut, like a murmur. Dersu sprang up and dashed out of the hut. In a moment he ran back, said we must arouse everyone immediately, as the river had flooded its banks and the cabin was surrounded by water. The men sprang up and slipped on their things. Two of them mixed their clothes and began to laugh.

" Why you laugh ? " cried Dersu angrily. " Soon you cry."

While we were pulling on our things the water began to soak through the walls and flooded the hearth. In the dim light we collected our bedding and went out to the mules. They were already standing up to their knees in water and looking round in terror. By the light of a torch of bark and resin we began to load them up. And, indeed, it was high time. The water had already washed out a deep channel behind the cabin, and if we had been a little later we should not have got through at all.

Dersu and Chan Bao had gone off somewhere and I, I must admit, was seriously alarmed. I ordered the men to keep together, and struggled to the hill which I had seen in the day. The murk, wind, and rain blinded us directly we turned the corner of the hut.

The downpour lashed our faces so that we could not open our eyes. One could not see one's hand before one's face. In the absolute darkness it seemed as though trees, hill, and water in the river were all swept along into the abyss, all blended with the rain into one solid, monstrous mass, sweeping forward with terrific velocity.

Among the men it was sheer confusion.

At that moment ahead I caught a glimpse of a spark of light. I guessed that Dersu and Chan Bao had succeeded in lighting a fire. Beyond the cabin was already a deep river. I told the men with the mules to hug the side opposite the current. It was only about a hundred and fifty paces to the fire, but it took us a long time to make it. In the darkness we crashed into fallen trunks, entangled ourselves in bushes, and then again fell into the water. It was racing down the valley, and I concluded that by the morning probably the whole forest would be flooded. At last we reached the hill.

Only then did I realize the forethought of my companions. Only then did I realize why they had been collecting wood all day. They had fixed two pieces of cedar bark on poles and under its shelter lit a fire.

Without loss of time we set to work to pitch tents. A lofty rock behind us sheltered us from the gale. There was, of course, no thought of sleep. Long we sat there by the fire and dried ourselves, while the weather raged more boisterously than ever and the roar of the waters increased.

At last it grew light. We could no longer recognize the place where the cabin had stood. Not a trace of it remained. The whole forest was under water. It even reached our bivouac, and it was time to think of moving up still higher. At a word the men understood what was necessary. Some took the tents and others cut brushwood to spread on the damp earth. Dersu and Chan Bao again started hauling wood. All this took us an hour and a half, during which the rain almost seemed to ease off a little. But that was only a momentary pause. Again the dense fog grew up, swiftly rising, and immediately after the drenching downpour with a roar renewed its vigour.

Such rain I have never seen, before or since. The neighbouring hills and the trees were all blotted out by a curtain of solid falling water. We shrank into our tents.

Suddenly there were cries of alarm. The danger threatened from the side where least expected. Down the gorge, near the mouth of which he had found some shelter, water was rushing. Luckily, on one side the drop was deeper. The water raced there and quickly eroded itself a deep channel. Chan Bao and I defended our precious fire, while Dersu and the soldiers struggled with the water. No one thought for a moment of keeping himself dry. If we could keep warm it was much to be thankful for.

Every now and then a dark spot of sky could be seen through

the fog. The clouds were scudding swiftly, but not in the direction of the wind.

" Bad," muttered Dersu, shaking his head. " Not finish soon."

Before evening we again went hunting for wood to lay in a supply for the night.

In the morning of 12 August a strong wind blew from the north-east but soon lulled. The downpour continued without a break. We were all worn out and could scarcely stand up from fatigue. One moment we had to grab the tent to hold it down, another to cover the fire, another to drag up wood. The water kept breaking through into the tent and we had to throw up dams to deflect it.

The sodden wood burned badly and smoked heavily. Our eyes were sore from smoke and want of sleep. They felt as though filled with sand. The wretched dogs crouched under the rock and did not lift their heads.

The river was a fearful sight. The speed of the current made one's head swim. It looked just as though the banks were racing past in the opposite direction to the water. The entire valley, from hill-side to hill-side, was filled with water. Monsters of the forest, their roots underwashed, crashed into the flood, dragging with them huge clumps of earth and many a shrub and sapling growing in it. Then the torrent picked up this fallen mass and swung it onward. With savage bursts the waters raced down the valley. Where some obstacle held it up the spot was marked by a cloud of yellow foam. Bubbles rose from the pools, floated down-wind, burst, and were replaced by fresh ones.

So one more day dragged by. In the evening the rain came with renewed force, and at the same time the gale increased in fury. All that night we spent in a kind of stupor. One would stagger up, but the others collapsed on their legs.

Thus passed the fourth night of the storm.

At daybreak as at dusk. The men, crouching in the tent under their overcoats, lay motionless. At the fire there remained only Dersu and Chan Bao, but even they, I could see, were feeling the fatigue of the strain. Myself I felt completely exhausted.

I wanted neither to eat, nor drink, nor sleep. I only wanted just to lie there, motionless.

About midday the sky seemed to clear a trifle, but the rain did not slacken.

Suddenly there appeared short but violent whirlwinds, each followed by a calm. They became fewer and fewer, but each succeeding one more violent.

" Soon finish," said Dersu.

The old man's words roused the men from their apathy. They arose and struggled to their feet. The rain was now falling in gusts, one moment a downpour, another sleet. This was at least a variation, and gave rise to hopes of change in the weather.

At dusk it began to ease off noticeably, and by the evening it stopped altogether. Little by little the sky began to clear, and here and there a star peeped out.

What joy it was for all when we could dry ourselves, brew tea and revel in it, lie on a dry couch, and sleep the soundest sleep of the just. That was a real rest.

The next morning we awoke late. Through the breaks in the clouds we could see the sun. He was hiding his face behind the clouds, as though unwilling to look upon the earth and see the havoc of the storm. On every side roaring cascades of muddy water came tumbling down the hills. The foliage of the trees and the grass on the ground were not yet dry and glistened as though varnished. The sunlight was reflected in the drops of water, which glittered in all colours of the rainbow. Nature once more returned to life. The clouds departed towards the east. Now the storm must be raging somewhere off the coasts of Japan or the southern extremity of Sakhalin.

All that day we stayed there, drying our things and resting. Man soon forgets his troubles. The soldiers began to laugh and chaff each other again.

The sky was purple-red that evening and the twilight long.

That night we turned in early. We needed our fill of sleep to make up for the past and to prepare for the future.

On 15 August all arose with the dawn. On the eastern horizon still lay a dark bank of clouds. I reckoned that Merzliakoff with the rest could not have gone far. The flood will have held him up somewhere near the Bilimbé. To join him involved crossing to the other bank, and that, if done at all, must be done as soon as possible, as farther down there would be more water in the river and the passage harder.

To carry out the idea we first went down the side of the valley, but were soon compelled to stop. The river had under-washed the rocks and the waters had carried down a mass of trunks and packed it all up into a great dam. On that side we could see a small hill not covered with water. It was necessary first of all to explore that. First went Chan Bao. Up to his waist in water, with a pole in his hand, he examined the opposite bank, feeling the bottom. His reconnaissance showed that there the river forks, a distance of about 30 yds. separating the two arms. The second branch was broad and deeper than the first, but free from float. He could not touch the bottom, as the strength of the current deflected his pole. Dersu and Chan Bao started felling a big poplar, and the men came to help them with a cross-cut saw. Standing over knee-deep in water, they worked with a will, and in about a quarter of an hour the tree began to crack, and fell with a crash into the water. The butt end began to creep down-stream, but quickly caught on some snag and was held. On that bridge we crossed the second branch. There remained some 60 yds. of submerged forest to cross. When we had satisfied ourselves that there was no stream, we returned.

Men can walk across, and baggage and saddles can be hauled over, but what about the mules? If they were let into the water the strength of the current would sweep them down into the floating timbers and barriers of fallen logs before we could lead them across on the halter.

Choosing the strongest halter, we made fast a rope to it and pulled the end across our bridge. When everything was ready the first mule was cautiously led into the river.

In the muddy water he sank till only his head was clear. The strong current caught him and carried him against the tree, and the water rose over the top of his head. The poor brute bared its teeth and began to gasp, but at that moment we dragged him to the bank. This first attempt was not altogether a success, so we then chose another place where the bank was more sloping. That time we had better luck.

Making our way through the submerged forest was no easy job. The mules sank up to their knees in the mud, fell into deep holes, and exhausted themselves.

It was not till dusk that we managed to reach the hills on the right side of the valley. The mules were dead beat, but the men were still more tired. To fatigue was added chill, and we had no means of warming ourselves. But the main thing was that we had succeeded in crossing the river.

The fine weather did not spoil us for long. In the evening of 16 August the fog appeared again and it began to drizzle. This sleet lasted all night and all the next day. We tramped all that day almost up to our knees in water.

At length it grew dark and I had already lost hope of reaching the mouth of the river that day, when suddenly we heard the sound of the waves breaking on the shore. It appeared that through the fog we had suddenly arrived at the coast and not recognized it until we saw seaweed under our feet and the white crests of the breakers.

I wanted to turn to the left, but Dersu advised us to bear to the right. He based his idea on the sight of human footprints in the sand. They were leading from the river Shakira towards the river Bilimbé and back. From this the Gold concluded that Merzliakoff's camp was on the right side.

I fired two shots into the air and at once heard an answering shot from the direction of the Shakira. In a few minutes we were together.

At once began mutual questioning, what

had happened and what had we seen. Long we sat and yarned that evening by the fireside.

The night was cold. The riflemen frequently stood up and warmed themselves by the fire. At daybreak the thermometer showed 42° F. When some sunshine had warmed the earth we all fell asleep again and slept till nine.

To cross the Bilimbé before the waters had fallen was out of the question. But there is a silver lining to every cloud. We were so greatly in need of rest; our mules looked half dead; we needed to patch and repair our clothing and footwear, to repair the saddles, to clean up our fire-arms. Besides all that, our supplies were beginning to run low. I decided upon some shooting and despatched a couple of riflemen to find some Chinese and buy stores.

The soldiers prepared for the journey, and I set off to the Bilimbé to see how much the water had subsided during the night. I had not gone a hundred yards before they called me back. I returned and saw a couple of Chinamen approaching the camp with pack-horses. They were men from the cabin of Dun Tavaiz, where I had intended to send my men. They told us that their employer knew that we could not cross the Bilimbé now, and so decided to send us some supplies. I was touched by this kindness, and wanted to give them a present, but they declined to accept anything.

The Chinamen stayed the night with us. I learned from them that there had been heavy floods on the Iodzyhé, where several men had been drowned. On the Sanhobé the floods had washed away a number of houses, but there had been no fatalities, though a great many horses and cattle had perished.

After bidding the Chinamen farewell, I went to the mouth of the Bilimbé. The sea had an unusual appearance here. For a distance of a couple of miles or more from the shore it was discoloured to a dirty yellow, and all over it was floating a mass of logs and trees. In the distance these looked like boats. A few of the trees had not lost their green foliage. Directly the wind changed all this floating timber was flung ashore.

After two days the water began to subside, and one could think of attempting to cross to the far bank.

The order to start the following day delighted my companions. Everybody got busy, collecting, arranging, and packing his kit and all his belongings.

After the storm the equilibrium of the atmosphere was restored and peace reigned over the face of nature. The evenings in particular were calm and still. The nights were cool.

When the last glimmer of sunlight had faded in the west and all around was enveloped in the darkness of night, we had occasion to observe an interesting atmospheric phenomenon. The sea was calm. Not a ripple. This smooth surface of the water seems to have a dull glimmer. Every now and then, all of a sudden, the whole surface of the ocean lit up, as though a sheet of lightning had flashed over it. These flashes vanished at one place and appeared at another, and died away over the horizon. The sky was so starry that it looked like a regular mist of stars, the Milky Way standing out with special brilliance. I cannot say whether this was due to the exceptional clearness of the air, or whether there was some causal connection between the two phenomena. We sat up late, admiring the beauty of the scene. The next morning the watch told me that the illumination of the sea had lasted all night and faded away only at daybreak.

CHAPTER XXV : A RISKY CROSSING

AFTER the thunder the weather improved and we made
fair progress.

I noticed that every time the path took us near to the
river, my companions talked anxiously to each other. The
reason soon became clear. As a result of the recent rains the
water in the Takemé had risen considerably, in fact enough to
prevent our fording it.

On consultation, we decided to try to cross on a raft and go
round only in the event of failure.

For this we needed to find a reach where the water was calm
and deep enough, and we found such a place soon enough above
the last rapids. The channel here was near the far bank, and
from our side a long sand-bank projected, now entirely covered
by water. Having felled three big firs, we trimmed off the
branches, sawed them in half, and made a tolerably solid raft
by lashing them together. We finished the job before dusk and
postponed the attempt till the next morning.

In the evening we discussed it over again, and decided that
when the raft was carried along the left bank Arinin and Chan
Bao should jump ashore first, while I flung the kit ashore and
Chan Lin and Dersu should steer the raft. Then I should jump
off, and after me Dersu, and the last to abandon the raft would
be Chan Lin.

The next day we acted accordingly. We placed our bundles
in the middle of the raft, the rifles on top, and took our positions
at the edges.

Scarcely had we pushed off when the current caught it and,
in spite of all our efforts, swept us far below the place where we
had counted on getting ashore. Directly it approached the far

bank Chan Bao and Arinin, picking up their rifles, jumped ashore. The reaction of this thrust her out into the middle of the stream again. While she was being carried down along the bank I started flinging the kit ashore. Dersu and Chan Lin exerted themselves to the very utmost to keep her as close inshore as possible, so that I might be able to land. I was just preparing to jump when suddenly Chan Lin's pole broke, and he fell head first into the water. He came up in a moment and swam ashore. Meanwhile I grabbed the spare pole and dashed to help Dersu. Ahead of us I saw a rock jutting out of the water. Dersu called to me to jump as quickly as possible, but, not knowing his idea, I went on working with the pole. Before I realized what was happening he picked me up in his arms and flung me into the water. I succeeded in grabbing a shrub and crawled ashore. At the same moment the raft struck the rock, spun round, was carried out again into the middle. Dersu remained on board alone.

We dashed down the bank, intending to hold out a pole to the Gold, but here the river made a bend and we could not reach the raft. Dersu made desperate efforts to bring it in under the bank again, but what was the strength of one man compared with the force of the current ! Thirty or forty yards ahead was the roar of the rapids. We could see that Dersu would not succeed in managing the raft and that the stream was sweeping him remorselessly into the cataract. Not far above the rapids there projected the branch of a sunken poplar. The nearer the rapids the swifter the stream, and Dersu's fate seemed inevitable. I dashed along the bank shouting to him. Through the thickets I could see him fling the pole away, stand on the edge of the raft, and, just at the moment when it swept past the poplar, spring at it like a cat and grip it in his arms.

In another moment the raft reached the rocks. Twice its ends stuck out of water, and then it was shattered to pieces. A cry of relief burst from me, but at that instant I realized the new problem. How could we get Dersu ashore ? And how long could he hold on ? The branch was inclined down-stream at an angle of about thirty degrees. Dersu clung firmly, gripping it with both arms and legs. Unfortunately, we had not a rope with us. It had all been used up in building the raft and been lost with it. What was to be done? There was not a moment to lose. His arms would be chilled, give way, and then . . .

We hurriedly conferred. Chan Lin called our attention to Dersu, who was waving some signs with his arms. Through the roar of the waters it was impossible to hear what he was shouting.

At last we grasped his meaning. He wanted us to cut down a tree. To fell a tree into the river opposite Dersu would be dangerous, as in falling it might knock him off his branch, so we had to choose one higher up. Choosing a big poplar, we started hacking at it with all our might, but then saw that Dersu was waving his arms to say no.

Then we went to a lime. Again he gave a negative sign. Then we stood by a big fir, and here he gave an affirmative sign. Now we understood him. A fir has not thick branches and so would not be jammed in the water, but would float.

During this I noticed that Dersu was showing us a strap. Chan Bao understood this. Dersu meant that the tree must be fastened. I tore open all the knapsacks to see what we could use for rope.

We took the slings of our rifles, our belts, and the straps of our boots. There was a spare strap in Dersu's sack. We tied them all together and made one end fast to the tree.

Then we worked desperately with our axes. The fir, rapidly undercut, began to droop. But a little more and it would fall into the river. Then Chan Bao and Chan Lin took the ends of the straps and fixed them round the stump. The current at once began to sweep the tree towards the rapids. It began to describe a circle from the middle of the river to the bank, and just as the tip swung past Dersu he grabbed the branches with both hands. I handed him a stick, and we dragged him ashore.

I thanked him for having pushed me overboard in the nick of time. Dersu was embarrassed, and started explaining that he had no choice, as if he had jumped and I been left on board, I should certainly have been killed, and now we were all safe and sound. He was quite right, but all the same he had risked his life to save me from risking mine.

Man soon forgets danger. The moment it is past he begins joking. Chan Lin simply roared with laughter and twisted himself into knots to illustrate how Dersu had clung to his branch. Chan Bao said that he had clung so tightly that he began to wonder whether he were not related to a bear. Dersu himself laughed at the picture of Chan Lin falling into the water, and they all laughed at me because I found myself on the bank without any memory of how I got there.

Then we set to work to collect our scattered kit, and by the time we had done that the sun had gone down behind the trees. That evening we sat long over the fire. Chan Bao and Chan Lin told us all over again how they sank in the water, and how they saved themselves from drowning. Gradually the conversation died down. We sat puffing at our pipes a little longer, and then one by one turned in, while I turned to write up my diary.

The next day on we went down the valley of the Takemé, and at three in the afternoon reached the sea without further incident. That was 22 September. How good it was to stretch out at full length on the nice clean matting in a house! The hospitable natives lavished their attention on us. One brought us some meat, others tea, and a third some dried fish. I had a good wash, put on clean clothes, and set to my work.

On the morning of 25 September we said good-bye to the Takemé and proceeded northwards. I invited Chan Lin to join us, but he declined. The sable season was coming on, and it was time for him to overhaul his traps and tools and get ready for the winter. I made him a present of a small *berdianka*, a rifle, and we parted good friends.

From the Takemé there are two trails towards the north, an inland road by the mountains, the other along the shore.

Merzliakov with the horses took the former, I followed the latter.

We came to the Kulumbé in about two hours and a half, which we forded. Then we climbed out on to a terrace, lit a fire, and set to work to dry ourselves. We were in a vantage position and, looking down, could easily see what was taking place in the water.

The autumn invasion of the dog-salmon had begun. Thousands upon thousands of fish covered the bottom of the river. Sometimes they remained motionless, but all of a sudden, as though startled at something, one would dash aside and then slowly return. Chan Bao fired a shot in and killed a couple of fish, which was ample for our supper.

On the northern edge of the valley, at the point where the river terrace passes into the hills, the trail is shut off by a lofty rock. Here we were obliged to climb. It was impossible to grip the stones, as they were loose and rolled out of their matrices. On the side of the cliff the trail hugs the cliff at a height of some 70 ft. above the sea. It is a risky business following straight along it, as the ledge is so narrow that one can only go sideways, clinging with the face to the wall and gripping every possible hold with the hands. Besides, the ledge itself is uneven and slopes downwards towards the sea. Many a traveller has lost his life here. The Udehé call the rock Kule Gapani and the Chinese Van Sin Laza, from the name of Van Sin, who was the first victim of rashness. It is dangerous to pass in boots, and men usually do it barefoot or in some dry and soft footwear. It is impassable in wet weather, or when dew or frost is on the ground.

Our boots were wet from fording the Kulumbé, so the passage by this difficult spot was postponed till the next day, and we hunted round for a good spot to camp. At that moment there appeared in the water not far from the shore some sort of animal. It raised its head and looked round with evident curiosity. It was a sea-bear.[1] These creatures spend most of their time in

[1] The North Pacific fur seal, *Arctocephalus ursinus*, L.

the water, but sometimes crawl out on to the rocks to rest. Their sleep is watchful, and they frequently open their eyes and look round. Hearing and sight are the best developed senses with them. Clumsy and awkward as they are on land, in the water they are extremely active, and in their natural element are brave and even impudent, going so far as to attack even man. The two outstanding features in their character are their inquisitiveness and love of music. The native hunters call them by whistling or by drumming with a stick on some metallic object.

Dersu called out something to the creature. It dived, but a moment later appeared again. Then he threw a stone at it. Again it plunged under water, but a second later rose to the surface again, thrust its head out, and stared intently in our direction. That irritated the Gold beyond endurance. He snatched the nearest rifle and fired. The bullet splintered a stone just near the animal.

" You missed him that time, old chap," I said to him.

" Me frighten him ; me no want kill," he answered.

I asked him why he wanted to drive it away. Dersu explained that the sea-bear was counting to see how many people had come to the shore. A man may count animals, but for a mere sea-bear to count men, that offended his hunter's pride.

The rest of that day Chan Bao and Dersu spent examining the pass, rolling down loose stones, and, where possible, cutting steps, while I sat till almost dusk plotting our trail.

The farther north we went the higher were the coastal terraces. At the foot of one we came upon a hut, belonging to some Koreans engaged in fishing and sable-trapping. Not far from the hut we saw some sable-traps, the so-called bridge trap. To build this, the Koreans make use of some storm-blown trunk flung across from one side of a stream to another. Sometimes they will fell a tree on purpose, if the locality is suitable and there is no other trunk handy. In the middle of the bridge thus made they put a fence of small branches intertwined, with a small opening left in it, in which they hang a hair noose. They shave off the sides of the trunk to prevent the sable climbing round that way. One end of the noose is made fast to a stick, which is just balanced on a small projection, with a weight, such as a stone, of 7 or 8 lb. attached to it. When a sable comes along and wants to cross the bridge it meets the barrier and tries to go round it, but the planed-off sides of the trunk prevent him. So then he tries to spring through the opening, is caught in the noose, drags it, and pulls the stick and weight off its support. The stone falls into the water and drags in the valuable animal with it. The Koreans look on this as the best method of trapping sables, as it never fails, and there is no instance of the animal having escaped. Besides, lying in the water, the body is preserved against the attacks of marauding crows or jays.

We continued our journey northward, and on 4 October the order was given to prepare for an expedition. This time I wanted to go up the river Amagu to its source, and then cross the ridge Karta and return to the coast down the Kulumbé.

The Old Believers settled there had told me that these rivers are full of rapids and the mountains covered with screes. They advised us to leave the mules behind in the village and go on foot, humping our packs. Then I decided to take only Dersu. Chan Bao and Rifleman Fokin would accompany us for two days and then we would relieve them of their spare provisions and carry on, while they returned.

I estimated that our supplies would last us for two-thirds of the journey, so arranged with Merzliakov to send an Udehé named Sala with a couple of riflemen to the rock Van-Sin-Laza to fix a dump of supplies in a prominent position.

The next day with bulging packs we set forth. When we had gone a mile we stopped to camp on a gravel bank. There was still an hour to sunset, so I put in the time with a gun on the stream Dunantsa.

The autumn was now in full swing. Every day the forest was assuming more and more a grey, monotonous, lifeless tint, reminding us of the approach of winter. Only the oaks still retained their foliage, but this too was turning yellow, which gave them a still more depressing effect. The shrubs, shorn of their exuberant garb, began to look extraordinarily alike. The black, chilled earth, under a carpet of fallen leaves, was plunged into a heavy sleep. Humbly, unprotestingly, the plants prepared for death.

I was so deep in meditation that I completely forgot why I had thus come out here in the falling light. Suddenly I was aroused by a loud noise behind me.  I spun round and caught sight of an un-couth, humpbacked animal with white legs, with its huge head extended, racing through the forest at a rapid trot. I raised my weapon, aimed and pulled, and the monster crashed. I then saw Dersu climb-ing down the cliff to the spot where the monster fell.

It was an elk, a young bull of about three years, and he must have weighed a good 500 lb. I was struck by his unwieldy, immensely powerful neck carrying a huge head, and great pendulous muzzle. The elk is a very wary brute. It is enough for him to be disturbed but once for him to desert a favourite spot for a long time. In retreating from the hunter he travels always at a trot, never at a gallop. He loves wallowing in marshy pools. When wounded he bolts, but in the autumn turns very savage, and not only defends himself valiantly, but even attacks the hunter. In doing so he rears up on his hind legs and, crossing his fore ones, tries to beat his enemy down with them, and then savagely tramples him underfoot. The Ussurian race hardly differs from the European, except that the antlers are different. They are not broad and palmated, and rather resemble those of the wapiti than those of the ordinary elk.

Dersu set to work to skin it and cut the meat into joints.

It was not a pleasing picture, but I could not help admiring my friend's work. He was a complete master of the knife, not making a single superfluous cut nor single unnecessary movement. It was evident that his hand was well trained to the job.

We agreed to take some of the meat with us, and let Chan Bao and Fokin collect the rest for the party.

After supper that night Rifleman Fokin and I turned in to sleep, while the Gold and Chan Bao arranged themselves on the other side. They undertook to look after the fire.

During the night I awoke. Round the moon was a broad haze, a sure sign of impending frost. And so it turned out. Before daybreak the temperature dropped and the water in the pools froze. Chan Bao and Dersu were the first to awake. They flung more wood on the fire, brewed tea, and only then called us.

What wonderful birds crows are ! How quickly they know when there is meat about ! Hardly had the rays of the sun gilded the mountain-tops, when a few of them put in an appearance round our camp. They croaked loudly to each other, and flitted from tree to tree. One perched quite near and began his ill-omened croaking.

" Ah, you brute of a bird ! Be off, or I'll soon settle your hash ! " muttered Fokin, stretching out his hand for his rifle.

" No need shoot," said Dersu, restraining him. " Him not hurt us ; crow too want dinner ; him come see, man here or not. Him fly off. We go . . . then him jump down . . . eat what left."

The reasoning was convincing to Fokin. He put his rifle down and no longer abused the crows, although they ventured even nearer to him than before.

I was tormented by thirst. Suddenly I caught sight of some whortleberries. They were touched with frost, and I began eagerly swallowing them. Dersu looked at me with curiosity.

" What him name ? " he asked, examining a few of the berries in his hand.

" Whortleberry," I answered.

" Really can eat him ? " he asked again.

" Very much so," I answered. " Do you mean to say you've never eaten any ? "

Dersu answered that he had seen them often enough, but never knew they were eatable.

The whortleberries were so numerous that whole patches of ground looked as though stained wine colour by them.

In the evening I was jotting down my observations, while Dersu was roasting a piece of venison on a spit. During supper I threw a piece of meat into the fire. Seeing this, Dersu hurriedly picked it out and flung it aside.

" Why throw good meat in fire ? " he asked crossly. " Much waste burn him. We go to-morrow, other man come here, eat. Throw meat in fire, all same throw away."

" But who will be coming this way to-morrow ? " I asked in turn.

" Who ! Racoon come, badger come, crow come ; no crow, then mouse come ; no mouse, then ant come. In *taigá* many sort man."

Then I understood. Dersu worried his head not only about men, not only about animals, even about such tiny creatures as ants. He loved the *taigá* itself with all its inhabitants, and took every kind of care of it.

CHAPTER XXVI : A FEARFUL STRAIN

AT daybreak the frost struck again. The moist ground was frozen so hard that it rang beneath our feet. Before starting we checked our stock of supplies. We had enough bread left for two days. I did not worry particularly about that, as I calculated that it was not very far round back to the sea, and Sala and the riflemen would have a supply-dump ready for us at the Van-Sin-Laza rock. As soon as the sun came out Dersu and I put on our things and started off in fine fettle.

The river Kulumbé is shut in by mountains and winds its course between cliffs. It is as though the mountains here were trying to shut the water off and throw obstacles in its path, but at every attempt the water got the upper hand and by sheer strength hewed its way through to the sea.

In the Kulumbé valley there is no trail, so we were obliged to cut through the rough. Not wishing to ford the stream, we tried to stay on one bank, but soon found out that this was impossible. The very first big rock forced us to cross to the other bank. I wanted to change my clothes, but Dersu advised me to go on walking in my wet things and so warm myself by the exercise. We had not gone another half-mile before we were compelled to ford the river again, back to the right bank, and then once more to the left, and again and again. The water was cold. It made our knees ache, as though squeezed in a vice.

Lofty hills hemmed in the valley on either side with their steep cliffs. To go round them was impossible, as that would have cost us a good four days' extra trek. Dersu and I decided to push straight on in the hope of striking an open valley beyond the cliffs. But it was not long before we found our mistake. Ahead there were cliffs again, and again we were obliged to ford.

" Ugh ! " growled Dersu. " We go all same otter. Go little way on bank, look-see water, dive, go on bank, dive again."

The comparison was very true. That is just the way otters travel.

Either we grew accustomed to the water, or else the sun warmed us, or perhaps a little of both, but after a time the fords seemed less trying and the water a little less cold. I stopped abusing it all, and Dersu stopped his growling. Instead of the straight line we had hoped for, our track became a zigzag. Like that we dragged on till midday, but before evening we came into a real gorge. It was nearly half a mile long, and here we had no choice but to walk down the river bed itself. Every now and then we came out on a sand-bank and warmed ourselves in the sun, and then back into the chilly water. At length I felt fatigue.

At one place we came to a piece of level bank between the cliffs, where the floods had piled up a mass of drift-wood. We halted here and the first thing we did was to light a big fire and prepare supper.

In the evening I counted up the fords. Over a distance of ten miles we had forded the stream thirty-two times, not counting the long walk through the water down the ravine.

That night the sky was again masked by clouds, and before daybreak there began a fine rain. That morning we were up earlier than usual, ate a snack, swallowed some tea, and were off again.

For the first four miles we walked farther in water than on land, but at long last the narrow, rocky gorge was passed and the mountains seemed to recede. I was delighted, supposing that the sea was now not far off, but Dersu called my attention to a bird of some sort which, he told me, lives only in the remotest forest, far from the sea, and before long I realized the truth of his reasoning. Once more the fords became more frequent and also deeper. Twice we lit bonfires merely to warm our chilled bones.

At midday we came across a freshly trodden path on a big

rock; it crossed the Kulumbé and led towards the north. Beyond the rock Dersu found an old bivouac. From the signs he read that Merzliakov had camped for a night here, when he came from the Takemé to Amagu.

We counted that if we followed the path we should come on to the river Naina, to the Koreans, but if we went straight on we should come out on the coast near the rock Van-Sin-Laza. We did not know the road to the river Naina, and, what is more, we did not know how long it would take to walk it. To the sea we calculated that we should reach it, if not that day, at least the following day about noon.

So we ate the last of our meat and marched on. About two the fine rain turned into a downpour, which forced us to stop before the proper time to take refuge under canvas. I was chilled to the marrow, my hands numbed, my fingers would not bend, my teeth chattered. As luck would have it, the firewood was damp and burnt badly. We set to work to dry our clothing. I felt dead beat and was shivering. Dersu took the last biscuit out of his pack and advised me to eat it. But

I could not face food. After drinking some tea I lay by the fire, but could not warm myself.

About eleven at night the rain stopped, but sleet continued. Dersu sat up all night nursing the fire.

Towards morning the sky cleared. There was so sharp a drop in temperature that the raindrops stopped trickling from the boughs and froze upon the twigs into icicles. The air became clear and transparent. The sun came out cold and livid.

I had a bad headache. I felt chilled to the marrow, and my bones ached. Dersu, too, complained of weakness and loss of strength. There was nothing to eat nor any desire. We drank some hot water and struggled on.

Before long we were forced once more into the water. This time it seemed colder than ever, and when we came out on the far bank it was a long time before we could warm ourselves. Then the sun came out from behind the mountains, and under its genial rays the chilled air began to feel a little warmer.

However much we tried to avoid fords, there was no other resource. But still, they became fewer. Three or four miles down the river they split into branches with eyots between, thickly overgrown with willows. Here there were plenty of hazel-hen. We shot, but did not succeed in killing any. Our hands were trembling, and we had no strength to aim. We plodded miserably on, one behind the other, in doleful silence.

Suddenly ahead of us it looked lighter. I thought it must be the sea, but a terrible disappointment awaited us when we came near. The forest lay upon the ground. It had all been smashed down by storms last year. It must have been that same blizzard of 20–22 October in the pass on the Sihoté-Alin. Evidently the centre of the typhoon had been here.

The choice for us was to make a detour round the wreckage of the forest, or to go by the eyots through the willows. Not knowing the extent of the wrecked area, we chose the latter alternative. The river was crammed with float, so we could cross without difficulty from one bank to the other. This great dam was nearly four miles long. Our progress was rather slow.

We constantly stopped to rest. Then the dam came to an end and there was open water again. I counted twenty-three fords and then lost count.

That afternoon we could scarcely drag our legs. I felt myself completely worn out. Dersu was ill, too. Once we caught sight of a boar, but had no heart for shooting. That day we camped early.

Here I collapsed. A fever shook me, and for some reason my face, feet, and hands were badly swollen. This time Dersu worked alone. Then I became unconscious. Vaguely I was aware of cold water on my head.

How long I remained in that condition I do not know. When I recovered consciousness I saw that I was covered with the Gold's jacket.

It was evening and stars were shining. Dersu was sitting by the fire. He looked worn out, exhausted.

Apparently I had been delirious for about twelve hours, and all that time Dersu had kept awake and looked after me. He put a damp cloth on my head and warmed my feet by the fire.

I asked for something to drink. Dersu gave me an infusion of some herb, nasty, with a sweetish taste. He insisted on my drinking it, as much as possible. Then we lay down both covered by the same canvas, and both fell asleep.

Next day was 13 October. Sleep had somewhat refreshed Dersu, but I felt completely worn out. Still, it was impossible to spend the day there. Of food we had not one crumb left. By dint of tremendous effort we struggled to our feet and trudged on down the river.

The valley was becoming broader and broader. The storm-fall and burnt ground were left behind. Instead of fir, cedar, and spruce, birch thickets became more frequent, with willow and larch like building timbers.

I staggered on like a drunken man. Dersu, too, had worn himself out and could scarcely drag his feet. Noticing lofty rocks ahead on the left bank, we managed to crawl across to the right in time. Here the Kulumbé split into eight channels, which made our passage considerably easier.

Dersu did all in his power to keep me up. Sometimes he tried to crack a joke, but from his face I could see how much he too was suffering.

Suddenly he called out : " Kaza ! Kaza ! " and pointed to a white bird flickering through the air. It was a sea-gull !

The hope that the end to our sufferings was near renewed my strength. But here again was another ford, back to the left bank of the Kulumbé, which was now flowing swiftly in one channel. Across the stream lay a long larch. It swayed terribly. This crossing took us a long time. Dersu first of all took the rifles and knapsacks across and then helped me.

At length we reached the rock. There, in a patch of oak scrub, we sat and rested awhile. There was another good mile to the sea.

Gathering the remains of our strength, we crawled onwards. Presently the oaks began to thin out, and there before us shone the sea.

Our exhausting journey was over. Here the soldiers were to bring us provisions. Here we could stay until we recovered completely. At six in the afternoon we reached the rock of Van-Sin-Laza.

But a bitter disappointment was awaiting us. There was no sign of supplies. We searched every nook and cranny, we hunted under fallen logs and behind great rocks, but found nothing.

There remained a single hope. Perhaps they had left the dump on the far side of the Van-Sin-Laza. The Gold decided to crawl over to see. But when he reached the top he saw that the dangerous ledge was covered with ice. He did not venture farther. Up there, he surveyed the sky-line and all around. There was nothing. When he came down he broke the news to me and at the same time made an effort to console me.

" No mind, captain," he said. " Near sea all time can find eat."

Then we went down to the shore and rolled over a stone. From under it out dashed a lot of little crabs; they scattered nimbly and quickly hid under other stones. We started catching them with our hands and in a few minutes had a couple of dozen. We found several sorts of shell-fish, which we ate raw, but the crabs we roasted. This did not make a full dinner but eased the severest pangs of hunger.

My fever passed, but the weakness remained. Dersu wanted to go shooting the next day, and so lay down early to sleep.

Worn out by the fatigue of the road, exhausted by fever, I lay beside him and fell asleep.

I caught a sound. The dawn threw a faint light on the sea and deserted shore.

Our fire was nearly out. I awoke Dersu and we started blowing up the embers. At that time a distant sound again caught my ears, something like a faint roar.

" There is a wapiti belling," I said to my friend. " Go along, you will shoot him."

Dersu started picking up his things, when he stopped, thought a moment, and then said :

" Him no wapiti; this time him no cry."

The sound was repeated, and now we could distinguish that it came from the sea. It sounded familiar to me, but I could not make up my mind where I had previously heard it.

Suddenly Dersu sprang up, pointed out to sea, and cried :

" Look-see, captain ! "

I looked and saw the torpedo-boat *Grozny*, my old friend, rounding the headland.

As though by arrangement, we both fired two shots into the air and flung seaweed on to the fire.

A column of white smoke rose from it.

The *Grozny* uttered two piercing whistles and turned towards us. They had seen us. At once it felt as though a whole mountain had rolled off our shoulders, and we both rejoiced like children.

In a few minutes we were on board, warmly welcomed by the captain. On returning from the Shantar Islands they had put in at Amagu and there learnt from Merzliakov that I had gone inland and was expected to come out on to the coast somewhere near the mouth of the Kulumbé. The Old Believers had told him that the Udehé Sala and a couple of riflemen had been detailed to leave a supply-dump by the rock Van-Sin-Laza, but during a storm their boat had been wrecked on a rock and all the cargo lost. They returned at once to Amagu to get fresh supplies and set off again to meet us, so then the captain decided to come for us himself. He reached the Takemé in the night and turned back, but at daybreak had come to the Kulumbé, blown his siren to advise us, and that was what I had taken for the belling of wapiti.

As we sat at table, with abundant food and a glass of tea, we never noticed that we had reached Amagu.

Here Merzliakov, pleading rheumatism, asked leave to go to Vladivostok, to which I readily consented. I let a couple of the riflemen go with him, and gave them orders to meet me with a big supply of provisions and warm clothing on the river Bikin.

In an hour the *Grozny* began to weigh anchor.

Standing on the beach, I could see the captain on his bridge. He waved his cap in good-bye.

Now all that was left of my detachment were Dersu, Chan Bao, and four riflemen who had not asked for leave to Vladivostok and volunteered to remain with me to the end of the expedition.

CHAPTER XXVII : THE LOWER KUSUN

I SPENT the next five days having a much-needed rest and making preparations for an expedition to the north along the coast.

Winter was drawing on. The gaunt skeletons of the trees had a lifeless appearance. Their beautiful summer foliage was now all brown and yellow, rotting on the ground. The problem of feeding the mules became harder than ever, and I decided to leave them with the Old Believers till the spring.

On the morning of 20 October we set out.

We reached the river about two in the afternoon. A stiff breeze was blowing off the sea, and the waves were noisily breaking on the beach, sucking back along the sand in a cloud of foam. From the mouth of the river a sand-bank stretched out to sea. Thoughtlessly I walked along it, when suddenly I felt a great weight tugging at my feet. I tried to retreat but to my horror found I could not stir from the spot. I was slowly sinking. " Quicksands ! " I yelled in an unnatural voice, and tried to support myself with my rifle, but even that began to be sucked down.

The soldiers did not understand my predicament and stared uncomprehendingly at my struggles, but at that moment Dersu and Chan Bao arrived on the scene, and at once dashed to my rescue. Dersu held out his gun-prop, while Chan Bao started throwing drift-wood at my feet. Gripping one log with my arm, I managed to free first one foot, and then the other, and with considerable effort succeeded in making my way back to terra firma.

Chan Bao told me that quicksands are fairly common along this coast. The tide undermines the sand and makes it dangerous to walk on, but when the movement subsides the sand is so firm that a man can walk on it and even a horse with a heavy pack. There was nothing to do but stop there and literally wait for time and tide.

At night the sea calmed down. Chan Bao had told the truth. Next morning the sand was so firm that we did not even leave footprints on it.

The path brought us to the edge of a lofty cliff, an old river terrace. The scrub and scattered trees had disappeared and before us was unrolled the broad valley of the Kusun. Nearly a mile ahead we could see some Chinese houses. When after a long trek human habitations appear in sight both man and beast step out with renewed vigour.

My dog dashed ahead and gazed attentively at some bushes by the roadside. We soon came to the fields. The corn had already been harvested and stacked. Suddenly Alpa pointed. ' Can it be a pheasant ? ' I thought, and held my gun ready.

I noticed that Alpa was in a great state of excitement; she kept looking back at me with an inquiring glance, whether she should go on or not. I gave a sign. She cautiously moved forward, vigorously sniffing the air. By the manner of her I  could tell it was not a pheasant, but something else. Suddenly, with a tremendous fluster, out flew three birds at once. I fired and missed. Their flight looked rather heavy; they flapped their wings rapidly, and soon planed down clumsily to the ground. I followed with my eyes and saw that they had come down in the yard of the nearest house, and realized that they were domestic fowls ! As the natives do not feed them they are obliged to forage for themselves outside and often stray quite a long distance from their homes.

The fowls and the path led us to the cabin of an old Udehé called Liurl. His household consisted of five men and four women.

The natives along the Kusun do not go in for market gardening themselves but employ Chinese to do it for them. They dress in a mixed fashion, partly Chinese, partly their own. They talk Chinese, and use their own language only when they want to keep anything secret.

Forty years ago the Udehé had been so numerous along the coast, old Liurl told us, that when the swans were flying from the Kusun to Olga Bay they turned black from the smoke coming out of the countless wigwams of the natives.

In the creeks of the Kusun we met an old sailor, a Manchu, by name Hei Ba-tou, which means Foreman of the Sea. He was an experienced navigator, and had sailed the Sea of Japan since his boyhood. His father had been engaged in maritime trade and brought his boy up to a seafaring life. Formerly he had been working the shores of southern Ussuria, but of later years he had moved up towards the north.

Chan Bao persuaded him to accompany us along the coast. It was decided that the next day the Udehé would take our baggage to the mouth of the Kusun and load it up in Hei Ba-tou's boat by the evening.

The morning of the second day I was up early and at once prepared for the start, as I knew from experience that unless you stir natives up they take ages over anything. I was not wrong. The Udehé first of all started mending their boots, then patching their boats, and so it was nearly midday before we started.

On the Kusun we had to say good-bye to Chan Bao. Circumstances demanded his return to the Sanhobé. He did not want to accept money from me, and promised to help again if I should come back to the coast next year. We shook hands and parted, I for the west, he for the south.

On the coast it is so mild in the daytime in the autumn that one can go about only in breeches and shirt, but in the evening it is necessary to pull on a sweater, and by night to roll up in a fur rug. So I arranged to send all my warm kit by boat, and took myself only a day's supply of food and my rifle. Hei Ba-tou was to bring his boat to the mouth of the Tahobé and wait for us there.

The lower reaches of the Tahobé are covered with thin woodland consisting of elm, lime, oak, and black birch. The more open country, more suitable for settlement, is a little higher up, a mile or two from the sea. Here we found a hut. I took the inhabitants at first for Udehé, and it was not till the evening that I learned that they were Solons.

Our new acquaintances differed but little in outward appearance from the Ussurian natives. They seemed to me to be a little shorter and broader in build; they were more lively and more expansive. They spoke Chinese and some jargon consisting of a blend of the Solon and Gold languages. The costume was like that of the Udehé, but a little less variegated and ornamental. The whole family consisted of ten. Now how had they turned up here all the way from Manchuria? My inquiries elicited the following story.

Formerly they had lived on the river Sungari, whence in their hunting they had wandered as far as the Hor, which falls into the Ussuri. When numerous bands of brigands put in their appearance in that district, the Chinese sent troops against them, and so the Solons found themselves between two fires. The brigands robbed them on one side and the troops persecuted everybody alike without distinction. So the Solons fled to the Bikin, and from there wandered across the Sihoté-Alin and ended up on the coast.

The next four days were given up to a survey of the Tahobé and Kumuhu. We invited one of the young Solons to come with us. He was a sturdy, beardless young fellow, by name Datsarl. He carried himself with dignity and looked down upon my riflemen with a superior air. I could not refrain from admiring his light step and the quickness and smartness of his movements.

We started on 23 October along the left bank, Dersu, Datsarl, and I ahead, while Zakharoff and Arinin brought up the rear.

Presently we saw a squirrel sitting on a trunk of a tree. It was squatting on its haunches, its tail lifted up behind, and was nibbling a cedar cone. On our approach it grabbed its cone and bolted up a tree, from the top of which it looked down on us in surprised curiosity. Solon crept up to the tree, called out,

and hit the tree with a stick with all his might. The startled squirrel dropped its nut and climbed still higher That was all the Solon wanted. He picked up the cone and walked on, without paying any more notice of the squirrel. The little creature jumped from branch to branch and snorted with anger at being thus impudently robbed of its dinner in broad daylight. We all laughed. Dersu had not seen this trick before, and made a note of it for future use when he should want some cedar cones.

" No be cross," he said, looking up at the squirrel to console it. " Us walk down here, how can find nut? You look-see up there, find plenty nut," he said, pointing to a huge cedar.

A mist hung over us all day. The sky was veiled as with a cobweb of layers of feathery clouds. There was a halo round the sun, which contracted gradually until it blended into a single livid spot. In the forest all was still and the breeze had already dropped among the tops of the trees.

This evidently made Dersu and the Solon anxious. They made some remarks to each other, and kept looking up at the sky.

" That's bad," said I ; " the wind is beginning to blow from the south."

" No," said Dersu. " Him go so," and he pointed to the north-east.

I felt that he was wrong, and started arguing.

" Look-see bird," replied the Gold. " Him look at wind."

And, in fact, on the top of a fir was perched a crow, facing the north-east. That was the most comfortable position for him, as the wind blew down his plumage, whereas if he had sat sideways or back to the wind, it would have blown up his feathers and he would have felt cold.

Towards evening the sky was covered with cloud, the radiation of warmth from the ground fell, and the temperature rose two or three degrees. All this was a bad sign. To be on the safe side we pitched our tents firmly and collected a big pile of wood. But our precautions were wasted, and the night passed uneventfully.

In the morning, directly I awoke, the first thing I did was to glance at the sky. The clouds were lying in parallel rows running from north to south.

There was nothing to wait for, so we picked up our packs and started up the Tahobé.

I counted on reaching the Sihoté-Alin that day, but the weather held us back. About midday a thick mist appeared again, and the mountains turned dark blue and grim. About four it started to rain in torrents, and that turned to snow, thick and wet. The path was whitened, and we could follow it with the eye far ahead, among the shrubs and logs. The wind became gusty and sharp.

It was time to camp. Not far from the river on the right bank there towered up a solitary rock, like a ruined castle with towers at the corners. At the foot grew a clump of birches. It looked a suitable spot, so we stopped to bivouac there for the night.

The men started collecting wood, and the Solon went to cut some poles and pegs for the tent. He had gone barely a hundred yards from the tent when he stopped, looked upwards, ran on a little farther, and then, running back to the camp, said something anxiously to Dersu. The Gold looked up at the rock too, spat, and dropped his axe.

They then both came to me and asked me to choose another

spot. When I asked why, the Solon said that when he started cutting a tree down, the devil threw two stones down at him from the top of the rock. Dersu and the Solon begged me so earnestly to change the site, and there was such alarm in their faces, that I consented and ordered the camp to be moved a little way down-stream, where we found a more suitable spot.

We all set to work together to get ready and collect firewood and build a big bonfire. Dersu and the Solon took a lot of time and trouble to build up a kind of fence. They cut down trees, stuck them in the ground, buttressed them with their gun-props, and did not even grudge their own clothing.

When I asked what all the trouble was about, Dersu explained to me that it was to prevent the devil on top of the rock seeing what was going on in our camp. I was much amused but did not smile for fear of hurting my friend's feelings.

My riflemen did not bother their heads whether the devil were watching them or not. They were far more interested in their supper.

In the evening the weather became worse. We crouched inside the tent and warmed ourselves with hot tea.

At eleven that night thick snow started falling and immediately after there was a flash in the sky.

" Lightning ! " cried the riflemen in one voice.

Before I could answer there was a sharp peal of thunder.

This mixture of thunder and snow lasted till two in the morning. The lightning flashed frequently, with a reddish tinge. The claps of thunder were heavy and rolling. One could almost feel the air and earth quiver under them.

This phenomenon, of a thunderstorm and snow at the same time, was so unusual that everybody kept looking up at the sky with curiosity, but the sky was dark, and only in the flashes could one catch a glimpse of heavy clouds, moving in a south-westerly direction.

One peal of thunder was simply deafening. The lightning kept playing around the rock where the devil had been sitting. At the same moment another sound mingled with the roar, the

crash of a landslide. The effect on the Solon was remarkable.
He lit another fire and crouched behind the screen. I glanced
at Dersu. He was upset, surprised, and also frightened. The
devil on the rock throwing stones, thunderstorm and snow
combined, the landslide on the hill, all that blended in his brain
into a single connected whole.

"Enduli hunt devil," he exclaimed in a tone of relief, and
started a brisk conversation with the Solon.

Enduli is a deity, according to the natives, who dwells so high
up that he very seldom comes down to the world of men.

Then the storm moved away, but the lightning long continued
to play about the sky, reflected widely from the horizon, so that
we could see the outlines of the hills quite clearly and the heavy
clouds intermixed with rain and snow. The roll of distant
thunder still reverberated dully from afar, making both air and
earth shudder.

After drinking some boiling hot tea the riflemen turned in,
but I sat late talking to Dersu by the fire, asking him all about
these devils and about thunder with snow. He answered me
readily enough.

Thunder, that is Agdy. When the devil stays too long in
one place, then the god Enduli sends thunder, and Agdy drives
the devil away. That is to say, at the spot where the storm
burst out the devil was sitting. When the devil had been chased
away, that is after the storm, there was peace around. Animals,
birds, fishes, insects, and the grass, all knew that the devil had
gone, and were happy and cheerful again.

As to the thunder and snow together, he said that previously
they used to have thunder and lightning only in summer, and
that it was the Russians who brought winter thunder with them.
This was the third winter thunderstorm that he could remember
in his lifetime.

Thus in chatting the time slipped by.

Daybreak. The hills began to stand out of the darkness,
forest-clad, and the devil's rock, and the bushes overhanging
the river. It all foretold dull weather. Then suddenly in the

east, unexpectedly, from behind the mountains there broke a purple dawn, reddening the gloomy sky. In the pink and golden glow every bush, every twig stood out clearly.

I gazed in admiration at the beauty of the play of light from the beams of the rising sun.

" Now, old man," I said to my companion, " it is high time for a snooze."

But Dersu was asleep.

Next day we all slept late. The sky was still covered with clouds, but they no longer had so menacing a look as during the night.

We ate a snack, drank some tea, and resumed our trek up the valley of the Tahobé, which was to bring us to the Sihoté-Alin. We counted it one more pass to the water-shed, but by dusk we were still short of the main crest, so stopped to camp in thick forest.

Towards evening the sky cleared and the night promised to be a cold one. I placed all my hopes in my rug and turned in some distance from the fire, giving up my place to the Solon, whose blanket was a miserable affair. But at three the cold awoke me. Roll myself up tightly as I could, it was of no avail. That cold air found its way in, and cut first my shoulder and then my feet. There was nothing else to do but get up.

Around all was dark. The fire was out. I collected the glowing embers and started blowing them into flame. In a few moments they broke into flame, and I could see round. Zakharov and Arinin were lying under cover of the canvas, and Dersu was sleeping in a sitting position, fully dressed.

While collecting some more wood I could see the Solon asleep in the corner, right away from the fire. He had neither blanket nor warm rug. He lay on a couch of fir twigs, covered only with his old cloak. Afraid that he would catch a chill, I shook him by the shoulder, but the Solon slept so soundly that only by effort could I awake him. Datsarl sat up, scratched his head, yawned, and rolled over on his other side in the same place and snored vigorously.

I warmed myself by the fire, and then turned in alongside the rifles and slept well.

Next morning we were up very early. Our stock of provisions was running low, and so there was no time to waste. Our breakfast consisted of roast squirrel, the remains of our rolls baked in the ashes, and mugs of scalding tea.

When we started the sun had only just peeped out. It was rising behind the tree and the bright beams illuminated the mountain peaks snow-capped. We crossed them and came out on to the river Kumuhu.

When a route laid down is approaching its end, everybody quickens pace. But in fact, in coming out on to the coast, we were gaining nothing. From the mouth of the Kumuhu we should again tramp down some mountain stream, again bivouac, pitch tents, collect firewood for the night, the same old programme, but still, at the end of a march is always something attractive. For that reason we all turned in early to sleep so as to be early to rise.

The next morning, directly the east began to redden, we arose as though at the word of command, and collected our kit for the road. I picked up a towel and went down to the river for a wash.

Nature was still drowsy, when everything is slumbering and revelling in the sweet repose before dawn. Thick mist was rising from the river, and a heavy dew had fallen. Then a gentle morning breeze blew through the trees. The mist began to move and appeared on the far bank. In camp everything was quiet, as the men were storing up strength with breakfast.

Suddenly my ear caught a crunch upon the gravel. Someone was walking along the stones. I looked up and saw two shadows, one tall, one short. It was a cow elk with her heavy-headed calf. She shook her head and began biting her flank. I stood admiring them, afraid the riflemen would see them. Suddenly the cow sensed danger and, pricking her huge ears, stared in our direction. Water was dripping from her lips, making circles ripple out on the smooth surface of the water. She shook herself, uttered a hoarse grunt, and dashed into the forest. At that moment the breeze dropped, and again the opposite bank was enveloped in mist. A shot rang out. Zakharov had fired and missed, whereat in my heart of hearts I was glad.

At last the sun came out. The wisps of mist took on an orange tint, and through them could be discerned the outlines of the bushes, trees, and mountains.

In half an hour we were on the road, chatting cheerfully as we walked.

In the flat country by the sea an Old Believer named Dolganov had set up, engaged in exploiting the natives who live along the banks of the rivers. We did not want to stop with a man who battened upon the poor, and so we pushed on straight to the coast, and at the mouth of the river found Hei Batou with his boat. He had reached the Kumuhu the same day that he had left the Kusun, and waited for us there a whole week.

In the evening the riflemen lit enormous bonfires. They were in a very cheerful mood, just as though they had arrived home. They were so accustomed to living on the trail that they never noticed its hardships.

We stayed there one day. We needed rest to renew our strength and repair our kit.

At last 1 November arrived, the first day of the first winter month.

CHAPTER XXVIII : IN THE HEART OF USSURIA

AT the river Kumuhu we parted with the Solon, who returned to his family, while we went on northwards.

The path which had so far taken us along the shore came to an end at the Kumuhu. From Cape Olympiad to the river Samarga in a straight line is nearly a hundred miles, but along the winding, rocky coast is nearer a hundred and fifty.

The mossy, coniferous forest covers the mountains like bristles on a brush and extends right down to the sea. This part of the country is considered very hard, and even the natives avoid it. The distance which can be done by boat in half a day can scarcely be covered in four by men on foot over the mountains.

Hei Ba-tou's boat could stop only in the mouths of rivers where there was no bar and at least one small creek.

In the morning I made the following arrangements, that Hei Ba-tou should sail across to the river Nahtohu and again wait for us there, while we would cross over by the river Holunku and then down the Nahtohu and back to the coast. I had everything ready overnight so that Hei Ba-tou could sail at dawn.

On the morning of 3 November I awoke early, dressed, and went out of my tent.

When the sun had risen above the horizon I could see the sail of Hei Ba-tou's junk far away out to sea.

I brewed tea and awoke my companions. After a good breakfast we picked up our packs and started.

It was growing colder and colder every day and the evenings were noticeably drawing in. To find shelter from the wind at night we buried ourselves in the densest thickets we could find. To collect enough wood we were obliged to stop to camp early, with the result that our day's marches were short, and a march which in summer would have taken us a day at this season took us twice as long.

On choosing a camp site, I told Zakharov and Arinin to pitch the tent, while Dersu and I went out for some shooting. Along both banks of the stream there remained here and there a narrow belt of living forest of aspen, alder, cedar, willow, birch, maple, and larch. We walked on, talking in an undertone, Dersu a little way ahead and I bringing up the rear. Suddenly Dersu signed to me to stop. I thought at first that he was listening, but soon saw it was something else. He was standing on tiptoe, leaning on one side, sniffing the air.

" Scent," he whispered. " Man here."

" What sort of man ? "

" Pig," answered the Gold. " Me smell find."

I sniffed vigorously, but in vain. I could detect nothing. Dersu cautiously advanced, and kept stopping to sniff, and like that we advanced a hundred paces or so. Suddenly something crashed off to one side. It was a wild sow with a young pigling, and at the same moment a few boars scattered. I fired and brought down the young pig.

On the way back I asked Dersu why he had not fired. He answered that he had not seen the pig but only heard the noise of their bolting. Dersu was upset. He swore aloud, and then suddenly pulled off his cap and began to beat his head with his fist. I laughed and chaffed him, saying that he could see better with his nose than with his eyes. I did not know it at the time, but that trifling incident was a warning of tragic events to come.

That young pig came in the nick of time, and for supper that night we feasted on fresh pork. We were all in the best of humour and laughed and cracked jokes merrily. Only poor old Dersu was off colour. He kept whining to himself, and then asking himself out loud why he had not seen the pigs.

We were now going without a guide, following the landmarks given us by the Solon. The hills and streams were so much alike that it was very easy to mistake one for another. I was very anxious about this, but Dersu paid no attention to it. He was so accustomed to the forest that to him it was a matter of indifference where he spent the night. For him one place was as good as another.

Directly we left camp we came to rising ground. From the first pass we could see the river valley. Beyond it rose another range with rounded hills. From up here there was a magnificent panorama. On one side, as far as the eye could reach, there extended more mountains, like enormous waves with white crests, fading away in mist towards the north. To the northeast we could see the Nahtohu, and beyond, to the south, the sea.

The cold, piercing wind did not allow us to stay there long admiring the beauty of the scene, and drove us down into the valley. At each step there was less and less snow, and soon we were walking on frozen moss. It crackled under our feet and remained pressed to the ground. I went ahead, with Dersu behind. Suddenly he ran up after me and began to examine the ground. Only then did I notice human footprints, going in the same direction as ourselves.

" Who has gone by here ? " I asked the Gold.

" Small foot. Russians no have foot like that ; Chinese no have too. Koreans no have too," he answered, and then added : " His . . . moccasin, toe up. Man gone by soon. Me think us soon catch him."

Other signs, quite invisible to us, showed him that the man was an Udehé out for sable, carrying a stick, an axe, a net for the sable, and, judging by his walk, he was a young man. Because he was going straight through the bush without paying attention to the shrubs and undergrowth and keeping to the open ground, Dersu concluded that he was returning to his camp. After consultation we decided to follow his tracks, especially as they were taking us in the right direction.

The forest came to an end and once more we came to a burnt-out area, through which we walked for an hour. Suddenly Dersu stopped and said he smelt smoke. And in about ten minutes we came to a brook and there saw a wigwam with a fire by its side.

When we were within a hundred paces of the wigwam a man sprang out, holding a rifle in his hand. It was Yanseli, an Udehé from the Nahtohu. He had only just returned from hunting and was getting his supper ready. His pack lay on the ground, with stick and axe lying across it.

I was curious to know how Dersu had divined that Yanseli was carrying a net. He answered that on the trail he had noticed a broken-off twig of rowan and alongside it, lying on the ground, a ring torn from the net. Dersu turned and asked the Udehé whether he was carrying a net. The man silently opened his bag and handed us a net. One of the middle rings was new.

Yanseli told us that we were on a brook that ran into the Nahtohu. With some little difficulty we persuaded him to come with us as guide. The chief attraction to him was not money, but some cartridges for his *berdianka*, which I promised to give him when we reached the coast.

The last few days had been particularly cold. Ice appeared along the edges of the stream, which facilitated our movements considerably. All the small streams were frozen and we made use of them as short cuts and soon reached the Nahtohu.

In the afternoon Yanseli led us on to a trail which followed down-stream by his sable-traps. I asked him who came trapping sable here. He told me that for ages this region had belonged to an Udehé called Monguli, and we should probably soon meet him. It so happened, for a mile or two farther on we caught sight of a man standing near one of the traps, looking at it intently. Seeing us approaching from the side of the Sihoté-Alin, he was alarmed at first and started to run away, but was reassured when he caught sight of Yanseli. As customary under such circumstances, we all stopped. The soldiers lit up their pipes, while Dersu and the Udehé started chatting.

" What's up ? " I asked Dersu.

" Chinaman stolen him sable," he answered.

According to Monguli, a Chinaman had passed that way two days previously, taken a sable out of the trap, and re-set it. I suggested that perhaps the trap was merely empty. In reply

Monguli pointed to a spot of blood, clear proof that the trap had acted.

"Perhaps it was not a sable," I suggested, "but only a squirrel."

"No," answered Monguli. "When the beam fell on the sable it gnawed the uprights. You can see his tooth-marks."

Then I asked him how he knew it was a Chinaman.

The Udehé replied that the man who stole the sable was dressed in Chinese fashion, and in the heel of his left boot one nail was missing.

These arguments were conclusive.

The last two days had been cold and windy. The bank ice on the streams had widened, and in places the two sides had met in the middle and thus made natural bridges, where one could cross freely from one side to the other.

In the open country we found three Udehé cabins. The local natives had taken to the Chinese type of hut only quite recently, and until a few years previously lived in their own type of hut and wigwam. Round the houses were some small gardens, worked by Chinese labour, who took half-share of the profits in their fur business.

From interrogation I learnt that the river Nahtohu is the northern limit of Chinese influence. There were only five men here, four who lived here permanently and one who had come from the Kusun.

All the males, includ'ng boys, carried two knives in their girdles, the usual type of hunting-knife, and also a small curved blade in the use of which they are very skilful, using it as a tool in place of awl, plane, drill, chisel, etc.

They had some unpleasant news for us. They told us that on 4 November our boat had sailed from the Holunku and vanished into thin air.

I remembered that on that day there had been a high wind. One of the Udehé had seen a boat of some sort out at sea struggling with the wind, which was blowing it farther and farther out.

For us this was an irreparable disaster. In that boat were all our belongings, our warm clothing, boots, and store of provisions. With us we had only the things in which we stood up and could carry, light autumn clothing, a single pair of moccasins, blanket, towel, tent canvas, guns, ammunition, and now a very limited supply of provisions. I knew that there were Udehé living farther north, but it was a long way to them, and they were so poor that it was hopeless to think for a moment that we could find refuge and food among them for all our detachment.

What was to be done?

Our heads filled with these depressing thoughts, we came to the thick, low-growing, coniferous scrub which separates the river fields of the Nahtohu from the sea.

As a rule, when we were arriving at a boat we were as cheerful as though coming home, but now the Nahtohu was as foreign to us and as desolate as any other river. We were sorry, too, about Hei Ba-tou, that fine old sailor, who by now was probably drowned.

We walked on in silence. All were occupied by the single thought. What should we do? The riflemen understood the gravity of the situation, out of which it was now my duty to extricate them.

At last it grew lighter. We could now see the sky through the trees, the forest abruptly ceased, and the sea appeared.

ONCE there used to be lagoons round the mouth of the Nahtohu, separated from the sea by a spit of land, but now they are represented by a mossy bog, covered with marsh Ledum, crakeberry, and bog whortleberry. The little bay into which the river empties is bounded by two capes. Here, at the foot of the cliffs, we pitched our camp.

In the evening Dersu and I sat by the fire and talked the situation over. Since the disappearance of the boat four days had passed. If she had been anywhere in the neighbourhood she would, by now, have put in an appearance. I suggested going down to the Amagu and wintering with the Old Believers, but Dersu disagreed with me. He counselled remaining on the Nahtohu, keeping ourselves by hunting, and getting skins for making new clothing. We could count on getting some dried fish and millet from the natives, he felt sure. But then other difficulties arose. In another couple of weeks our light autumn clothing would be quite inadequate. But still, Dersu's suggestion was sound, and we adopted it.

After supper the riflemen turned in to sleep, but Dersu and I sat late over the fire, discussing the situation still further.

I suggested going to the Udehé huts, but Dersu was in favour of stopping on the coast, first because here it was easier to find food and, secondly, he had not yet given up hope of Hei Ba-tou's return.

If the latter were alive he would certainly return, would look for us on the shore, and, if he did not find us, might go on farther. In that case we should be waiting for nothing. It was impossible to disagree with him.

Gloomy thoughts one after another chased through my brain and gave me no peace.

To return to headquarters without having completed my task would be dreadful. On the other hand, to start on a winter expedition without due provision was the height of imprudence.

The riflemen, learning that we were stopping there for a considerable time and perhaps even for the whole winter, set to work to collect drift-wood and fix up winter quarters. That was a sound idea. They improvised a stove with slabs of stone and a chimney in the Korean fashion, out of a hollow tree. On the roof they piled moss with turf. Inside the hut they strewed the floor with pine needles and dry grass. Altogether they succeeded in making the hut quite snug.

The next day Dersu and I started for a walk down the coast

southwards in the hope of finding some trace of Hei Ba-tou and, incidentally, of getting some game.

We walked along the shore discussing what might have happened to the old sailor who had thus disappeared. It was the hundredth time we had thrashed it out, and we had always come to one and the same conclusion. We decided that we must make some boots and return to the Old Believers on the Amagu.

My dog Alpa was running on ahead, about a hundred and fifty paces in front of us. Suddenly I realized that there were two creatures ahead, Alpa and something else, like a dog, but dark-coloured, hairy, and short-legged. It was running along near the cliffs with heavy, clumsy leaps and seemed to be trying to overtake the dog. When level with Alpa, the hairy thing took up a defensive attitude. Then I saw it was a wolverine, or glutton, the biggest of all the weasel tribe. This cunning brute lives in the mountain forests where there are plenty of roe, and especially of musk-deer. It will sit motionless for hours on a branch or rock near the game track, waiting for its prey. It knows the habits of its victim accurately, its favourite paths and habits. It knows, for instance, that when the snow is deep the musk-deer always runs in the same circle, so as not to have the trouble of trampling down a fresh one. Consequently, when it has frightened one, it chases it until it has completed a ring. Then it climbs on to a branch and waits till the deer comes round again. If this does not succeed it wears the creature down, following it persistently until it drops from fatigue. If during the hunt it sees another it does not attack it, but continues its hunt after the first, even if out of sight.

Alpa stopped and stared inquisitively at her unexpected neighbour. I was going to shoot, but Dersu stopped me, reminding me that we must economize our ammunition. As usual he was quite right. So I called off the dog, and the wolverine ran off, soon disappearing in a gully.

Choosing a site to bivouac, we piled our things and walked off in different directions in the hope of shooting something to eat.

We did not have long for hunting. When we met again the day was nearing its end. The sun was peeping at us from behind the mountain-tops, its rays penetrating into the thickest forest, lighting up the trunks of the limes, the conical tops of the firs, and the hairy cones of the cedars with a golden glow. From one side of us there came a piercing scream.

" Musk-deer ! " whispered Dersu in reply to my look of inquiry.

A couple of minutes later I caught sight of the creature, rather like a roe but a good deal smaller and darker in colour, and from its jaws there hung a pair of slender, curved tusks. Trotting along a hundred paces or so, the creature stopped, turned its head in our direction, and froze in an expectant attitude.

" Where is it ? " asked Dersu.

I pointed to it with my hand.

" Where ? " he asked again.

I started directing his gaze with my hand along the line of

prominent objects, but however much I tried he could not see anything. Dersu quietly raised his rifle, gazed attentively at the spot where I had showed him the animal, fired . . . and missed. The sound of the shot re-echoed through the forest and died away in the distance. The startled musk-deer dashed off on one side and disappeared into the thickets.

" Got ? " asked Dersu, and I could see from his expression that he could not see the result of his shot.

" No," I told him. " This time you have missed. The musk-deer has bolted."

" What ! Me not hit ! " he cried in alarm.

We walked up to the spot where the animal had been standing. There was no blood-spoor. There was no doubt about it. Dersu had missed. I began to chaff my friend a bit, but Dersu sat down on the ground and placed his rifle across his knees and began to think. Suddenly he sprang to his feet, slashed a big blaze on a tree, and walked away a couple of hundred yards. I thought he was going to show me what he could do, and that his miss was purely a chance. But at that distance the mark on the tree was hard to see, and he was obliged to come nearer. At last he chose a spot, set up his prop, and started to aim. Dersu aimed a long time. Twice he removed his head from the backsight and, it seemed, could not make up his mind to pull the trigger. At last he fired and dashed up to the tree.

From the way his arms dropped I knew at once that he had missed. When I went up to him I noticed that his cap was lying on the ground, his rifle too. The wild look in his widely open eyes was staring into space. I touched him on the shoulder. Dersu started and began talking swiftly :

" Before no man no-can find animal before me. All time me see him first. Me shoot . . . all time make hole in him shirt. My bullet no time never go by. Now me fifty-eight year. Eye all gone bad, no-can see. Shoot musk-deer, no-can hit. Shoot tree, no-can hit. Me no want go to Chinese. Me no-can know their work. How me go on live ? "

Then I suddenly realized how out of place was my chaff. For him, dependent upon his shooting for his living, the decline of his eyesight meant destruction. The tragedy was heightened by the fact that Dersu was utterly alone in the world. Where could he go ? What could he do ? Where could he lay his weary, aged head ?

I felt a wave of inexpressible pity surge over me.

" Never mind," I said to him. " You have helped me very much indeed, and many a time you have saved me from disaster. I am heavily in your debt. You will always find a roof for your head where I am, and a loaf of bread. We will live together."

Poor Dersu fussed around and began collecting his things. He picked up his old rifle and gazed at it, like a thing that was no more of any use to him.

Near the stream we parted, Dersu returning to the camp, while I went on hunting.

I wandered about the forest a long time without seeing anything and at last, feeling tired, I turned back. Suddenly something stirred in some bushes. I froze and held my rifle ready. Again a gentle rustle, and out from a clump of alders there quietly strolled a roe. It began to browse, and paid no attention to me whatever. I aimed quickly and fired. The animal crashed forward and rolled over with its muzzle on the ground. It was quite dead. I pulled off my girdle, strapped the roe's legs together, and slung it on my shoulder. I felt something warm trickle down my neck. It was blood. Then I dropped my trophy on the ground and called out to Dersu, and before long heard his answering cry. He came without his rifle, and we slung the roe on a pole and carried it between us.

By the time we reached camp it was evening.

After the shooting I felt tired. At supper I talked to Dersu about Russia, advised him to give up his life in the *taigá*, so full of danger and privation, and come and live with me in a town. But he remained silent, pondering deeply.

At last I felt my eyelids were gluing together. I rolled up in my blanket and fell asleep.

During the night I awoke. It was long after midnight. It seemed to me that all nature was slumbering.

By the fire was sitting Dersu. At first glance I could see that he had not laid down to sleep. He was glad I was awake, and started brewing tea. I noticed that the old fellow was in an excited state, that he waited on me with extra attention, and did everything he could to keep me awake.

I humoured him and said I did not feel sleepy. Dersu flung more wood on the fire and built up a big blaze. Then he stood up and began to talk, in a solemn voice.

" Captain," he said. " Now me talk, you listen all time."

He began to relate how he had lived formerly, how he had been left all alone in the world, and earned his living by the chase. His rifle always saved the situation for him. He sold antlers and in exchange with the Chinese took ammunition, tobacco, and material for clothing. It never entered his head that his eyes might fail, or that it was impossible ever to buy new ones for all the money in the world. It was now some six months that he had noticed that his eyesight was growing weaker. He thought it would pass away, but to-day had shown that his hunting was over. It terrified him. Then he remembered my words, that with me he would always find a shelter and a loaf of bread.

" Thank you, captain, big thank you."

Then suddenly he went down on his knees and bowed his head to the ground. I dashed forward to pick him up, and started telling him that it was the other way round, that I owed my life to him, and if he came to live with me it would give me very great pleasure. To distract him from his gloomy thoughts I suggested brewing another lot of tea.

" Wait, captain. Me not finish talk."

Then he continued to relate the story of his life. He told me how, when he was still a young man, he had learnt from an old Chinaman how to hunt for ginseng and learnt its signs.

He had never sold any roots, but taken them with him to the upper reaches of the Lefu and planted them there. The last time he had visited his plantations was fifteen years ago. The roots had all taken well; there were altogether twenty-two of them. He did not know if they were all right still; they probably were, as they were planted in a most remote spot, far from any trace of human movement.

" That all to you," he concluded his long speech.

I was astonished. I began to urge him to sell those roots to the Chinese and get the money, but Dersu insisted.

" Me no need," he explained. " Me little life left. Soon finish, soon die. Me very much want give you *pantsuy*, ginseng."

In his eyes there was such an imploring expression that it was irresistible. My refusal hurt him. I agreed, but made him give me his word that at the end of the expedition he would come back with me to Khabarovsk. Dersu consented.

We decided to go up to the Lefu in the spring and look for the priceless roots.

Dersu flung still more wood on the fire. The bright flame flickered upwards and lit up the bushes and cliffs with a ruddy glow, the silent witnesses of our talk and the mutual obligations we had undertaken.

Then in the east appeared a belt of rose. Dawn was beginning. The embers were smoking; it seemed as though the fire had entered inside them.

" Let us have a little sleep now," I said to my companion.

He stood up, arranged the canvas, and we both lay down and, pulling the blanket over us, slept the sleep of the dead.

When we awoke the sun was already high. It was a bright, frosty morning. The water in the pools was covered with a thin sheet of ice and in it the outlines of the bushes were reflected as though in a mirror.

We hurriedly ate a piece of cold meat, swallowed some tea, picked up our packs, and started back to camp.

We found them all at home. Arinin had killed a sea-lion and

Zakharov a sea-bear, so we now had an abundant supply of meat and leather.

From 12 to 16 November we stayed there. During this time the riflemen went out to collect whortleberries and cedar-nuts.

Dersu bartered the two raw hides with the Udehé for one dressed elk-skin. He then made the native women cut him out a pair of moccasins, which he sewed himself, separately for each foot.

On the morning of the 17th we said good-bye to the Nahtohu and started tramping back to the settlement of Old Believers. As we left I cast a last glance out to sea in the hope that I might catch a glimpse of the sail of Hei-Ba-tou's junk. But the sea was deserted. The wind was blowing off the land, and so it was calm along the shore, but farther out there were big waves. I waved my hand and gave the signal to march.

It was a sad business, going back, but there was nothing else we could do.

The return journey passed without incident, and on 23 November we came to the Kusun.

CHAPTER XXX : THE *TAIGA* IN WINTER

AFTER a short rest with the natives on the Kusun I wanted to go on, but they advised me to stop and spend the night indoors with them. The Udehé said that after a quiet spell and frosty weather they must inevitably expect a gale. The local Chinese, too, were alarmed and kept looking towards the west. I asked what was the trouble. They pointed to the crest of Kiamo, which was covered with snow. Only then did I notice that the ridge, up till now sharply outlined and clear, had turned vague and misty, with hazy contours. It was as though the mountains were smoking. According to the natives, the gale from the range of Kiamo would reach the coast in a couple of hours.

The Chinese lashed the roofs of their houses to the nearest stumps and trees and the fences of their wheat-fields they covered with nets woven of grass.

And in fact about two in the afternoon the wind sprang up, at first gentle and steady, but increasing in strength. With it it brought a sort of mist. This was snow, dust, and dried leaves lifted into the air and carried off by the wind. Towards evening it attained its maximum intensity. I went out with the anemometer to measure its strength, but a gust smashed the screw of the apparatus and nearly blew me off my feet. Out of the corner of my eye I had a glimpse of a board hurtling through the air and of a great piece of bark ripped off somebody's roof. Near the cabin stood a two-wheeled Chinese *arba* cart. The hurricane blew it right across the yard and dashed it against the fence. A haystack that had been badly built vanished without trace in a few minutes.

Towards morning the typhoon abated somewhat. Violent gusts alternated with moments of calm. When it had blown itself out I no longer recognized the scene. One cabin was blown flat. Another had a wall blown in. The ground was strewn with uprooted trees.

It was necessary to carry on, whether we wanted to or not. My comrades were tired, but the Chinese were so hospitable that I decided to stay another day there, and I did rightly. That evening a young Udehé arrived at full speed from the coast with splendid news. Hei Ba-tou had returned with his junk and all our stores were intact. My companions cried " Hurrah ! " and shook hands all round in their delight, and I myself was so delighted that I felt I wanted to dance a jig.

The next morning the moment it was light we were down on the shore. Hei Ba-tou was as delighted as we. The soldiers crowded round him and bombarded him with questions. It appeared that the typhoon had carried him across right to the coast of Sakhalin. Hei Ba-tou kept his head and struggled all the time to keep as close as possible to the shore, as otherwise he would have been carried right away to Japan. From the island of Sakhalin he had managed to make his way back to the mainland, and then sailed southwards along the coast. At the mouth of the Nahtohu he heard from the natives that we had left for the Amagu and so he had started at once to catch us up. He had laid up for last night's storm, and then reached the Kusun in a day's sail.

At once a new plan took shape in my head. I decided to make my way up the Kusun to the Sihoté-Alin and come down the Bikin. We now had everything we needed, provisions, instruments, warm clothing, boots, and ammunition.

Hei Ba-tou also decided to spend the winter on the Kusun. His voyage out to sea had been exhausting. There was a lot of floating ice along the coast, and the mouths of the rivers were frozen.

The men started unloading the boat without delay. When the mast, sail, and rudder were dismantled they dragged her up the shore and put her on wooden rollers, supporting her with posts on both sides.

The next day we started building sledges. We got three from the natives, but were obliged to make three ourselves.

Zakharov and Arinin were good carpenters, and a couple of Udehé helped them. Dersu was given general charge of the work, and it was interesting to note how apt were all his suggestions and criticisms. The riflemen were accustomed to him by now, never argued with him, and did not start a piece of work without his approval. Ten days were spent on that job.

We had by this time become great friends with the Kusun Udehé, and knew them all by name as well as by sight.

On 25 November Dersu, Arinin, and I went on a fishing expedition to the mouth of the Kusun with the natives. The Udehé took some torches made of rushes and heavy wooden mauls. Between some streams on one of the islands, all overgrown with aspen, alder, and willows, we found some strange sort of constructions covered with grass. I recognized them at once as the work of Japanese hands. They were fish-poachers' huts, snugly hidden both from the land side and from the sea. We made use of one of them.

In the creeks the water was well frozen. The ice was smooth as a mirror, clean, and transparent. Through it we could clearly distinguish the shallow parts and the deep pools, the weeds, stones, and waterlogged trunks. The natives cut some holes through the ice and let down a double net. When it was dark they lit their rush torches and ran in the direction of the holes, every now and then hammering on the ice with their mauls. Terrified at the light and noise, the bewildered fish dashed forwards and were caught in the nets.

We had a good catch.

The Udehé let down their nets and beat up the fish from another direction, then crossed to a small lake, from there to the stream, to the river, and the creek.

By ten we had finished. A part of the natives went home, and the rest spent the night on the fishing-ground. Among these was a man named Logada, an old acquaintance of mine from last year. Now it was a cold and windy night and the cold could be felt even near the fire. About midnight I happened to think of Logada, missed him, and asked where he was. One of them said he was sleeping outside. I slipped on my things and went out to see. It was dark and the keen wind cut like a knife. I walked a little way along the river and came back and told them I could not see a fire anywhere. The Udehé answered that Logada slept without a fire.

" What do you mean, without a fire ? " I asked incredulously.

" Yes," they answered calmly.

Fearing that something had happened to Logada, I took a lantern and went out again to look for him. A couple of Udehé came to keep me company. Along the bank, some fifty paces from the hut, we found Logada asleep on a couch of dry grass.

His hair was spangled with hoar-frost, and his back white. I shook him vigorously by the shoulder. He sat up and began pulling the rime off his eyelashes. As he was not shivering, evidently he did not feel cold.

" Aren't you cold ? " I asked him in astonishment.

" No," he answered. " What's up ? "

His friends told him that I had been worried about him and gone out to look for him in the dark. Logada replied that it was crowded and stuffy inside the hut, and so he had decided to sleep outside. Then he rolled himself up tightly in his jacket, lay down on the grass, and fell asleep.

I went back to the cabin and told Dersu about it.

" No matter, captain," replied the Gold. " These man no fear cold. Him live all time on mountain, hunt sable. Where night catch him there him sleep. Him always warm him back on moon."

When it was light the Udehé went off fishing again, but this time employed a different method. Over the hole through the ice they put up a little skin tent which shut out the light on all sides. The sun's rays penetrated the clear ice and lit up the bottom, with the result that the men in the little tents could see the stones, shells, sand, and weeds. A harpoon let down into the water did not quite reach the bottom. They put up four of these little tents, all right up against each other, and a man crawled inside each with a harpoon. The rest of the party then began quietly driving the fish in that direction. When a fish passed under one of the tents, the man inside struck with his harpoon. This method was even more successful than the night fishing.

By 2 December the riflemen had finished their job. For final clearing up I allowed them another day, and on the afternoon of the 4th we started loading the sleighs, leaving only our bedding for the next morning.

The Chinese came to see us off with flags, rattles, and rockets.

During the past two days the river had frozen splendidly. The ice was even, smooth, and glistened like a looking-glass.

Our train consisted of eight sleighs, each carrying three hundredweight. We had no sledge-dogs, as I had not enough money to buy them, and in any case I doubt whether we could have found enough on the Kusun. So we were obliged to haul the things ourselves. The weather was favourable, and the sleighs slid lightly over the ice. Everybody was cheerful, full of fun and laughter.

That day we reached the mouth of the river Buy, which the Chinese call Ulengu. Here we parted from the Kusun and turned towards the Sihoté-Alin.

Near the mouth of the Ulengu there lived an Udehé called Suntsai, famous as a hunter and for his skill in handling boats on the rapid mountain rivers. He willingly accepted my invitation to come with us to the Sihoté-Alin on condition that I stopped a day at his place. He said he wanted to send off his brother on a hunting expedition, and to make his own preparations for a long journey.

In the evening he entertained us royally with *stroganina*, that is raw fish sliced in thin flakes and spiced. On the table was served up an entire frozen *lenok*, one of the salmon family, which runs to 15 or 20 lb. in weight. We discarded the European's prejudice against raw fish and did it justice.

The next four days we spent in the passage of the Ulengu,

which rises in the Sihoté-Alin and flows towards the south-east. Owing to the inevitable forest fires which occur ever from year to year the mountains are bare of trees. Only along the banks of the river are there any, and on the eyots between the channels.

From the appearance of the frozen river one would think that the Ulengu would have deep water in summer, but in fact this is not the case. The water that comes down from the mountains in spring soon rushes down without leaving noticeable traces behind, but in winter the state of affairs is quite different. The water fills all the holes, bays, and creeks and then freezes. Fresh layers of ice are formed on top which keep increasing and spreading. This considerably lightened our road. In big rivers the fallen trees are carried down by the water, but in the smaller ones they remain where they fall. Knowing this, we took a supply of axes with us and a couple of cross-cut saws. With the help of the soldiers we quickly cut through obstacles and hacked open a trail.

The nearer we came to the pass the more water there was on top of the ice, and such places could be distinguished from some distance by the evaporation rising from them. To avoid them it was necessary to drag ourselves along the hill-sides, which cost us a great effort and much time. It was particularly advisable to take care to avoid wetting one's feet. In such cases the native footwear cannot be improved upon; it is made of fish skin sewn with sinew.

Here there occurred an incident which detained us for nearly a whole day. At night we did not notice how close the water had come to the bivouac, and one sleigh was frozen in. We were obliged to dig it out with axes and then thaw the runners over the fire and repair the cracked places. From this experience we learnt not to leave the sleighs standing on the ice, but to raise them on wooden rollers.

Every day the trail became harder and harder. Many a time we found ourselves in a thick patch of forest, or on stony screes all littered with fallen trunks. Dersu and Suntsai went ahead with axes, cutting down bushes and small trees where they would interfere with the progress of the sleighs, or packing holes with them, and slopes where there was danger of the sleighs turning turtle.

The farther we penetrated into the mountains, the thicker the snow. On every side, wherever we looked, there was nothing but the gaunt and blackened trunks of trees, stripped of bark and branches. These burnt-out forests are a depressing sight, indeed. Not a footprint to be seen, not a bird. .

Then Dersu, Suntsai, and I walked ahead. The riflemen followed slowly, and we could hear their voices behind us. At one spot I stopped to have a look at the minerals in the rocks protruding through the snow. A few minutes later, when I overtook the party, I saw that they were alarmed at something, and attentively examining something at their feet.

" What's the matter ? " I asked Suntsai.

" One Chinaman go back three day," answered Dersu. " We find him track."

And, in fact, here and there could just be discerned a faint human footprint, almost obscured by the snow. They noticed that the tracks were irregular, in zigzags, that the Chinaman had often sat down, and two bivouacs of his were quite near each other.

" Him sick," they decided.

We pushed on. The tracks kept following the river. We could see that the Chinaman had made no attempt to climb over the fallen trunks, but had gone round them. We followed them for about half an hour, when the tracks turned off sharply to one side. We followed them. Suddenly from a neighbouring tree there flew off two crows.

" Ah ! " exclaimed Dersu. " Man die ! "

There, some fifty paces from the river, we saw the Chinaman. He was sitting on the ground, leaning against a tree. The right

elbow was resting on a stone, and his head was inclined to the left. On his right shoulder sat a crow. At our approach the bird flapped off from the corpse.

The dead man's eyes were open and dusted with snow. On examining the ground my companions came to the conclusion that he had felt ill and decided to camp for the night, taken off his pack, and tried to pitch his tent, but his strength failed him, and he sat down at the foot of the tree and died. Suntsai and Dersu stayed to bury him, and we went on.

All that day we worked hard without dropping our arms, without even stopping for dinner, but we did not make more than six miles. The fallen timber, the top ice, the hummocky bogs, the holes among the rocks, blinding snow-drifts, all combined, formed such obstacles that in eight hours' hard work we covered no more than three miles. Towards evening we were approaching the crest of the Sihoté-Alin. The barometer showed us an altitude of 2230 ft.

The next day, as I was having a look round, I noticed a thick column of steam rising in one place. I called Dersu and Suntsai and we went to see what it was.

It turned out to be a hot spring, of iron and sulphuretted hydrogen. The rock around was all stained red from the iron, with a white, calcareous incrustation. The natives were well aware of the existence of this hot spring on the Ulengu as a favourite place for elk, but they carefully concealed the knowledge from the Russians.

From the frozen steam rising from the spring the neighbourhood was white with hoar, the stones, the bushes, and the prone trees were clad in a dainty mantle, all glistening in the sun like diamonds. Unfortunately, owing to the cold, I was unable to take a sample of the water for chemical analysis.

While we were examining the hot springs, the riflemen broke camp and loaded the sledges. Then at once began the ascent of the Sihoté-Alin. First of all we carried all the baggage up and then dragged up the empty sleighs.

The eastern slope of the Sihoté-Alin is completely bare, and it would be hard to imagine a more uninviting place than the source of the Ulengu. It was hard to believe that there had ever been a living tree here. Here and there a charred stump remained standing upon its roots. Suntsai told us that once there had been a great many elk here, which gave the river its native name of Buy, meaning elk, but since the forest was burnt down all animal life had fled and the whole valley of the Ulengu turned into a desert.

The sun had already completed the greater part of his journey across the sky by the time the riflemen arrived with the last sleigh. We loaded them up and started without further delay.

The trees covering the Sihoté-Alin are short and old. The choice of a camp site in such a district always offers difficulty. You either come on to stones mingled with the roots of trees, or else upon some great prone trunk all hidden by moss. The question of firewood is more troublesome still. To the townsman it may seem strange that there should be any difficulty about firewood in the midst of a forest, but in fact there is. Fir, spruce, and larch all throw out sparks, which are liable to set fire to the tent, clothing, and blankets ; alder is poor stuff, full of moisture and giving more smoke than flame; there is left only birch. But in the coniferous forests of the Sihoté-Alin birches occur only here and there. Luckily, Suntsai knew the district well, and he quickly found all we wanted for camp, so I gave the signal to stop.

The riflemen started pitching the tent, while Dersu and I went to see if we could shoot something or even get on the trail of an elk. Not far from the camp I caught sight of three birds like hazel-hen. They were strutting about the snow without paying attention to us. I was just going to shoot, when Dersu stopped me.

" No need shoot, captain," he said. " Can catch him so-how."

I was astonished when he walked up to the birds without any particular care, and still more so when I saw that the birds were not afraid of him, any more than domestic poultry, but walked off on one side, without undue haste. Presently he came within four yards of them. Then Dersu took his knife and, without paying any more attention to the birds, started cutting a young fir sapling, trimmed it, and at the end tied a slip knot. He then walked up to the birds and put the noose over the head of one of them. The captured bird fluttered and flapped its wings. The other two, coming to the conclusion that it was about time they flew off, settled on a larch near by, one on a low bough, the other rather high up. Thinking that they must by now be thoroughly frightened, I was just going to shoot when Dersu stopped me again saying that it was easier to catch them on a tree than on the ground. He walked up to the larch and quietly raised the stick, trying not to make a noise. In trying to slip the noose over the head of the lower bird, he chanced to hit it on the beak with the end of the stick. The bird simply shook its head and began staring in our direction. In a minute it was fluttering helplessly on the ground at our feet. The third bird was perched so high up that it was out of reach from the ground. Dersu started climbing the tree. The young larch was thin and flexible and began swaying violently. The silly bird, instead of flying away, clung to the branch with its claws, trying to balance itself. As soon as he could reach it, Dersu hooked the noose over its head, and the third one too was pulled down. Like that Dersu got us three birds for dinner without firing a shot. Then I noticed that they were bigger and darker than the common hazel-hen, and the cock bird had red brows over the eyes, like blackcock. They were what the Old Believer settlers have

called *dikushka*,[1] the 'wild bird,' found in Ussuria only in the coniferous forests of the Sihoté-Alin, southwards, to the source of the Armu. It certainly is an appropriate name that the Old Believers have given it, unless it is from the fact that they inhabit only the wildest and remote places. The contents of the crops showed that they feed on pine needles and whortleberries. When we came to camp it was dark. A fire was burning in the tent, so that it looked like a great lantern with a candle alight inside. The smoke and steam, lit up by the flames, rose in a thick column. Dark figures were moving inside.

That evening we celebrated our crossing of the Sihoté-Alin. For supper we had roast *dikushka*, followed by hot chocolate, and wound up with tea with rum. Before we turned in I entertained the riflemen with one of the tales of Gogol.

Here we parted with Suntsai. The rest of the journey we could do alone, and the stream would bring us to the Bikin. All the same, Dersu asked him a mass of questions about the way.

When the sun was up we struck camp, packed the sleighs, put on our warmest things, and started down the mountain torrent, a mass of cascades and boulders and fallen trees.

That morning we could feel how the Sihoté-Alin cut us off from the sea, as the thermometer showed us 63° of frost Fahrenheit.

The farther we went from the Sihoté-Alin, the lower dropped the temperature. It is well known that in coastal regions it is often warmer on the tops of mountains than in the valleys. Evidently, the farther from the sea we were, the deeper we entered into a region of cold air.

Whirlwinds of snows twisted down the river. They rose unexpectedly as though at a signal, spun on one side, and then suddenly dropped.

Walking against the wind with a hard frost is trying work. We kept stopping to warm ourselves with a fire, with the result

---

[1] *Falcipennis falcipennis*, Hartlaub=*canadensis*, var. *franklini*, Middendorff, a member of the grouse family.

that for the whole day we did not manage to cover more than six and a half miles. We stopped to camp at a spot where the river split into three channels.

We trudged on for five days without particular incident, and on the 20th reached the Bikin. Here we were about two hundred and twenty miles from the railway.

At dusk we came to a group of three Udehé huts. The appearance of unknown people out of the ' blue ' startled the natives, but when they recognized Dersu in the party they were reassured and received us warmly. This time we did not pitch tent, but slept in the huts.

We had now been tramping in the *taigá* for two weeks. From the way the riflemen and Cossacks were attracted by the sight of human habitations, I realized that they felt the need of longer rest than a mere night's bivouac in the forest, so I decided to spend a day with the natives. When they heard this the riflemen made themselves at home in the huts. There was no fatigue duty for them, no need to cut fir branches, or haul firewood. They took off their boots and started cooking supper.

At dusk two young Udehé hunters returned and told us that they had come across spoor of wild pig near the huts, and they decided to organize a drive the next day. It promised to be interesting, and I decided to go with them. That evening they made their preparations, fixing their straps on their ski and sharpening their spears.

As we were to start at daybreak we all turned in early after supper. It was still dark, when I felt someone shake me by the shoulder and awoke. The fire was blazing merrily in the hut. The natives were all ready and only waiting for me. I dressed quickly, shoved a biscuit or two in my pocket, and off we went.

The Udehé went ahead and I followed. After following the river some way down they turned aside, and then up a low hill and down into another small valley. Here they consulted, and then started on again, but in silence.

In half an hour it was quite light. The sun's rays, illuminating the peaks, announced the break of day. At that moment we were just reaching the spot where the young man had seen the tracks the previous day.

It is to be observed that in summer pigs sleep by day and feed by night. In the winter it is the other way round; they are lively by day and rest at night. That meant that the herd had not gone far.

The tracking began.

For the first time in my life I saw what a speed natives maintain on ski in the forest. I was soon left behind and before long completely lost them from sight. It was useless to attempt to overtake them, so I simply followed their tracks at my ease. After about half an hour, feeling a bit tired, I sat down for a breather.

Suddenly I heard a noise behind me. I turned sharply and saw a couple of boar crossing my track at a trot. I raised my rifle and fired, but missed. The startled brutes dashed off on one side. Not finding any blood-spoor, I decided to follow them.

After about twenty minutes I overtook the boars. They were evidently tired from going through the deep snow. Suddenly they sensed danger and both at once, as though at the word of command, spun round to face me. From the movement of their jaws and the sound that reached me, I knew they were gnashing their tusks. Their eyes were blazing, their nostrils distended, their ears pricked forward. If there had been one boar I would perhaps have fired, but before me I saw two tuskers. There was no doubt that they were galloping towards me.

I held my fire and decided to wait for a better opportunity. They stopped gnashing their teeth, raised their muzzles, and began to sniff the wind, then turned round slowly and trotted on. Then I cut off and overtook them. The boars stopped again. One of them started ripping off the bark of a fallen trunk with his tusks. Suddenly both brutes were alert, uttered a short grunt, and started making tracks to my left. At that moment I caught sight of four Udehé, and from the expression on their faces I knew that they had seen the boars. I joined them, bringing up the rear. The pigs could not go far. They stopped and turned to defend themselves. The natives surrounded them in a ring and began to close in. That compelled the brutes to face first in one direction and then in another. At length they could not stand it any longer and charged.

The natives struck with their spears with extraordinary skill. One boar was wounded in the neck, while the spear passed right under the shoulder-blade of the other. The first one charged. A young Udehé tried to hold him on his spear, but I heard a dry, cracking sound. The boar had sheared the spear in half with one blow of his tusks, as though the stout wood were but a reed. The man lost his balance and fell. The boar

turned and charged straight at me. Instinctively I fired at him, point-blank. Luckily the bullet struck him right on the head.

Only then did I notice that the young Udehé whose spear had been broken was sitting in the snow pressing with his hand a wound in his foot, from which the blood was flowing freely. When the brute had struck at the spear he had ripped his foot with his tusk, and the man himself had not noticed it. I made him a bandage, while the others quickly collected firewood to make a bivouac. One of them stopped with the wounded man, another went for a sleigh, and the rest continued their hunt.

The young man's wound did not call forth any excitement in the huts. His wife laughed and chaffed him. Incidents like this are so frequent that nobody pays any attention to them.

There is not an Udehé who does not bear on his body the marks of the tusks of a boar or claws of a bear.

During the day the riflemen had repaired the damage done to the sledges and the women had darned the clothes and moccasins. To ease the work for my men, I hired a couple of natives with dog-sleighs to come with us to the next hamlet.

Next morning I left the Udehé. Then a rather amusing thing happened. I gave each man ten roubles, to one a ten-rouble note, to another two five-rouble notes. The first was annoyed. I thought that he was dissatisfied with the pay, and pointed out that his companion was obviously delighted. But it turned out quite the reverse. He was upset because I had given him only one note, but given his companion two. I had forgotten that they did not understand money. In order to give satisfaction to the man, instead of one ten-rouble note I gave him three three-rouble notes and one one-rouble. This upset the man to whom I had given two five-roubles, and to make the peace I had to give them all exactly alike.

CHAPTER XXXI : TIGER !

THE next day we continued our journey. We were all in the best of humour after the day's rest and stepped out bravely. That day we made over eleven miles and stopped to bivouac near a cabin inhabited by a couple of old sable-trappers, one an Udehé, the other a Chinaman.

We very much wanted to go up the Horsky pass, and I started making inquiries about the way. Our new Udehé acquaintance Kitenbu consented to come with us as guide. He was a man, I should say, of about sixty. His hair was streaked with threads of grey and his face was lined with wrinkles.

Kitenbu at once began making his preparations. He took a blanket, a goat skin, and a very much repaired old rifle, a *berdianka*. I took a kettle, notebook, and a sleeping-bag, while Dersu took his bit of tent canvas, tobacco, and provisions. Besides us three there were two other members of our little detachment, my dog Alpa and Kitenbu's dog, a greyish, sharp-muzzled mongrel with pointed ears, called Kady.

In the morning the weather turned fine. We counted on reaching a trapper's cabin on the far side of the pass by the evening, but our hopes were not fulfilled. In the afternoon films of clouds crept over the sky, rings appeared round the sun,  and the wind began to rise. I wanted to turn back already, but Dersu reassured me, saying there would not be a typhoon but only a strong wind which would drop the next day. And so it was. About four in the afternoon the sun was obscured in either cloud or mist, you could not tell which. The air was filled with a fine, powdery snow. The rising wind blew in our faces and cut like a knife.

When it grew dusk we had reached the pass. Here Dersu stopped and began to discuss something with the Udehé. As I approached I gathered that the old man had strayed from the trail, and for fear of losing the way they decided to spend the night in the open.

" Captain," said Dersu, turning to me. " To-day us no find cabin ; must make camp."

" All right," I said. " Choose a good spot."

We went into the thickest patch of forest for the sake of shelter from the gale, and settled down at the foot of an enormous cedar, probably nearly 70 ft. high. Dersu took his axe and went for firewood, while the old man began cutting fir twigs for a couch and I lit the fire.

We did not finish our jobs till half-past six, and then we were all very tired, but directly the fire burst into a blaze we felt snug. Now we could change our boots, dry our clothes, and think of supper. In half an hour we were drinking tea and discussing the weather.

My Alpa had not such a thick coat as Kady. She felt the cold and, exhausted from the long day, squatted by the fire with closed eyes, as though dozing. The native dog, used since puppyhood to all sorts of privations, paid little attention to the discomforts of life on the trail. Rolling herself into a ball, she lay down on one side of the camp and went to sleep. She was powdered thickly with snow. Every now and then she stood up to shake herself, and settled down again on the other side, tucking her muzzle under her belly, trying to warm herself with her own breath.

Dersu was sorry for Alpa, and always made her a couch of fir twigs and dry grass before turning in himself. If he could not lay his hands on either, he would lend her his jacket. Alpa appreciated this, and whenever we stopped she would look for Dersu, paw him, and do all she could to attract his attention. And directly Dersu picked up the axe she squatted down and patiently waited his return with an armful of nice dry, springy fir twigs.

We ourselves were just as tired as the dogs, so immediately after supper we piled up a big fire and turned in.

We arranged ourselves round the fire, each in his own place. I took the lee side, and Dersu settled himself sideways to the wind. He rigged himself up a sort of little tent, and flung an overcoat over his shoulder. The old Udehé turned in at the foot of the cedar and covered himself with his blanket. He undertook to keep watch and make the fire up all night. Cutting an armful of fir twigs, I spread my sleeping-bag upon them and made myself very comfortable. The cedar sheltered me from the wind on one side, and on the other was the fire.

It is always depressing in a deep forest in bad weather. You always think that the first tree to come down will be the one under which you are sleeping. In spite of my fatigue it was some time before I could fall asleep. The wind worked up to such a pitch of fury that it flung itself like a wild beast at everything that stood in its way. It was particularly violent against the trees, and it developed into a regular battle between the monsters of the forest and the unbridled elements. The gale came in gusts, tore, and then deflected and moaned, giving the impression that we were in the heart of a gigantic whirlwind. The gale was describing an enormous circle, returning to our bivouac and attacking our great cedar, as though trying with all its might to fling it to the ground. But it did not succeed. The giant of the forest frowned, but only swayed from side to side. I fancied I heard someone fling more wood on the fire and the crackling of the branches as the flames leapt up, fanned by the wind, and then all was confusion and I dozed off. About midnight I awoke. Dersu and Kitenbu were awake, discussing something between themselves. By the intonation of their voices I gathered that they were alarmed at something.

' Probably the cedar is swaying and bending, and threatening to come down,' was the thought that flashed through my drowsy brain.

I quickly thrust my head out of the opening in my sleeping-bag and asked what had happened.

324

" Nothing, captain," answered Dersu, but I noticed from the ring in his voice that all was not well, but that he did not wish to alarm me.

The fire was burning brightly. Dersu was sitting by it, screening his face from the heat with his hand as he arranged the wood and collected the embers together. Old Kitenbu was stroking his dog. Alpa was sitting alongside me and, apparently, shivering from the cold.

The wood in the fire was blazing. The black shadows and red tongues flickered over the ground, dancing together, one moment darting off away from the fire, the next shrinking and blending with it, and playing on the boughs ·of the trees and hummocks of snow.

" Nothing, captain," said Dersu again. " You can sleep ; we sit so talk."

I did not persist, covered my head again, and dozed off.

About half an hour later I awoke again. Voices had disturbed me.

' Something wrong,' I thought, and crept out of my bag.

The gale had dropped a little. Here and there a few stars were twinkling. Every gust of the wind swept dry snow over the ground so violently that it made a noise, as though it were sand. Round the fire I could see my companions. Kitenbu was standing up and listening to something. Dersu was standing sideways, leaning on his elbow, staring into the darkness. The dogs were awake too. They crouched up to the fire, seemed to try to settle down, but at once sprang up again restlessly and moved to another spot. They sensed something and kept looking in the direction where the two men were staring.

The wind fanned the fire vigorously, shooting a thousand sparks into the air and wafting them away among the trees.

" What is it, Dersu ? " I asked the Gold.

" Pig," he answered.

" Well, what of that ? "

Wild pig moving in the forest, that is natural. The brutes

were moving, hit upon our camp, and showed their displeasure by their grunts.

Dersu made a gesture of impatience.

" How you, captain, live many years in *taigá*, still no-can understand nothing. Pig no want go by night."

Then in the direction where the two men were staring could be heard the crackle of broken twigs and characteristic snorting of pig. Not far from our bivouac they were coming down from higher ground and making the circuit of a conical hill.

" Then why do pig move about at night," I asked Dersu.

" Him no go all for nothing. Other man hunt him."

I thought he meant some Udehé, and was inwardly surprised at them being out in the forest on ski by night. But suddenly I remembered that by ' man ' Dersu comprised not only human beings, and then I at last understood. Wild boars fear one animal only, the tiger.

That meant the great carnivore was near.

I did not wait for tea, but dragged my bag nearer the fire and dropped off to sleep again.

I felt that I had been asleep a long time.

Suddenly something heavy fell on my chest, and at the same instant I heard the yells of dogs and a desperate cry from Dersu :

" Quick ! "

Instantly I flung off the flap of my bag.

Snow and dried leaves covered my face. At the same instant I caught a glimpse of a long shadow flit past the fire. The weight on my chest was Alpa.

The fire was almost out, only a few embers still glowing in it. The wind scattered the ashes and sprinkled sparks about the snow. Dersu was sitting on the ground, leaning his arms on the snow, holding one across his heart, as though to steady its beating. Old Kitenbu was lying prone on the ground, without moving.

It was some moments before I could collect my thoughts and realize what had happened or what I ought to do. With some difficulty I pushed the dog off me, crawled out of my bag, and went up to Dersu.

" What's up ? " I asked him, shaking him by the shoulder.

" Amba ! Amba ! " he answered in a terrified voice. "Amba come right in our camp. Amba take dog."

Then I noticed that the Udehé dog was missing.

Dersu stood up and began replenishing the fire. Directly the flames brightened up the old man pulled himself together. He stared round from side to side in terror, and had the look of a man crazed. At another time he would have looked comical.

Now it was I who retained my self-control, because I had been asleep and not seen what happened. But presently our roles changed. When Dersu recovered his calm I became alarmed. What guarantee was there that the great brute would not attack a man ?

How had it all happened, and why had no one fired ?

It appeared that Dersu had awakened first. The dogs disturbed him as they kept jumping first to one side, then to the other, of the fire. To escape the tiger Alpa had jumped right on to Dersu's head. Half asleep, he had thrust him off and at that instant seen the tiger at his very side. The monster quietly picked up the dog, without hurrying itself, just as though it knew that no one could interfere, and carried him off into the forest. Terrified at the shock, Alpa dashed through the fire and landed right on my chest. At that moment I heard Dersu's cry.

Instinctively I picked up my rifle, but did not know in what direction to shoot. Suddenly in the bushes behind I heard a rustle.

" Here ! " whispered Kitenbu, pointing away from the cedar.

" No, there ! " said Dersu, pointing in exactly the opposite direction.

The rustle was repeated, but this time on both sides at once. The wind was whispering in the tree-tops, and that interfered with the sound. At one moment it seemed to me as though I did hear the sound of broken twigs, and could even see the creature, but a moment later I realized that it was only a tree. The growth all round was so dense that even by day no one could see through it.

" Dersu," I said to the Gold. " Climb that tree; from up there you'll have a look."

" No," he answered. " Me no-can do. Me old man. Now no-can climb tree no-how."

The old Udehé also refused to climb a tree. So I decided to climb up the cedar myself. The trunk was smooth and even and covered with snow on the weather side. By dint of the greatest effort I managed to crawl up about half a yard, but my hands were numbed and I fell back to the ground.

" No need," said Dersu, looking up at the sky. " Night soon finish."

He picked up his rifle and fired a shot into the air. Just at that moment there was a sharp gust of wind. The report died away, drowned by a sudden gust of wind.

We made up a big fire and started brewing tea.

All this time Alpa clung close to me, and then to Dersu, and at the slightest sound shuddered and looked round in terror. For forty minutes we sat round the fire, sipping tea and comparing impressions.

At last it began to grow light, and the wind dropped quickly, but the frost intensified. Dersu and Kitenbu went into the thicket. They reported, from examination of the spoor, that nine pigs had passed, and that the tiger was sick and old. He had prowled round the camp for a long time, and only attacked the dog when the fire had completely gone out.

I suggested leaving our things in camp and following up the spoor of the tiger. I thought Dersu would say no and was surprised when he agreed.

The Gold began to explain to me that in the *taigá* a tiger

requires a great deal of food. This one had been hunting wild pig, but, coming upon humans, had stolen a dog.

" Such Amba may shoot, yes," he explained. " Shoot him no sin," he concluded, winding up quite a long speech.

The storm had completely dropped. The age-old firs and cedars had lost their wintry garb, but the ground was encumbered by great drifts and hummocks of snow. The sun's beams played over them and this dressed the grim forest in holiday array.

From our camp the tiger had gone back upon his own tracks, and these brought us to a huge prone trunk. The tracks went right under it.

" No hurry," said Dersu to me. " No need go straight. Need go round, good look-see." Then suddenly he cried : " Gone ! " and quickly turned back in the direction of the fresh spoor.

Here it was clear that the tiger had sat for a long time in one place. The snow was trampled down. He had put the dog down and listened to hear whether he were being followed. Then he had gone on farther with it.

We tracked him for three hours. He did not go straight but chose places where the snow was thinner, where the vegetation was denser, and there were big piles of fallen timber. At one place he had jumped on to a log and sat there a long time, until something had alarmed him and he had sprung off and crawled several yards on his belly. He had stopped from time to time and listened. When we began to overtake him he went off at first by great bounds, and then at a walk, and then a trot.

At last Dersu stopped and consulted Kitenbu. In his opinion it was better to turn back, as the tiger had not been wounded, the snow was not deep enough, and it was waste of time to go on farther after him.

What struck me as strange and incomprehensible was that the tiger had not eaten the dog, but carried it along with him. As though in answer to my thought, Dersu said that this was not a tiger but a tigress, and that she was taking the dog to her cubs.

She would not lead us to her lair, but take us astray into the hills until we were far away. With such reasoning it was impossible to argue.

When we had decided to return to our camp site, Dersu turned to the direction in which the tiger had gone and called out : " Amba ! You got no face ! You one big thief, worse than dog. Me no afraid of you. Another time see you, then shoot ! "

Then he lit his pipe and turned back on our trodden path.

A little distance short of our camp site it so happened that I was going ahead, and Kitenbu and Dersu had dropped behind. When I reached the top of the pass I thought I saw something dash downhill away from our camp.

In a minute we reached the spot.

All our things were scattered about and ripped open. Of my sleeping-bag there remained but a few pieces. The tracks in the snow showed that the place had been sacked by a pair of wolverines. I had caught a glimpse of them as I was coming up.

Collecting what was left of our belongings, we dropped quickly from the pass. It was easy going downhill as our old ski tracks, though snowed over, stood well. We simply raced along them and by evening had rejoined the detachment.

Some Udehé were standing near the rock Sinopku. From them I learnt that on the Bikin they were looking for somebody, and that a police sergeant was leading a search party, but owing to the deep snow they had turned back. I did not then know that it was I for whom they were looking.

The natives told us that farther on there were two empty huts.

" What is the place called ? " I asked them.

" Beisilaza-datani," answered one of them.

" How many miles ? " Zakharov asked him.

" A mile and a half," answered the Udehé confidently.

I asked him to come with us and he agreed gladly. We bought some elk venison from them, some fish and bear's fat, and set out.

When we had gone well over two miles I asked the guide how much farther.

" Not far," he answered.

Then we went another three, but the huts seemed bewitched, receding from us as fast as we overtook them. It was time to stop to camp, but it would be silly to dig out a camp in the snow when there were huts near. So I asked again how far still.

" Near," he answered.

At each bend in the river I thought I should see the huts, but we came to bend after bend and never a sight of them. Like that we went a good five miles.

Suddenly it occurred to me to ask our guide how many miles it was still to Beisilaza-datani.

" Five," he answered in the same confident tone.

Then the riflemen sat down and began to swear. It turned out that our guide had not the faintest notion of what a verst, or a mile, means. Natives never measure distance like that, but always by time, a half-day journey, a two-day journey, and so on.

So then I gave the signal to stop and bivouac. The Udehé assured us that the huts were then quite near, but by now nobody believed him. The men started hurriedly scraping away the snow, hauling wood, and pitching the tents. We were very late and darkness overtook us still at work. All the same, the camp was made very comfortable.

The last day of 1907 we devoted to crossing to the last point on the Bikin. Here there were only Chinese living.

The Chinese killed a pig, prepared plenty of wine for us, and implored me to spend the next day with them. Our supply of provisions by now had quite run out and the prospect of seeing in the New Year in more civilized surroundings appealed to my companions. I willingly accepted the Chinamen's invitation, but made the riflemen promise that they would not drink a lot of wine. They kept their word, and I did not see any of them a little bit the worse for drink.

The next day was bright and frosty. In the morning I paraded my command, and proposed a toast to the health of all who had helped our expedition and rendered our task easier. Cries of " Hurrah ! " resounded through the forest. Chinamen came running out from the neighbouring huts on hearing the noise, and when they heard what it was all about, started buzzing their rattles.

Hardly had we separated and gone to our respective huts and sat down to supper when we heard the sound of bells outside. The Chinese came with the news that the police sergeant had arrived. In a few minutes a man in a heavy fur coat came into the hut, and the police sergeant was bewitched into Merzliakov.

We embraced. The conversation was lively. It turned out that there was no police sergeant at all, but it was he who had wanted to come to meet me, but postponed the idea on account of the deep snow.

W E reached Khabarovsk in the evening of 7 January. The riflemen reported to their companies and Dersu and I went to a flat, where my friends came to see us. They all looked at Dersu with surprise and curiosity. He too did not feel quite on his own plane and rather out of his element, and it was a long time before he could settle down to this new form of life.

I allotted a little room to him, where we put a bed, a wooden table, and a couple of stools. These, it appeared, were quite unnecessary to him, as he preferred to squat on the floor, or more often on the bed, tucking up his legs in Turkish fashion.

When he went to bed, in addition to a straw mattress and padded quilt, he spread his goat skins underneath, in his old way.

His favourite place was the corner near the stove. He sat by the pile of firewood and stared by the hour into the fire. In a room everything was unfamiliar to him, and only the burning wood recalled his native *taigá*. When the wood burned badly he grew angry with the stove, and muttered :

" Bad man, him no want burn."

Once the idea struck me to make a record of Dersu's talk on a phonograph. He quickly understood what was wanted of him, and made a long speech into the receiver which filled up almost the whole cylinder. Then I changed the film for a pronouncing one, and turned on the machine again. Dersu, on hearing his own voice coming back again out of the machine, was not in the least surprised, and not a muscle of his face stirred. He listened attentively to the end, and then said :

" Him," pointing to the apparatus, " talk true, not leave one word."

Dersu was incorrigible. He humanized even the phonograph. Sometimes I would go and sit and have a chat with him. We used to yarn together over all our adventures on our expeditions. These talks gave us both a great deal of pleasure.

But on coming home from the field there is always a mass of work to attend to, drawing reports of field work and statement of accounts, plotting our route, working out the collections, and so on. Dersu noticed that I used to sit the livelong day at the table and write.

" Me did think," he said. " Captain sit so," and he made the motion of being seated, " eat, judge men, no other work. Now me understand. Captain go mountain . . . work ; come back town . . . work. Now no-can walk."

Once when I went into his room I found him dressed to go out, with his rifle in his hand.

" Where are you going ? " I asked him in surprise.

"Go shoot," he said, and then, noticing the surprise in my eyes, started explaining that there was a lot of dirt accumulated in the barrel, and that if he fired a shot the bullet would pass down the rifling and clean it all out ; after that he would only need to clean it out with a rag.

The prohibition of shooting within the town was an unpleasant surprise for him. He turned his beloved old *berdianka* over in his hands and, with a deep sigh, put it back in the corner. This incident seemed to upset him terribly.

The next day, when passing his room, I saw his door ajar. Something had happened, and I went in softly. Dersu was standing by the window muttering to himself. Men who live a solitary life in the *taigá* become accustomed to express their thoughts aloud.

" Dersu ! " I cried to him.

He turned round. A rather bitter smile was playing on his lips.

" What's the matter ? " I asked him.

" Me here," he said, " all same duck. How man can live in box ? " and he pointed to the walls and ceiling. " Man must live in mountain, all time go, shoot."

Dersu was then silent, turned again to the window, and watched the people in the street.

He was homesick for his lost liberty.

'It can't be helped,' I thought. 'He'll live it down and grow used to a house.'

It once happened that some small job was necessary in his room, to repair the stove and plaster the ceiling. I told him that he could move into my office for a couple of days, and go back to his own room as soon as it was ready.

"No mind, captain," he replied. "Me can sleep in street. Make tent, light fire, no hurt, no matter."

To him it all seemed so simple, and it took a lot of trouble to get that idea out of his head.

He was not offended, but did not like all the restrictions of town life. You cannot pitch a tent in the street, or light a fire, or shoot a rifle, because it would interfere with somebody else.

Once he was present when I was buying firewood, and he was tremendously struck that I paid for it.

"What!" he cried. "Plenty wood in forest. What for give money for nothing?"

He abused the contractor, called him 'bad man,' and tried his best to persuade me that I was being swindled. I tried to make it clear to him that I was paying not so much for the wood as for all the labour in getting it there, but it was useless. Dersu could not reconcile himself to that, and that evening he did not light his stove. Next day, to save me from expense, he went out to the park to fell a tree for me. They arrested him and drew up a report. Dersu protested in his own fashion and made a scene. So then they took him to the police station. Then they rang me up and told me about it and I smoothed things over. But however hard I tried, I never succeeded in explaining to him that he must not cut down trees in the town.

This incident made a profound impression on him. He realized that in a town a man cannot live just as he wishes, but how other people wish. Strangers surrounded him on every side and hampered him at every step. The old fellow became pensive and solitary ; he grew thinner, seemed to decline, and to age rapidly.

The next incident completely upset his equilibrium. He saw me pay for water.

" What ! " he cried. " Must also pay water ! Look-see river," pointing to the Amur. " There plenty much water. . . . How can . . . ? "

He did not complete the sentence, but bolted to his room.

That evening I was sitting writing in my office. Suddenly I heard a door gently creak. I turned round and saw Dersu standing in the doorway. I saw at once that he wanted to ask me something. His face expressed embarrassment and alarm. Before I could utter a question, he flung himself on his knees and said :

" Captain, please . . . let me go mountain ! Me no-can live in town ; buy wood, buy water too ; cut wood . . . man swear."

I raised him to his feet and made him sit on a chair.

" Where are you going ? " I asked him.

" There ! " and he pointed to the Hekhtsir range, visible in the blue distance.

I hated parting with the old fellow, but I hated to keep him. I was obliged to give way. But I made him promise that in a month he would come back, and then we would go off again together. I wanted to arrange for him to live with some native friends. I wanted him to spend another couple of days with me so that I could fit him up with cash, clothes, and supplies. But it turned out otherwise.

Next morning, as I passed his room, I noticed that his door was open. I looked in. His room was empty.

Dersu's departure was a terrible blow to me. I felt as though something had been torn out of my breast. A vague uneasiness crept over me. I felt anxious, afraid of something, and I felt a presentiment that I should never see Dersu again. I was upset all that day and unable to concentrate on my work. At last I flung down the pen, put on my coat, and went out to the camp.

Outside spring was already in the air, and the snow was thawing rapidly. From white it was turning to dirty brown, as though bespattered with soot. On the sunny side of the great clumps of snow like snowballs there were little ridges of ice. They melted in the daytime and dripped, but froze again at night. Water was already flowing in the gutters and canals. It was bubbling merrily, as though hastening to bring to every withered herb the glad news that it was awake again and now busy bringing back life to nature.

Some riflemen returning from musketry told me that on the road they had met a strange man with a pack on his back and a rifle in his hand. He was striding along cheerfully, singing to himself. Obviously it was Dersu.

A couple of weeks after his departure I received a telegram from a friend.

' Man you sent into *taigá* found murdered.'

' Dersu ! ' I thought instantly.

Then I remembered that to prevent him being detained by the police in town I had given him my card and written on the back that his passport was in my custody. They had probably found this card on him and so telegraphed to me.

The next day I left by rail for Korforovskaya, a station on the south · side of the Hekhtsir range. There I learnt that some workmen had seen Dersu on the road in the forest. He was walking with his rifle in his hand and talking to a crow perched on a tree.

It was almost dark when the train arrived, so I decided to start for the scene of the crime next morning.

But that night I could not sleep. A crushing grief lay on my heart. I felt that I had lost my nearest friend. What had we been through together ! How many a time had he saved me from a desperate situation !

To distract myself I tried to read, but could not. My eyes passed mechanically over the letters, but in the brain I could see only the picture of Dersu imploring me to set him at liberty. I blamed myself for having brought him to a town. But whoever could have thought things would have turned out as they did?

At nine I started.

It was the end of March. The sun was already high in the heavens, warming the earth with his beams. The air was still fresh with the night frost, especially in the shade, but from the melted snow, the water in the brooks, and the cheerful appearance of the trees, it was clear that the cold of night no longer inspired dread.

A little track led me into the forest. About a mile in, a little to the right of the path, I saw a fire with three figures sitting by it. In one of them I recognized the police inspector. A couple of workmen were digging a grave and by their side on the ground, covered with a mat, lay something. I recognized the moccasins.

" Dersu ! Dersu ! " the cry was wrung from my breast.

The workmen looked at me in surprise. I did not want to betray my emotion to these strangers, so I went off to one side, sat on a stump, and gave full rein to my grief.

The ground was frozen still, and the men were burning a fire in order to thaw it, and every now and then dug out a spadeful. Five minutes later the inspector came up to me. He had such a cheerful expression that he looked as though he had come to a party.

Judging from the evidence, Dersu had been killed in his sleep. The murderers had searched him for his money and stolen his rifle.

In an hour and a half the grave was ready. The men brought up Dersu and took off the mat. A ray of sunshine forced its way through the thick branches of the firs and lit up the dead man's face. The eyes were open, gazing at the sky. The expression was that of a man who had forgotten something and was making an effort to remember it. The men picked up the body, put it in the grave, and started heaping earth on it.

" Farewell, Dersu," I said quietly. " In the *taigá* thou wert born and in the *taigá* thou hast completed thy reckoning with life."

In twenty minutes, on the spot where they had let down the body of the Gold, there rose a hummock of earth.

The men had finished their job. They lit their pipes, picked up their tools, and started for the station after the inspector.

I sat down by the road and buried myself in memories of the friend whom I had lost.

As in the cinema, all the pictures of our past life together were unrolled before the eyes of my memory.

At that moment there flew up a nuthatch. It perched on a branch near the grave, looked confidingly at me, and twittered.

' Peaceful man,' and I thought how Dersu had talked of the feathered inhabitants of the forest. The pretty little bird flew off into the trees. Then I felt again the renewed pang in my heart.

I moved on a little way, and looked round, so as to remember the spot where they had buried Dersu. Two huge cedars stretched their sheltering boughs over his resting-place, visible from afar.

" Farewell, Dersu, old friend ! " I said for the last time, and turned to walk back to the station.

In the summer of 1908 I left on another expedition, my third, which lasted nearly two years.

In the winter of 1910 I returned to Khabarovsk and at once took the train to Korforovskaya to visit the grave of my friend.

I no longer recognized the spot. Everything had changed. A whole township had sprung up round the station and on the flanks of the Hekhtsir granite quarries had been opened up ; they were felling the forest for sleepers. Several efforts I made to locate the grave, but in vain. My cedar landmarks had vanished. New roads had been made. There were quarry faces, dumps, embankments . . . all around bore the signs of another life.

THE END

GLOSSARY

AGDY. ' Thunder ' in the tongue of tribes of the *taigá* of Ussuria.

AMBA. ' Devil.' The native tribes use the same word for ' tiger.' The tiger in Ussuria was regarded as divine, both by aborigines and Chinese, as the Lord of the *taigá*, who protects the ginseng.

ARBA. A Chinese two-wheeled cart.

BERDIANKA. The Russian service rifle in use from about 1875 until 1891.

BUDA. The Russian name for *gumisa*, or Chinese millet.

BURKA. A black, shaggy, sleeveless mantle or cloak in general use in the Caucasus. It is suitable in mountain regions with treacherous climate. It is made of sheepskin. The word is Caucasian, probably Georgian.

BUY. The Gold name for the elk. It can hardly be more than a coincidence that it so closely resembles the familiar Indo-European root meaning ' bull.'

CHOLDONI. Brigands.

DABA. A coarse, blue material, used for clothing by the Chinese in Ussuria.

DIKUSHKA. In Russian the ' wild thing,' the name used in Ussuria for a bird of the grouse family, *Falcipennis falcipennis*, Hartlaub.

GAR. The Russian word for a burnt-out forest ; also called ' *pal* ' in other parts of Siberia.

GINSENG. The root of a plant, *Panax ginseng*, one of the natural order *Araliaceæ*, a native of Manchuria, Korea, and Ussuria. In great demand in China as a medicine. Manchurian ginseng was once considered the finest, and became so scarce that an imperial edict was issued to protect it. The Korean form then became most esteemed. Related species have been imported from America but are not considered so good, nor can it be cultivated with success. The price varies from 6 or 12 dollars an ounce to as much as 300, and even 400 dollars an ounce. It is believed, however, that its virtues are purely psychological, and there is no evidence that it has any real pharmaceutical properties. It is the object of a whole mass of folk-lore, but the superstition that it rejuvenates old men and the impotent probably arose from the fancied resemblance of the forked root to the figure of a man. It is analogous to the mandrake of the Hebrews.

341

GLOSSARY

GNUS. The Russian word for ' abomination,' applied by the settlers to the countless swarms of biting flies, mosquitoes, and midges which make life in the *taigá*, to those unaccustomed to it, a burden at certain seasons. Pronounced ' *gnooce*.'

GOLD. The people of the Manchurian branch of the Tungus-Manchurian tribe. They call themselves ' Nanai.' They live along the basin of the Amur from Khabarovsk to Mariinsk, along the Ussuri and its tributaries, and also in Chinese territory. About five thousand Golds live in Russian territory. Their main occupation is in hunting and fishing. They have a certain indigenous culture seen in their picturesque costumes.

The tribes of the Ussurian *taigá* enjoy an excellent reputation for their ' truly noble qualities.' Unfortunately, like so many Asiatic aborigines, they had been for many years steadily decreasing under the pressure of Russian and Chinese culture, and their chief enemies, namely scarlet fever, smallpox, and famine.

Our hero, Dersu Uzala, in every way confirms the wonderful testimonial given to his people in the passage quoted.

The Tungus, closely related to the Golds, are described by the Russian writer Maximov as ' the Frenchmen of the North,' owing to their bright and lively disposition.

GORBUSHA. The Humpback Salmon of Americans and Canadians ; the Russian word ' *gorbusha* ' means the same thing. The scientific name is *Salmo gorbusha*, Wahlbaum. It is a native of the North Pacific, from the Behring Straits to Korea on the Asiatic coast and to the Sacramento River on the American. In the breeding season the exaggerated hump and elongated jaws of the male give this fish a grotesque appearance. According to Berg, it is not a big fish, not exceeding 8 lb. in weight.

HUNHUZ. The name, apparently Chinese, given to wandering bands of brigands.

K'ANG. In houses in the northern parts of China and Korea heating is effected by flues enclosed in a built-in platform running round the rooms at a convenient height above the ground to serve as seat or bed.

KANGU. The Spirit of the Mountains in Gold folk-lore.

KASHA. A food in Russia ; the most frequent kind is made of buckwheat.

KAZA. The Gold word for ' sea-gull.'

KETA. The Dog Salmon of the Americans, *Salmo keta*, an inhabitant of the North Pacific, ranging as far south as San Francisco on the American side, and the river Tumen-ul on the Asiatic. The flesh, which is bright red, is largely eaten in smoked and frozen form throughout Siberia. It is the author of the coarse-grained, scarlet caviare which in recent years has appeared on the London market. In Russia this caviare is regarded as much inferior to that of the sturgeon.

GLOSSARY

KUROSLEP. The Russian name of the Scarlet Pimpernel, *Anagallis arvensis*. It is curious that, although this pretty little plant enjoyed high repute for medicinal virtues in Europe from classical times, the Russian name bears witness to the fact that there existed a belief that it produces blindness in poultry.

LENOK. A kind of trout occurring in all Siberian rivers. The scientific name is *Brachymystax lenok*, Guenther. It is good eating and runs to 15 lb. or slightly more.

LOTSA. The name applied by Manchurian natives to the Russians.

LUDEVA. A strongly built fence or barrier of trees and bushes, built by Chinese hunters, often extending over many miles. At intervals there are openings with pitfalls beneath, carefully concealed by a network of branches, shrubs, and grass. The quantity of game, particularly wapiti, roe, and musk-deer, killed in this manner is shocking.

MALMA. The Far Eastern race of the Alpine char, *Salvelinus alpinus malma*, Wahlb. Unlike its relatives, it is a sea fish, mounting the rivers to spawn. It is excellent to eat, but is not big, seldom exceeding 2 ft. or 2 ft. 3 in. in length.

UDEHÉ. A tribe of Tungus affinity, related to the Golds, generally alluded to in this book by the name Taz, which was often applied by Russians to the aborigines of the Far East. They are mainly engaged in fishing and hunting. There are a few thousand of these attractive people, but, as this book shows, they have suffered terribly under the pressure of the higher culture and industry of the Chinese.

OROCHONS are a tribe related to the above. They are few in number, live along the Amur, and are engaged in reindeer-breeding.

PANTSUY. The Gold word for ginseng, q.v.

PURGA. The Russian word for a violent snowstorm or blizzard, with a severe gale and very low temperature.

SHUGA. Lumps of frozen snow, mingled with ice, which appear in autumn, floating down northern rivers, a sure sign of impending frost. The word is Siberian dialect. In Russia it is called *salo*, i.e. tallow, from the resemblance to solidifying fat.

SOLONS. A small tribe of Tungus living mainly in China, engaged chiefly in hunting. In Russia the census of 1897 showed only fifteen Solons in Russian territory.

SOSHKI. A wooden prop, used to support the barrel of a heavy rifle when the hunter is taking aim. They are in general use in northern and central Asia, and for heavy, old-fashioned weapons they are indispensable.

STAROSTÁ. In pre-revolutionary Russia the head-man of a village, or bailiff.

343

GLOSSARY

TAIGÁ. The vast forest of northern Asia, which extends from the Urals to the Sea of Okhotsk, a distance of about 2500 miles from west to east, and about 700 to 800 from south to north. Outwardly gloomy and lifeless, it is full of game and other animals. Its characteristics are vividly described in this book, but the *taigá* of Ussuria is far richer and more diversified than that of central Siberia, owing to the admixture of a large number of Oriental and Southern forms of flora and fauna.

UNTY. Moccasins or knee-boots made of fur.

VESELUSHKA. Literally, the cheerful little bird, the Russian name of the dipper, *Cinclus cinclus*.

VIAZIGA. The dried backbone of the sturgeon, in Russia considered a delicacy.

WAPITI ANTLERS in velvet. The Chinese use them as medicine and attribute to them the power of rejuvenation.

INDEX

P

R

INDEX